PRAISE, WORSHIP AND LYRICS SONGBOOK

PRAISE, WORSHIP, AND LYRICS SONGBOOK
COPYRIGHT © 2023 BY SHILOH VESSELS
All Rights Reserved

No part of this publication may be reproduced, distributed, or transmitted in any form or other electronic or mechanical methods, without the prior written permission of Shiloh Vessels, except with brief quotations embodied in critical reviews and certain other non-commercial uses. Except otherwise indicated, all scriptural quotations are from the King James Version of the Bible and used with permission granted.

This book is intended for educational purposes only and should not be misconstrued as professional advice or opinions. As a reader, you agree to hold harmless the author and publisher for any errors or omissions and agree that the content is for educational purposes only. The content of this songbook does not reflect the views of Absolute Author Publishing House.

Publisher: Absolute Author Publishing House
Editor: Shiloh Vessels
Cover Designer: Shiloh Vessels

Paperback ISBN: 978-1-64953-919-9

Disclaimer: Shiloh Vessels hereby declare that we do not own the rights to the music/songs. All rights belong to the owner. No Copyright infringement intended.

My worship is to God Almighty alone. In the presence of God, there is fullness of joy and liberty. Because of this deep understanding, I crave the manifestation of the presence of God. I have a part to play as a praise and worship minister, the part is called prepare, and then I invite the Holy Spirit to take full control. The songbook is designed and arranged in such a way that it can pull up any set category to minister. I give God the glory for the grace and privilege to worship His Holy Name.

Agatha Mba

This is an answered prayer that we never knew we needed. This divine book and exceptional idea make the life of choristers and ministers easy. This book introduces a variety of song choices and patterns that glorify God. I'm in awe and grateful for this blessing!

Precious Deborah Omotayo

A novel and collegial arrangement of Praise and Worship songs at your fingertips, inspired by the Holy Spirit. Beneficial to everyone who has breath to systematically praise the living God with ease of reference. To Him alone be all the glory".

Preston Barovbe

Worship is what I do to HONOUR and reference God Almighty for who He is, His mercies, and to praise Him for His mighty acts. Worship is also a moment of privilege and great humility to know that I have been graced by this Mighty God to be in his awesome presence and pour out my gratitude. The creation of the songbook and collection of songs was an experience that brought God to the forefront of our minds. Each song was a masterpiece of God's goodness, mercy, greatness, kindness, majesty, sovereignty, and above all His love toward us all. May His name be forever praised.

Tosin Durojaiye

Worshipping God has completely changed my life. I understand through scripture how spiritual and intimate an experience worshipping God truly is. There is nothing like being in His presence and singing praises to Him. David, in Psalms 34:1, said it perfectly, I will bless the Lord at all times: His praise shall continually be in my mouth. To Adonai, our Lord and Master be all the praise.

Rachel Shonde

Table of Contents

INTRODUCTION	1
ACKNOWLEDGMENT	3
PART A CONTEMPORARY PRAISE AND WORSHIP	4
ONE WORSHIP SONG AND 5 PRAISE SONGS AND LINKS	
SET 1 – SET 36	5-40
PART B AFRICAN PRAISE AND WORSHIP	41
ONE WORSHIP SONG AND 5 PRAISE SONGS AND LINKS	
SET 1 – SET 40	42-82
PART C MIXED CONTEMPORARY AND AFRICAN PRAISE AND WORSHIP	83
ONE WORSHIP SONG AND 5 PRAISE SONGS AND LINKS	
SET 1 – SET 42	84-125
PART D HIGH PRAISE – THANKSGIVING	126
SIX PRAISE SONGS & LINKS	
SET 1 – SET 42	127-129
PART E KINGDOM ADVANCEMENT SONGS	130
SIX PRAISE SONGS & LINKS	
SET 1 – SET 42	131-133
PART F CONTEMPORARY ANOINTING SONGS	134
SIX PRAISE SONGS & LINKS	
SET 1 – SET	135-139

PART G MINISTRATION SONG RECOMMENDATION	140
ALL ROUND REST	141
ENOUGH IS ENOUGH	142
SHOWERS OF BLESSING	143
COVENANT DAY OF FAVOUR	144
NEW DAWN BANQUEST	145
FINANCIAL FORTUNE BANQUEST	146
COVENANT FAMILY DAY	147
COVENANT DAY OF FRUITFULNESS	148
BREAKING INVISBLE BARRIERS	149
NEXT LEVEL BANQUEST	150
COVENANT DAY OF OPEN DOORS	151
ENCOUNTER OF DESTINY	152
BREAKING GENERATION CURSES	153
COVENANT DAY OF VENGEANCE	154
COVENANT DAY OF SETTLEMENT	155
COVENANT DAY OF RESTORATION	156
COVENANT DAY OF EXEMPTION	157
COVENANT DAY OF BUSINESS AND CARREER BREAKTHROUGH	158
COVENANT DAY OF MARITAL BREAKTHROUGH	159
MINISTRATION SONG AND LINKS	160

INTRODUCTION

Without counsel, purposes are disappointed. But in the multitude of counsel, they are established. Proverbs 15:22. This Praise and Worship Songbook was established in the year 2023 by the inspiration of the Holy Spirit and the collective will of Shiloh Vessels members. The scope was for members of the choir to select a wide range of praise and worship songs and bring them into one place, making songs selection easier.

Previously, the song selection process was a task for the praise and worship leaders, especially for new and upcoming leaders. For example, when we practiced there were times when songs did not flow together due to the difference in song bit and structure. Instrumentalists would wait for the readjustment of the songs before practice resumed,

It was evident during the preparation stage, that there was lack of readily available songs or lyrics to select. When songs were made available, they were disorganized and not easily accessible, it took much effort to sequentially bring songs together. This prompted the leadership to work towards compiling an easy-to-use songs book, as an asset of help the current members and future newcomers to the Choir.

Praise and Worship songs were sourced along with their lyrics and links to the song's performance. We then arranged each song to flow into a sequence by rhythm, beat, and genre. We then set out to create a platform and space where anyone can access the songs listed from anywhere in the world, via an E-Book version, or hardcopy version.

This Praise and Worship Songbook will eradicate wrong song choices. It will enhance the communication between ministers and instrumentalists.

We believe this songbook will be a blessing to the body of Christ, young and old, as we sing praises to Abba Father together.

Song selection process for praise and worship was a bit of a task for praise and worship leaders, especially for new and upcoming praise and worship leaders. As we begin to practice the songs selected by the lead minister, we find out that the songs do not flow together due to the difference in song bit and structure the instrumentalists will wait for the re-adjustment of the songs before practice resume. And because of this issue practice is delayed unnecessary, so we decided to do something about it.

It was evident during the preparation stage, that there was lack of readily available songs or lyrics to select and practice from, efficiently and effectively. When songs were made available, they were disorganized and not easily accessible, it took much effort to sequentially bring songs together. This prompted the leadership to work towards compiling an easy-to-use songs book, as an asset of help the current members and future newcomers to the Choir.

It was evident during the preparation stage, that there was lack of readily available songs or lyrics to select and practice from, efficiently and effectively. When songs were made available, they were disorganized and not easily accessible, it took much effort to sequentially bring songs together. This prompted the leadership to work towards compiling an easy-to-use songs book, as an asset of help the current members and future newcomers to the Choir.

Praise and Worship songs were sourced along with their lyrics and links to the song's performance. We then arranged each song to flow into a sequence by rhythm, beat and genre. We then set out to create a platform and space where anyone can access songs list from anywhere in the world, via the E-Book version, or via the hardcopy.

This Praise and Worship Songbook will eradicate wrong song choices, time wasting and lack of proper preparation between ministers and instrumentalists. We believe this songbook will be a blessing to the body of Christ, young and old, as we sing praises to our Heavenly Father.

ACKNOWLEDGEMENT

We must start by thanking the Holy Spirit for the inspiration to write this first-of-its-kind songbook. We thank God for WCI Croydon Church, without whom we would not have the opportunity to produce this book. We want to acknowledge and appreciate the Agatha Mba, Precious Omotayo, Preston Barovbe, Oluwatosin Durojaiye, and Rachel Shonde for their valuable contributions, from early drafts to giving advice on the book cover and keeping everyone focused on the end goal. More grace and anointing to you all.

PART

A

CONTEMPORARY PRAISE AND WORSHIP - SET 1

WORSHIP-:

AT THE CENTER OF IT ALL

PRAISE-:

1. OPEN THE EYES OF MY HEART LORD
2. BLESSED JESUS WE'VE COME TO GIVE PRAISE
3. BLESSED BE THE NAME OF THE LORD
4. I KNOW YOU RESCUED MY SOUL
5. ARISE, ARISE, ARISE

WORSHIP & PRAISE LYRICS

AT THE CENTER OF IT ALL

AT THE CENTER OF IT ALL
IT'S YOU I SEE X 2
THERE IS POWER IN YOUR NAME
MIRACLES HAPPEN IN YOUR NAME
AS WE LIFT OUR VOICE IN PRAISE
IT'S YOU I SEE X 2
YOU ARE BIGGER, STRONGER, HIGHER, GREATER

LINK: https://youtu.be/_GzvFn-oyII

OPEN THE EYES OF MY HEART LORD

OPEN THE EYES OF MY HEART, LORD
OPEN THE EYES OF MY HEART, I WANT TO SEE YOU
TO SEE YOU HIGH AND LIFTED UP
SHININ' IN THE LIGHT OF YOUR GLORY
POUR OUT YOUR POWER AND LOVE
AS WE SING HOLY, HOLY, HOLY

LINK: https://youtu.be/fadU7b9aa78

BLESSED JESUS WE'VE COME TO GIVE PRAISE

BLESSED JESUS
WE'VE COME TO GIVE PRAISE
YOU SRE WORTHY
AND BLESSED BE YOUR NAME
WE LOVE YOU LORD
WE LOVE YOU LORD

LINK: https://youtu.be/tHQxyREYj-c

BLESSED BE THE NAME OF THE LORD

BLESSED BE THE NAME OF THE LORD x2
BLESSED BE THE NAME OF THE LORD, MOST HIGH
THE NAME OF THE LORD IS, A STRONG TOWER
THE RIGHTEOUS RUN INTO IT AND THEY ARE SAVED
THE NAME OF THE LORD IS, A STRONG TOWER
THE RIGHTEOUS RUN INTO IT AND THEY ARE SAVED

LINK: https://youtu.be/bYrcrP1ysjw

I KNOW YOU RESCUED MY SOUL

I KNOW HE RESCUED MY SOUL; HIS BLOOD HAS COVERED MY SIN
I BELIEVE, I BELIEVE, MY SHAME, HE'S TAKEN AWAY
MY PAIN IS HEALED IN HIS NAME, I BELIEVE, I BELIEVE,
I'LL RAISE A BANNER 'CAUSE MY LORD HAS CONQUERED THE GRAVE.
MY REDEEMER LIVES (4X)

LINK: https://youtu.be/3gIYEDzSyok

ARISE, ARISE, ARISE

ONE THING WE ASK OF YOU, ONE THING THAT WE DESIRE
THAT AS WE WORSHIP YOU, LORD COME AND CHANGE OUR LIVES
SO, ARISE, ARISE, ARISE, ARISE, ARISE, TAKE YOUR PLACEBE ENTHRONED ON OUR PRAISE, ARISE
KING OF KINGS, HOLY GOD, AS WE SING ARISE
ARISE, ARISE, ARISE

LINK: https://youtu.be/RFoe8ZgNZEI

CONTEMPORARY PRAISE - PRAISE AND WORSHIP – SET 2

WORSHIP-:

WE BOW DOWN AND WORSHIP, YAHWEH

PRAISE-:

1. EVERY PRAISE TO OUR GOD
2. CREATOR OF THE UNIVERSE
3. JESUS YOUR MY FORM FOUNDATION
4. HOLY ARE YOU LORD, (AWESOME GOD)
5. YOU ARE THE REASON WHY I LIFT MY HANDS

WORSHIP & PRAISE LYRICS

WE BOW DOWN AND WORSHIP, YAHWEH

WE BOW DOWN AND WORSHIP, YAHWEH
YAHWEH, YAHWEH, YAHWEH
YAHWEH, YAHWEH, YAHWEH
WE BOW DOWN AND WORSHIP, YAHWEH
WE BOW DOWN AND WORSHIP, YAHWEH

LINK: https://youtu.be/q0A6nHOspkc

EVERY PRAISE TO OUR GOD

EVERY PRAISE IS TO OUR GOD
EVERY WORD OF WORSHIP, WITH ONE ACCORD
EVERY PRAISE, EVERY PRAISE
IS TO OUR GOD
SING HALLELUJAH TO OUR GOD
GLORY HALLELUJAH IS DUE OUR GOD
EVERY PRAISE, EVERY PRAISE, IS TO OUR GOD

LINK: https://youtu.be/X48B8AbkmbA

CREATOR OF THE UNIVERSE

CREATOR OF THE UNIVERSE WHAT CANT YOU DO
WHAT CAN'T YOU DO WHAT CAN'T YOU DO
WHAT CAN'T YOU DO JESUS, NAME ABOVE EVERY
NAME ABOVE EVERY OTHER NAME EVERY OTHER NAME
WHAT CAN'T YOU CHANGE, WHAT CAN'T YOU CHANGE JESUS
LIFT YOUR HANDS AND SAY YOU'RE ABLE
YOU ARE ABLE GREAT AND MIGHTY GREAT AND MIGHTY GOD
YOU'RE ABLE JESUS

LINK: https://youtu.be/HPqDaKajSnQ

HOLY ARE YOU LORD, ALL CREATION CALL YOU LORD

HOLY ARE YOU LORD, ALL CREATION CALL YOU GOD
WORTHY IS YOUR NAME, WE WORSHIP YOUR MAJESTY
AWESOME GOD, HOW GREAT THOU ART
YOU ARE GOD, MIGHTY ARE YOUR MIRACLES
WE STAND IN AWE OF YOUR HOLY NAME
LORD WE BOW AND WORSHIP YOU

LINK: https://youtu.be/qnLvi392hhE

JESUS YOU ARE MY FIRM FOUNDATION

JESUS, YOU'RE MY FIRM FOUNDATION, I KNOW I CAN STAND SECURE;
JESUS, YOU'RE MY FIRM FOUNDATION, I PUT MY HOPE IN YOUR HOLY WORD,
I PUT MY HOPE IN YOUR HOLY WORD.
I HAVE A LIVING HOPE, I HAVE A FUTURE;
GOD HAS A PLAN FOR ME, OF THIS I'M SURE(2X)

LINK: https://youtu.be/KVPsW4csPs0

YOU ARE THE REASON WHY I LIFT MY HANDS

YOU ARE THE REASON WHY I LIFT MY HANDS
WHY I LIFT MY VOICE
WHY I SING TO YOU
YOU ARE THE REASON I'M ALIVE TODAY
I AM HERE TO SAY
IT'S ALL BECAUSE OF YOU
YOU ARE THE REASON x4

LINK: https://youtu.be/49omWdzQ9eI

CONTEMPORARY PRAISE AND WORSHIP - SET 3

WORSHIP-:

NO OTHER NAME LIKE THE NAME OF JESUS

PRAISE-:

1. ARISE, ARISE, ARISE
2. CASTING CROWN, LIFTING HANDS
3. LORD YOU ARE GOOD AND YOUR MERCIES ENDURES FORVER
4. EVERY PRAISE IS TO OUR GOD
5. WATER HE TURNED INTO WINE

WORSHIP & PRAISE LYRICS

NO OTHER NAME IS THE NAME OF JESUS

NO OTHER NAME BUT THE NAME OF JESUS (3X)
IS WORTHY OF GLORY AND WORTHY OF HONOR
AND WORTHY OF POWER AND ALL PRAISE
HIS NAME IS EXALTED FAR ABOVE THE EARTH
HS NAME IS HIGH ABOVE THE HEAVENS
HIS NAME IS EXALTED FAR ABOVE THE EARTH
GIVE GLORY AND HONOR
AND PRAISE UNTO HIS NAME
LINK: https://youtu.be/QUgzowKz4Gw

ARISE, ARISE, ARISE

ONE THING WE ASK OF YOU, ONE THING THAT WE DESIRE
THAT AS WE WORSHIP YOU, LORD COME AND CHANGE OUR LIVES
ARISE, ARISE, ARISE, ARISE, ARISE, TAKE YOUR PLACE
BE ENTHRONED ON OUR PRAISE, ARISE
KING OF KINGS, HOLY GOD, AS WE SING ARISE
ARISE, ARISE, ARISE

LINK: https://youtu.be/RFoe8ZgNZEI

CASTING CROWNS

CASTING CROWNS, LIFTING HANDS
BOWING HEARTS, IS ALL WE'VE COME TO DO
ADONAI, ADONAI, ADONAI, YOU REIGN ON HIGH
WE WILL RISE, IN YOUR NAME, ADONAI, YOU REIGN ON HIGH

LINK: https://youtu.be/2P-FIceZIDo

LORD YOU ARE GOOD AND YOUR MERCY ENDURETH FOREVER

LORD YOU ARE GOOD AND YOUR MERCY ENDURETH FOREVER x2
PEOPLE FROM EVERY NATION AND TONGUE
FROM GENERATION TO GENERATION
WE WORSHIP YOU HALLELUJAH, HALLELUJAH
WE WORSHIP YOU FOR WHO YOU ARE

LINK: https://youtu.be/708opj5poOc

EVERY PRAISE TO OUR GOD

EVERY PRAISE IS TO OUR GOD
EVERY WORD OF WORSHIP, WITH ONE ACCORD
EVERY PRAISE, EVERY PRAISE
IS TO OUR GOD
SING HALLELUJAH TO OUR GOD
GLORY HALLELUJAH IS DUE OUR GOD
EVERY PRAISE, EVERY PRAISE, IS TO OUR GOD

LINK: https://youtu.be/X48B8AbkmbA

WATER YOU TURN INTO WINE

WATER YOU TURNED INTO WINE, OPENED THE EYES OF THE BLIND
THERE'S NO ONE LIKE YOU, NONE LIKE YOU
INTO THE DARKNESS YOU SHINE, OUT OF THE ASHES
WE RISE, THERE'S NO ONE LIKE YOU, NONE LIKE YOU
OUR GOD IS GREATER, OUR GOD IS STRONGER
GOD YOU ARE HIGHER THAN ANY OTHER
OUR GOD IS HEALER, AWESOME IN POWER OUR GOD, OUR GOD

LINK: https://youtu.be/NJpt1hSYf2o

CONTEMPORARY PRAISE & WORSHIP - SET 4

WORSHIP-:

YOU ARE ALPHA AND OMEGA

PRAISE-:

1. OPEN THE EYES OF MY HEART LORD
2. WATER HE TURNED INTO WINE
3. I KNOW HE RESCUED MY SOUL
4. JESUS YOUR MY FIRM FOUNDATION
5. BLESSED BE THE NAME OF THE LORD

WORSHIP & PRAISE LYRICS

YOU ARE ALPHA AND OMEGA

YOU ARE ALPHA AND OMEGA
WE WORSHIP YOU OUR LORD
YOU ARE WORTHY TO BE PRAISED
WE GIVE YOU ALL THE GLORY
WE WORSHIP YOU OUR LORD
YOU ARE WORTHY TO BE PRAISED

LINK: https://youtu.be/hLzX3rpbfSA

OPEN THE EYES OF MY HEART LORD

OPEN THE EYES OF MY HEART, LORD
OPEN THE EYES OF MY HEART, I WANT TO SEE YOU
I WANT TO SEE YOU, TO SEE YOU HIGH AND LIFTED UP
SHININ' IN THE LIGHT OF YOUR GLORY
POUR OUT YOUR POWER AND LOVE
AS WE SING HOLY, HOLY, HOLY

LINK: https://youtu.be/fadU7b9aa78

WATER YOU TURN INTO WINE

WATER YOU TURNED INTO WINE, OPENED THE EYES OF THE BLIND
THERE'S NO ONE LIKE YOU, NONE LIKE YOU
INTO THE DARKNESS YOU SHINE, OUT OF THE ASHES WE RISE, THERE'S NO ONE LIKE YOU, NONE LIKE YOU
OUR GOD IS GREATER, OUR GOD IS STRONGER
GOD YOU ARE HIGHER THAN ANY OTHER
OUR GOD IS HEALER, AWESOME IN POWER OUR GOD, OUR GOD

LINK: https://youtu.be/NJpt1hSYf2o

I KNOW YOU RESCUED MY SOUL

I KNOW HE RESCUED MY SOUL; HIS BLOOD HAS COVERED MY SIN
I BELIEVE, I BELIEVE, MY SHAME, HE'S TAKEN AWAY
MY PAIN IS HEALED IN HIS NAME, I BELIEVE, I BELIEVE,
I'LL RAISE A BANNER 'CAUSE MY LORD HAS CONQUERED THE GRAVE.
MY REDEEMER LIVES (4X)

LINK: : https://youtu.be/3gIYEDzSyok

JESUS YOU ARE MY FIRM FOUNDATION

JESUS, YOU'RE MY FIRM FOUNDATION, I KNOW I CAN STAND SECURE;
JESUS, YOU'RE MY FIRM FOUNDATION, I PUT MY HOPE IN YOUR HOLY WORD,
I PUT MY HOPE IN YOUR HOLY WORD.
I HAVE A LIVING HOPE, I HAVE A FUTURE;
GOD HAS A PLAN FOR ME, OF THIS I'M SURE(2X)

LINK: https://youtu.be/KVPsW4csPs0

BLESSED BE THE NAME OF THE LORD

BLESSED BE THE NAME OF THE LORD x2
BLESSED BE THE NAME OF THE LORD, MOST HIGH
THE NAME OF THE LORD IS, A STRONG TOWER
THE RIGHTEOUS RUN INTO IT AND THEY ARE SAVED
THE NAME OF THE LORD IS, A STRONG TOWER
THE RIGHTEOUS RUN INTO IT AND THEY ARE SAVED

LINK: https://youtu.be/bYrcrP1ysjw

CONTEMPORARY: PRAISE AND WORSHIP – SET 5

WORSHIP-:

WHO IS LIKE UNTO THEE OH LORD

PRAISE-:

1. JESUS YOUR MY FIRM FOUNDATION
2. WATER HE TURNED INTO WINE
3. HALLELUJAH FOR THE LORD OUR GOD THE ALMIGHTY REIGNS
4. HOLY ARE YOU LORD (AWESOME GOD)
5. YOU REIGN, YOU ANCIENT ZION'S KING, KADOSH, KADOSH

WORSHIP & PRAISE LYRICS

WHO IS LIKE UNTO THEE OH LORD

WHO IS LIKE UNTO THEE OH LORD
AMONG THE GODS WHO IS LIKE THEE
GLORIOUS IN HOLINESS
FEARFUL IN PRAISES DOING WONDERS
HALLELUJAH

LINK: https://youtu.be/YqA1RaGM4G8

JESUS YOU ARE MY FIRM FOUNDATION

JESUS, YOU'RE MY FIRM FOUNDATION, I KNOW I CAN STAND SECURE;
JESUS, YOU'RE MY FIRM FOUNDATION, I PUT MY HOPE IN YOUR HOLY WORD,
I PUT MY HOPE IN YOUR HOLY WORD.
I HAVE A LIVING HOPE, I HAVE A FUTURE;
GOD HAS A PLAN FOR ME, OF THIS I'M SURE(2X)

LINK: https://youtu.be/KVPsW4csPs0

WATER HE TURNED INTO WINE

WATER HE TURNED INTO WINE , OPENED THE EYES OF THE BLIND
THERE'S NO ONE LIKE YOU, NONE LIKE YOU
INTO THE DARKNESS YOU SHINE, OUT OF THE ASHES WE RISE, THERE'S NO ONE LIKE YOU, NONE LIKE YOU
OUR GOD IS GREATER, OUR GOD IS STRONGER
GOD YOU ARE HIGHER THAN ANY OTHER
OUR GOD IS HEALER, AWESOME IN POWER OUR GOD, OUR GOD
LINK https://youtu.be/NJpt1hSYf2o

HALLELUJAH FOR THE LORD OUR GOD THE ALMIGHTY REIGNS

HALLELUJAH, HALLELUJAH
FOR THE LORD OUR GOD THE ALMIGHTY REIGNS
HALLELUJAH, HALLELUJAH
FOR THE LORD OUR GOD THE ALMIGHTY REIGNS
HOSSANA HALLELUJAH x3

LINK: https://youtu.be/HRPtXuFpV9U

HOLY ARE YOU LORD (AWESOME GOD)

HOLY ARE YOU LORD
ALL CREATION CALL YOU GOD
WORTHY IS YOUR NAME, WE WORSHIP YOUR MAJESTY
AWESOME GOD, HOW GREAT THOU ART
YOU ARE GOD, MIGHTY ARE YOUR MIRACLES
WE STAND IN AWE OF YOUR HOLY NAME
LORD, WE BOW DOWN AND WORSHIP YOU

LINK: https://youtu.be/qnLvi392hhE

YOU REIGN, YOU ANCIENT ZION'S KING

YOU REIGN, YOU ANCIENT ZION'S KING
KADOSH, KADOSH, YOU ARE MIGHTY ON YOUR THRONE
OH SING, OH FOUNTAIN OF THE HILL, I AM KADOSH,
YOU ARE MIGHTY ON YOUR THRONE
REIGN FORTH, OH SPIRIT OF THE HILL, THAT IS KADOSH, YOU ARE MIGHTY ON YOUR THRONE

LINK: https://youtu.be/Jj-S6xk-Q4M

CONTEMPORARY: PRAISE AND WORSHIP – SET 6

WORSHIP-:

WE GIVE YOU GLORY LORD, AS WE HONOUR YOU

PRAISE-:

1. EVERY PRAISE IS TO OUR GOD
2. WE LIFT OUR HANDS IN THE SANCTUARY
3. LORD YOU ARE GOOD AND YOUR MERCY ENDURES FOREVER
4. IF YOU CALL TO HIM, OH SING FOR JOY TO GOD OUR STRENGTH
5. ARISE, ARISE, ARISE

WORSHIP & PRAISE LYRICS

WE GIVE YOU GLORY LORD

WE GIVE YOU GLORY LORD AS WE HONOUR YOU
WE GIVE YOU GLORY LORD AS WE HONOUR YOU
YOU ARE WONDERFUL, YOU ARE WORTHY OH LORD
YOU ARE WONDERFUL, YOU ARE WORTHY OH LORD

LINK: https://youtu.be/vHxBleOPX_M

EVERY PRAISE TO OUR GOD

EVERY PRAISE IS TO OUR GOD
EVERY WORD OF WORSHIP, WITH ONE ACCORD
EVERY PRAISE, EVERY PRAISE
IS TO OUR GOD
SING HALLELUJAH TO OUR GOD
GLORY HALLELUJAH IS DUE OUR GOD
EVERY PRAISE, EVERY PRAISE, IS TO OUR GOD

LINK: https://youtu.be/X48B8AbkmbA

WE LIFT OUR HANDS IN THE SANCTURARY

WE LIFT OUR HANDS IN THE SANCTURARY
WE LIFT OUR HANDS TO GIVE THE GLORY
WE LIFT OUR HANDS TO GIVE THE PRAISE
AND WE WILL PRAISEYOU FOR THE REST OF OUR DAYS
YES, WE WILL PRAISE YOU FOR THE REST OF OUR DAYS

LINK: https://youtu.be/iv68ruS6DVE

LORD YOU ARE GOOD AND YOUR MERCY ENDURETH FOREVER

LORD YOU ARE GOOD AND YOUR MERCY ENDURETH FOREVER x2
PEOPLE FROM EVERY NATION AND TONGUE
FROM GENERATION TO GENERATION
WE WORSHIP YOU, HALLELUJAH, HALLELUJAH
WE WORSHIP YOU FOR WHO YOU ARE

LINK: https://youtu.be/708opj5poOc

IF YOU CALL TO HIM

IF WE CALL TO HIM, HE WILL ANSWER US
IF WE RUN TO HIM, HE WILL RUN TO US
IF WE LIFT OUR HANDS, HE WILL LIFT US UP
COME NOW PRAISE HIS NAME, ALL YOU SAINTS OF GOD.
OH SING FOR JOY TO GOD OUR STRENGTH (2X)

LINK: https://youtu.be/Dd6QpIoIXFc

ARISE, ARISE, ARISE

ONE THING WE ASK OF YOU, ONE THING THAT WE DESIRE
THAT AS WE WORSHIP YOU, LORD COME AND CHANGE OUR LIVES
SO, ARISE, ARISE, ARISE, ARISE, ARISE, TAKE YOUR PLACEBE ENTHRONED ON OUR PRAISE, ARISE
KING OF KINGS, HOLY GOD, AS WE SING ARISE
ARISE, ARISE, ARISE

LINK: https://youtu.be/RFoe8ZgNZEI

CONTEMPORARY: PRAISE AND WORSHIP – SET 7

WORSHIP-:

YOU ARE HOLY (AWESOME GOD)

PRAISE-:

1. WE WANNA SEE JESUS LIFTED HIGH
2. CREATOR OF THE UNIVERSE
3. PRAISE YE THE LORD OH MY LORD
4. HOSSANA IN THE HIGHEST, LORD WE LIFT UP YOUR NAME
5. I WILL BLESS THE LORD, OH MY SOUL (HE HAS DONE GREAT THINGS)

WORSHIP & PRAISE LYRICS

HOLY ARE YOU LORD (AWESOME GOD)

HOLY ARE YOU LORD
ALL CREATION CALL YOU GOD
WORTHY IS YOUR NAME, WE WORSHIP YOUR MAJESTY
AWESOME GOD, HOW GREAT THOU ART
YOU ARE GOD, MIGHTY ARE YOUR MIRACLES
WE STAND IN AWE OF YOUR HOLY NAME
LORD, WE BOW DOWN AND WORSHIP YOU

LINK: https://youtu.be/qnLvi392hhE

WE WANNA SEE JESUS LIFTED HIGH

WE WANNA SEE JESUS LIFTED HIGH
THE BANNER THAT FLIES ACROSS THE LAND
THAT ALL MEN MIGHT SEE THE TRUTH AND KNOW
HE IS THE WAY TO HEAVEN
WE WANT TO SEE, WE WANT TO SEE
WE WANT TO SEE JESIS LIFTED HIGH
STEP BY STEP WE ARE MOVING FORWARD
LITTLE BY LITTLE WE ARE TAKING GROUND
EVERY PRAYER A POWERFUL WEAPON
STRONGHOLDS COME TUMBLING DOWN AND DOWN
AND DOWN AND DOWN

LINK: https://youtu.be/Glqypn3a9XE

CREATOR OF THE UNIVERSE

CREATOR OF THE UNIVERSE WHAT CANT YOU DO
WHAT CAN'T YOU DO WHAT CAN'T YOU DO
WHAT CAN'T YOU DO JESUS, NAME ABOVE EVERY
NAME ABOVE EVERY OTHER NAME EVERY OTHER NAME
WHAT CAN'T YOU CHANGE, WHAT CAN'T YOU CHANGE JESUS
LIFT YOUR HANDS AND SAY YOU'RE ABLE
YOU ARE ABLE GREAT AND MIGHTY GREAT AND MIGHTY GOD
YOU'RE ABLE JESUS

LINK: https://youtu.be/HPqDaKajSnQ

HOSSANA, HOSSANA IN THE HIGHEST

HOSSANA, HOSSANA, HOSSAN IN THE HIGHEST
HOSSANA, HOSSANA, HOSSAN IN THE HIGHEST
LORD WE LIGT UP YOUR NAME
WITH THE HEAT FULL OF PRAISE
BE EXALTED OH LORD MY GOD
HOSSANA IN THE HIGHEST

LINK: https://youtu.be/iG5y_Gd3oZc

PRAISE YE THE LORD OF MY SOUL

THIS IS THE DAY HE HAS MADE
HALLELUJAH
HALLELUJAJ
PRAISE YE THE LORD

LINK: https://youtu.be/n5bCj5VetwI

I WILL BLESS THE LORD, OH MY SOUL

I WILL BLESS THE LORD, OH MY SOUL
I WILL BLESS THE LORD, OH MY SOUL
AND ALL THAT IS WITHIN ME
BLESS HIS HOLY NAME
HE HAS DONE GREAT THINGS x3
BLESS HIS HOLY NAME

LINK: https://youtu.be/lYuibQ_tgDk

CONTEMPORARY: PRAISE AND WORSHIP- SET 8

WORSHIP-:

OH BE LIFTED ABOVE ALL OTHER GODS

PRAISE-:

1. CREATOR OF THE UNIVERSE
2. PRAISE YE THE LORD OH MY SOUL
3. HOSSANA IN THE HIGHEST
4. WATER HE TURNED INTO WINE
5. EVERY PRAISE IS TO OUR GOD

WORSHIP & PRAISE LYRICS

OH, BE LIFTED ABOVE ALL OTHER GODS

OH, BE LIFTED
ABOVE ALL OTHER GODS
WE LAY OUR CROWNS
AND WORSHIP YOU
ALL GLORIOUS GOD
WE PRAISE YOUR NAME
WE LAY OUR CROWNS
AND WORSHIP YOU
LINK: https://youtu.be/yH1FJEQBzss

CREATOR OF THE UNIVERSE

CREATOR OF THE UNIVERSE WHAT CANT YOU DO
WHAT CAN'T YOU DO WHAT CAN'T YOU DO
WHAT CAN'T YOU DO JESUS, NAME ABOVE EVERY
NAME ABOVE EVERY OTHER NAME EVERY OTHER NAME
WHAT CAN'T YOU CHANGE, WHAT CAN'T YOU CHANGE JESUS
LIFT YOUR HANDS AND SAY YOU'RE ABLE
YOU ARE ABLE GREAT AND MIGHTY GREAT AND MIGHTY GOD
YOU'RE ABLE JESUS
LINK: https://youtu.be/HPqDaKajSnQ

PRAISE YE THE LORD OF MY SOUL

PRAISE YE THE LORD OF MY SOUL
THIS IS THE DAY HE HAS MADE
HALLELUJAH
HALLELUJAJ
PRAISE YE THE LORD

LINK: https://youtu.be/n5bCj5VetwI

HOSSANA, HOSSANA IN THE HIGHEST

HOSSANA, HOSSANA, HOSSAN IN THE HIGHEST
HOSSANA, HOSSANA, HOSSAN IN THE HIGHEST
LORD WE LIGT UP YOUR NAME
WITH THE HEAT FULL OF PRAISE
BE EXALTED OH LORD MY GOD
HOSSANA IN THE HIGHEST

LINK: https://youtu.be/E1X-VDCMyAc

WATER HE TURNED INTO WINE

WATER HE TURNED INTO WINE , OPENED THE EYES OF THE BLIND
THERE'S NO ONE LIKE YOU, NONE LIKE YOU
INTO THE DARKNESS YOU SHINE, OUT OF THE ASHES WE RISE, THERE'S NO ONE LIKE YOU, NONE LIKE YOU
OUR GOD IS GREATER, OUR GOD IS STRONGER
GOD YOU ARE HIGHER THAN ANY OTHER
OUR GOD IS HEALER, AWESOME IN POWER OUR GOD, OUR GO
LINK: https://youtu.be/NJpt1hSYf2o

EVERY PRAISE TO OUR GOD

EVERY PRAISE IS TO OUR GOD
EVERY WORD OF WORSHIP, WITH ONE ACCORD
EVERY PRAISE, EVERY PRAISE
IS TO OUR GOD
SING HALLELUJAH TO OUR GOD
GLORY HALLELUJAH IS DUE OUR GOD
EVERY PRAISE, EVERY PRAISE, IS TO OUR GOD

LINK: https://youtu.be/X48B8AbkmbA

CONTEMPORY - PRAISE AND WORSHIP - SET 9

WORSHIP-:

WE BOW DOWN AND WORSHIP YAHWEH

PRAISE-:

1. OPEN THE EYES OF MY HEART LORD
2. YES LORD, YES LORD AMEN, (AM TRADING)
3. ARISE, ARISE, ARISE
4. CREATOR OF THE UNIVERSE
5. TAKE ALL THE PRAISE (I HAVE COME TO SAY THANK YOU LORD)

WORSHIP & PRAISE LYRICS

WE BOW DOWN AND WORSHIP, YAHWEH

WE BOW DOWN AND WORSHIP, YAHWEH
YAHWEH, YAHWEH, YAHWEH
YAHWEH, YAHWEH, YAHWEH
WE BOW DOWN AND WORSHIP, YAHWEH
WE BOW DOWN AND WORSHIP, YAHWEH

LINK: https://youtu.be/q0A6nHOspkc

OPEN THE EYES OF MY HEART LORD

OPEN THE EYES OF MY HEART, LORD
OPEN THE EYES OF MY HEART, I WANT TO SEE YOU
TO SEE YOU HIGH AND LIFTED UP
SHININ' IN THE LIGHT OF YOUR GLORY
POUR OUT YOUR POWER AND LOVE
AS WE SING HOLY, HOLY, HOLY

LINK: https://youtu.be/fadU7b9aa78

YES LORD, YES LORD, AMEN, (AM TRADING)

I'M TRADING MY SORROWS
I'M TRADING MY SHAME
I'M LAYING THEM DOWM
FOR THE JOY OF THE LORD
I'M TRADING MY SICKNESS
I'M TRADING MY PAIN
I'M LAYING THEM DOWM
FOR THE JOY OF THE LORD
YES LORD, YES LORD x3
YES, YES LORD
LINK: https://youtu.be/YYRc0JeQuC0

ARISE, ARISE, ARISE

ONE THING WE ASK OF YOU, ONE THING THAT WE DESIRE
THAT AS WE WORSHIP YOU, LORD COME AND CHANGE OUR LIVES
SO, ARISE, ARISE, ARISE, ARISE, ARISE, TAKE YOUR PLACEBE ENTHRONED ON OUR PRAISE, ARISE
KING OF KINGS, HOLY GOD, AS WE SING ARISE
ARISE, ARISE, ARISE

LINK: https://youtu.be/RFoe8ZgNZEI

CREATOR OF THE UNIVERSE

CREATOR OF THE UNIVERSE WHAT CANT YOU DO
WHAT CAN'T YOU DO WHAT CAN'T YOU DO
WHAT CAN'T YOU DO JESUS, NAME ABOVE EVERY
NAME ABOVE EVERY OTHER NAME EVERY OTHER NAME
WHAT CAN'T YOU CHANGE, WHAT CAN'T YOU CHANGE JESUS
LIFT YOUR HANDS AND SAY YOU'RE ABLE
YOU ARE ABLE GREAT AND MIGHTY GREAT AND MIGHTY GOD
YOU'RE ABLE JESUS
LINK: https://youtu.be/HPqDaKajSnQ

TAKE ALL THE PRAISE

I HAVE COME, TO SAY THANK YOU LORD
I HAVE COME, TO GIVE BACK TO YOU
I HAVE COME, TO SAY THANK YOU LORD
TAKE ALL THE PRAISE x3
TAKE ALL THE PRAISE, YOU DESERVE

LINK: https://youtu.be/07dgTV33pTA

CONTEMPORARY – PRAISE AND WORSHIP - SET 10

WORSHIP-:

YOU DERSEVE IT (MY HALLELUJAH BELONGS TO YOU)

PRAISE-:

1. BLESSED BE THE NAME OF THE LORD.
2. HOSANNA, HOSANNA, HOSSANA IN THE HIGHEST.
3. CREATOR OF THE UNIVERSE, WHAT CAN'T YOU DO
4. WE WANNA SEE JESUS LIFTED HIGH
5. HOLY ARE YOU LORD, ALL CREATION CALL YOU GOD

WORSHIP & PRAISE LYRICS

YOU DERSEVE IT

MY HALLELUJAH BELONGS TO YOU
MY HALLELUJAH BELONGS TO YOU
MY HALLELUJAH BELONGS TO YOU
MY HALLELUJAH BELONGS TO YOU
YOU DESERVE IT x 6

LINK: https://youtu.be/zxL1m0uG8x4

BLESSED BE THE NAME OF THE LORD

BLESSED BE THE NAME OF THE LORD x2
BLESSED BE THE NAME OF THE LORD, MOST HIGH
THE NAME OF THE LORD IS, A STRONG TOWER
THE RIGHTEOUS RUN INTO IT AND THEY ARE SAVED
THE NAME OF THE LORD IS, A STRONG TOWER
THE RIGHTEOUS RUN INTO IT AND THEY ARE SAVED

LINK: https://youtu.be/bYrcrP1ysjw

HOSSANA, HOSSANA, HOSSANA IN THE HIGHEST

HOSSANA, HOSSANA, HOSSAN IN THE HIGHEST
HOSSANA, HOSSANA, HOSSAN IN THE HIGHEST
LORD WE LIGT UP YOUR NAME
WITH THE HEAT FULL OF PRAISE
BE EXALTED OH LORD MY GOD
HOSSANA IN THE HIGHEST

LINK: https://youtu.be/E1X-VDCMyAc

CREATOR OF THE UNIVERSE

CREATOR OF THE UNIVERSE WHAT CANT YOU DO
WHAT CAN'T YOU DO WHAT CAN'T YOU DO
WHAT CAN'T YOU DO JESUS, NAME ABOVE EVERY
NAME ABOVE EVERY OTHER NAME EVERY OTHER NAME
WHAT CAN'T YOU CHANGE, WHAT CAN'T YOU CHANGE JESUS
LIFT YOUR HANDS AND SAY YOU'RE ABLE
YOU ARE ABLE GREAT AND MIGHTY GREAT AND MIGHTY GOD
YOU'RE ABLE JESUS

LINK: https://youtu.be/HPqDaKajSnQ

WE WANNA SEE JESUS LIFTED HIGH

WE WANNA SEE JESUS LIFTED HIGH
THE BANNER THAT FLIES ACROSS THE LAND
THAT ALL MEN MIGHT SEE THE TRUTH AND KNOW
HE IS THE WAYTO HEAVEN
WE WANT TO SEE, WE WANT TO SEE
WE WANT TO SEE JESIS LIFTED HIGH
STEP BY STEP WE ARE MOVING FORWARD
LITTLE BY LITTLE WE ARE TAKING GROUND
EVERY PRAYER A POWERFUL WEAPON
STRONGHOLDS COME TUMBLING DOWN AND DOWN AND DOWN AND DOWN

LINK: https://youtu.be/Glqypn3a9XE

HOLY ARE YOU LORD (AWESOME GOD)

HOLY ARE YOU LORD
ALL CREATION CALL YOU GOD
WORTHY IS YOUR NAME, WE WORSHIP YOUR MAJESTY
AWESOME GOD, HOW GREAT THOU ART
YOU ARE GOD, MIGHTY ARE YOUR MIRACLES
WE STAND IN AWE OF YOUR HOLY NAME
LORD, WE BOW DOWN AND WORSHIP YOU

LINK: https://youtu.be/qnLvi392hhE

CONTEMPORARY – PRAISE AND WORSHIP- SET 11

WORSHIP-:

BE GLORIFIED, BE GLORIFIED

PRAISE-:

1. TAKE ALL THE PRAISE, I HAVE COME TO SAY THANK YOU
2. BLESSED BE THE NAME OF THE LORD
3. ARISE, ARISE, ARISE
4. EVERY PRAISE IS TO OUR GOD
5. HELLALUYAH FOR THE LORD OUR GOD THE ALMIGHTY REIGNS

WORSHIP & PRAISE LYRICS

BE GLORIFIED, BE GLORIFIED

BE GLORIFIED, BE GLORIFIED
BE GLORIFIED, BE GLORIFIED
BE GLORIFIED, IN THE HEAVEN
BE GLORIFIED, IN THE EARTH
BE GLORIFIED, IN THIS TEMPLE
JESUS, JESUS
BE THOU GLORIFIED

LINK: https://youtu.be/xXFvwkGlneA

TAKE ALL THE PRAISE

I HAVE COME, TO SAY THANK YOU LORD
I HAVE COME, TO GIVE BACK TO YOU
I HAVE COME, TO SAY THANK YOU LORD
TAKE ALL THE PRAISE x3
TAKE ALL THE PRAISE, YOU DESERVE

LINK: https://youtu.be/07dgTV33pTA

BLESSED BE THE NAME OF THE LORD

BLESSED BE THE NAME OF THE LORD x2
BLESSED BE THE NAME OF THE LORD, MOST HIGH
THE NAME OF THE LORD IS, A STRONG TOWER
THE RIGHTEOUS RUN INTO IT AND THEY ARE SAVED
THE NAME OF THE LORD IS, A STRONG TOWER
THE RIGHTEOUS RUN INTO IT AND THEY ARE SAVED

LINK: https://youtu.be/bYrcrP1ysjw

ARISE, ARISE, ARISE

ONE THING WE ASK OF YOU, ONE THING THAT WE DESIRE
THAT AS WE WORSHIP YOU, LORD COME AND CHANGE OUR LIVES
SO, ARISE, ARISE, ARISE, ARISE, ARISE, TAKE YOUR PLACEBE ENTHRONED ON OUR PRAISE, ARISE
KING OF KINGS, HOLY GOD, AS WE SING ARISE
ARISE, ARISE, ARISE

LINK: https://youtu.be/RFoe8ZgNZEI

EVERY PRAISE TO OUR GOD

EVERY PRAISE IS TO OUR GOD
EVERY WORD OF WORSHIP, WITH ONE ACCORD
EVERY PRAISE, EVERY PRAISE
IS TO OUR GOD
SING HALLELUJAH TO OUR GOD
GLORY HALLELUJAH IS DUE OUR GOD
EVERY PRAISE, EVERY PRAISE, IS TO OUR GOD

LINK: https://youtu.be/X48B8AbkmbA

HALLELUJAH FOR THE LORD OUR GOD THE ALMIGHTY REIGNS

HALLELUJAH, HALLELUJAH
FOR THE LORD OUR GOD THE ALMIGHTY REIGNS
HALLELUJAH, HALLELUJAH
FOR THE LORD OUR GOD THE ALMIGHTY REIGNS
HOSSANA HALLELUJAH x3

LINK: https://youtu.be/HRPtXuFpV9U

CONTEMPORARY PRAISE AND WORSHIP - SET 12

WORSHIP-:

LORD, WE PROCLAIM YOU NOW

PRAISE-:

1. THANK YOU LORD (DON MOEN)
2. WATER YOU TURN INTO WINE
3. PRAISE YE THE LORD OH MY SOUL
4. HOLY ARE YOU LORD, ALL CREATION CALL YOU LORD
5. HOSSANA IN THE HIGHEST

WORSHIP & PRAISE LYRICS

LORD, WE PROCLAIM YOU NOW

LORD, WE PROCLAIM YOU NOW OF YOUR MIGHTY POWER
AND YOUR AWESOME MAJESTY
LORD, COME UPON US NOW
AND RELEASE YOUR POWER
AND LET YOUR PRENSENCE FALL (OH, LORD)
OH, LORD
OH, LORD
RELEASE YOUR POWER
AND LET YOUR PRESENCE FALL
LINK: https://youtu.be/yilGRPQ5FJc

THANK YOU, LORD (DON MOEN),

I COME BEFORE YOU TODAY
AND THERE'S JUST ONE THING THAT I WANT TO SAY
THANK YOU, LORD
THANK YOU, LORD
FOR ALL YOU'VE GIVEN ME
FOR ALL THE BLESSINGS THAT I CANNOT SEE
THANK YOU, LORD
THANK YOU, LORD
WITH A GREATFUL HEART, WITH A SONG OF PRAISE
WITH AN OUTSTRECTCHED ARM, I WILL BLESS YOUR NAME
THANK YOU LORD x3
LINK: https://youtu.be/K44trVhtZX4

WATER YOU TURN INTO WINE

WATER YOU TURNED INTO WINE, OPENED THE EYES OF THE BLIND
THERE'S NO ONE LIKE YOU, NONE LIKE YOU
INTO THE DARKNESS YOU SHINE, OUT OF THE
ASHES WE RISE, THERE'S NO ONE LIKE YOU, NONE LIKE YOU
OUR GOD IS GREATER, OUR GOD IS STRONGER
GOD YOU ARE HIGHER THAN ANY OTHER
OUR GOD IS HEALER, AWESOME IN POWER OUR
GOD, OUR GOD
LINK: https://youtu.be/NJpt1hSYf2o

PRAISE YE THE LORD OF MY SOUL

THIS IS THE DAY HE HAS MADE
HALLELUJAH
HALLELUJAJ
PRAISE YE THE LORD

LINK: https://youtu.be/n5bCj5VetwI

HOLY ARE YOU LORD (AWESOME GOD)

HOLY ARE YOU LORD
ALL CREATION CALL YOU GOD
WORTHY IS YOUR NAME, WE WORSHIP YOUR MAJESTY
AWESOME GOD, HOW GREAT THOU ART
YOU ARE GOD, MIGHTY ARE YOUR MIRACLES
WE STAND IN AWE OF YOUR HOLY NAME
LORD, WE BOW DOWN AND WORSHIP YOU

LINK: https://youtu.be/qnLvi392hhE

HOSSANA, HOSSANA IN THE HIGHEST

HOSSANA, HOSSANA, HOSSAN IN THE HIGHEST
HOSSANA, HOSSANA, HOSSAN IN THE HIGHEST
LORD WE LIGT UP YOUR NAME
WITH THE HEAT FULL OF PRAISE
BE EXALTED OH LORD MY GOD
HOSSANA IN THE HIGHEST

LINK: https://youtu.be/E1X-VDCMyAc

CONTEMPORARY PRAISE AND WORSHIP - SET 13

WORSHIP-:

YOU DESERVE THE GLORY AND THE HONOR

PRAISE-:

1. OPEN THE EYES OF MY HEART LORD
2. HOLY, HOLY, HOLY (X2) HOLY IS THE LORD GOD ALMIGHTY
3. WE LIFT OUR HANDS IN THE SANCTUARY
4. EVERY PRAISE IS TO OUR GOD
5. MASTER OF THE UNIVERSE

WORSHIP & PRAISE LYRICS

YOU DESERVE THE GLORY AND THE HONOR

YOU DESERVE THE GLORY AND THE HONOR
LORD, WE LIFT YOUR IN WORSHIP
AS WE LIFT HOLY NAME
FOR YOU ARE GREAT< YOU DO MIRACLE SO GREAT
THERE IS NO ONE ELSE LIKE YOU
THERE IS NO ONE ELSE LIKE YOU

LINK: https://youtu.be/LLseRHq-dA0

OPEN THE EYES OF MY HEART LORD

OPEN THE EYES OF MY HEART, LORD
OPEN THE EYES OF MY HEART, I WANT TO SEE YOU
TO SEE YOU HIGH AND LIFTED UP
SHININ' IN THE LIGHT OF YOUR GLORY
POUR OUT YOUR POWER AND LOVE
AS WE SING HOLY, HOLY, HOLY

LINK: https://youtu.be/fadU7b9aa78

HOLY, HOLY, HOLY (X2) HOLY IS THE LORD GOD ALMIGHTY

HOLY, HOLY, HOLY (X2)
HOLY IS THE LORD GOD ALMIGHTY
WORTHY TO RECEIVE GLORY
WORTHY TO RECEIVE HONOUR
WORTHY TO RECEIVE ALL OUR PRAISE TODAY PRAISE HIM
PRISE HIM, AND LIFT HIM UP

LINK: https://youtu.be/a0C8rhd472Y

WE LIFT OUR HANDS IN THE SANCTUARY

WE LIFT OUR HANDS IN THE SANCTUARY
WE LIFT OUR HANDS TO GIVE YOU THE GLORY
WE LIFT OUR HANDS TO GIVE YOU THE PRAISE
AND WE WILL PRAISEYOU FOR THE REST OF OUR DAYS
YES, WE WILL PRAISE YOU FOR THE REST OF OUR DAYS

LINK: https://youtu.be/iv68ruS6DVE

EVERY PRAISE TO OUR GOD

EVERY PRAISE IS TO OUR GOD
EVERY WORD OF WORSHIP, WITH ONE ACCORD
EVERY PRAISE, EVERY PRAISE
IS TO OUR GOD
SING HALLELUJAH TO OUR GOD
GLORY HALLELUJAH IS DUE OUR GOD
EVERY PRAISE, EVERY PRAISE, IS TO OUR GOD

LINK: https://youtu.be/X48B8AbkmbA

MASTER OF THE UNIVERSE

YOU ARE THE MASTER, MASTER OF THE UNIVERSE
CONQUEROR AND KING, LORD! MASTER OF THE UNIVERSE
YOU ARE THE EMPEROR ALWAYS, YOU ARE THE HEIR
OVER PRINCIPALITIES, YOU ARE THE HEIR, OVER
POWERS, YOU ARE THE HEIR, OVER RULERS, YOU ARE THE MASTER
MASTER OF THE UNIVERSE

LINK: https://youtu.be/kJ48XEDMBoY

CONTEMPORARY PRAISE AND WORSHIP – SET 14

WORSHIP-:

GREAT ARE YOU LORD

PRAISE-:

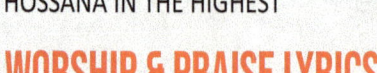

1. ARISE, ARISE, ARISE
2. I KNOW HE RESCUED MY SOUL
3. WATER HE TURNED INTO WINE
4. HALLELUYAH, FOR THE LORD OUR GOD THE ALMIGHTY REIGNS
5. HOSSANA, HOSSANA, HOSSANA IN THE HIGHEST

WORSHIP & PRAISE LYRICS

GREAT ARE YOU LORD

HOLY, HOLY, GOD ALMIGHTY
IT'S A PRIVILEGE TO WORSHIP YOU
MAKER OF ALL UNIVERSE
IT'S AN HONOUR JUST TO STAND BEFORE YOU
GREAT ARE YOU LORD
GREATLY TO BE PRAISED
GREAT ARE YOU LORD
GREATLY TO BE PRAISED
GREAT ARE YOU LORD

LINK: https://youtu.be/0ORTihWykSA

ARISE, ARISE, ARISE

ONE THING WE ASK OF YOU, ONE THING THAT WE DESIRE
THAT AS WE WORSHIP YOU, LORD COME AND CHANGE OUR LIVES
SO, ARISE, ARISE, ARISE, ARISE, ARISE, TAKE YOUR PLACEBE ENTHRONED ON OUR PRAISE, ARISE
KING OF KINGS, HOLY GOD, AS WE SING ARISE
ARISE, ARISE, ARISE

LINK: https://youtu.be/RFoe8ZgNZEI

I KNOW YOU RESCUED MY SOUL

I KNOW HE RESCUED MY SOUL; HIS BLOOD HAS COVERED MY SIN
I BELIEVE, I BELIEVE, MY SHAME, HE'S TAKEN AWAY
MY PAIN IS HEALED IN HIS NAME, I BELIEVE, I BELIEVE,
I'LL RAISE A BANNER 'CAUSE MY LORD HAS CONQUERED THE GRAVE
MY REDEEMER LIVES (4X)

LINK: https://youtu.be/3gIYEDzSyok

WATER YOU TURN INTO WINE

WATER YOU TURNED INTO WINE, OPENED THE EYES OF THE BLIND
THERE'S NO ONE LIKE YOU, NONE LIKE YOU
INTO THE DARKNESS YOU SHINE, OUT OF THE ASHES
WE RISE, THERE'S NO ONE LIKE YOU, NONE LIKE YOU
OUR GOD IS GREATER, OUR GOD IS STRONGER
GOD YOU ARE HIGHER THAN ANY OTHER
OUR GOD IS HEALER, AWESOME IN POWER OUR GOD, OUR GOD

LINK: https://youtu.be/NJpt1hSYf2o

HALLELUYAH, FOR THE LORD OUR GOD THE ALMIGHTY REIGNS

HALLELUJAH, HALLELUJAH
FOR THE LORD OUR GOD THE ALMIGHTY REIGNS
HALLELUJAH, HALLELUJAH
FOR THE LORD OUR GOD THE ALMIGHTY REIGNS
HALLELUJAH, HOSSANA HALLELUJAH x3

LINK: https://youtu.be/HRPtXuFpV9U

HOSSANA, HOSSANA IN THE HIGHEST

HOSSANA, HOSSANA, HOSSAN IN THE HIGHEST
HOSSANA, HOSSANA, HOSSAN IN THE HIGHEST
LORD WE LIGT UP YOUR NAME
WITH THE HEAT FULL OF PRAISE
BE EXALTED OH LORD MY GOD
HOSSANA IN THE HIGHEST

LINK: https://youtu.be/E1X-VDCMyAc

CONTEMPORARY PRAISE AND WORSHIP – SET 15

WORSHIP-:

HERE I AM TO WORSHIP

PRAISE-:

1. I KNOW HE RESCUED MY SOUL
2. ARISE, ARISE, ARISE
3. PRAISE YE THE LORD OH MY SOUL
4. OOO GLORY TO YOUR NAME (SHOUT IT LORD)
5. EVERY PRAISE TO OUR GOD

WORSHIP & PRAISE LYRICS

HERE I AM TO WORSHIP

LIGHT STEPPED DOWN INTO DARKNESS
OPENED MY EYES, LET ME SEE
BEAUTY THAT MADE THIS HEART ADORE YOU HOPE
OF A LIFE SPENT WITH YOU
HERE I AM TO WORSHIP
HERE I AM TO BOW DOWN
HERE I AM TO SAY THAT YOU'RE MY GOD

LINK: https://youtu.be/6CKCThJB5w0

I KNOW YOU RESCUED MY SOUL

I KNOW HE RESCUED MY SOUL; HIS BLOOD HAS
COVERED MY SIN
I BELIEVE, I BELIEVE, MY SHAME, HE'S TAKEN AWAY
MY PAIN IS HEALED IN HIS NAME, I BELIEVE, I BELIEVE,
I'LL RAISE A BANNER 'CAUSE MY LORD HAS CONQUERED
THE GRAVE
MY REDEEMER LIVES (4X)

LINK: https://youtu.be/3glYEDzSyok

ARISE, ARISE, ARISE

ONE THING WE ASK OF YOU, ONE THING THAT WE DESIRE
THAT AS WE WORSHIP YOU, LORD COME AND
CHANGE OUR LIVES
SO, ARISE, ARISE, ARISE, ARISE, ARISE, TAKE YOUR
PLACEBE ENTHRONED ON OUR PRAISE, ARISE
KING OF KINGS, HOLY GOD, AS WE SING ARISE
ARISE, ARISE, ARISE

LINK: https://youtu.be/RFoe8ZgNZEI

PRAISE YE THE LORD OF MY SOUL

THIS IS THE DAY HE HAS MADE
HALLELUJAH
HALLELUJAJ
PRAISE YE THE LORD

LINK: https://youtu.be/n5bCj5VetwI

OOO GLORY TO YOUR NAME (SHOUT IT LORD)

I WILL SING OF YOUR MERCY AND YOUR LOVE
OF GOODNESS AND TOUR GRACE
HALLELUJAH
OH, OH, OH, GLORY TO YOUR NAME
I SHOUT IT LOUD, GLORY TO YOUR NAME x2

LINK: https://youtu.be/69q_xxMfIeQ

EVERY PRAISE TO OUR GOD

EVERY PRAISE IS TO OUR GOD
EVERY WORD OF WORSHIP, WITH ONE ACCORD
EVERY PRAISE, EVERY PRAISE
IS TO OUR GOD
SING HALLELUJAH TO OUR GOD
GLORY HALLELUJAH IS DUE OUR GOD
EVERY PRAISE, EVERY PRAISE, IS TO OUR GOD

LINK: https://youtu.be/X48B8AbkmbA

CONTEMPORAY: PRAISE AND WORSHIP - SET 16

WORSHIP-:

HALLELUJAH, YOU HAVE WON THE VICTORY

PRAISE-:

1. HALLELUJAH FOR THE LORD GOD ALMIGHTY REIGNS
2. WATER HE TURNED INTO WINE
3. GOD IS ABLE TO DO JUST WHAT HE SAYS HE WILL DO
4. CREATOR OF THE UNIVERSE
5. OOO GLORY TO YOUR NAME (SHOUT IT LORD)

WORSHIP & PRAISE LYRICS

HALLELUJAH, YOU HAVE WON THE VICTORY

HALLELUJAH, YOU HAVE WON THE VICTORY
HALLELUJAH, YOU HAVE WON IT ALL FOR ME
DEATH COULD NOT HOLD YOU DOWN
YOU ARE THE RISEN KING, YEAH
YOU'RE SEATED IN MAJESTY, YEAH
YOU ARE THE RISEN KING

LINK: https://youtu.be/w3wBpKVugqg

HALLELUYAH, FOR THE LORD OUR GOD THE ALMIGHTY REIGNS

HALLELUJAH, HALLELUJAH
FOR THE LORD OUR GOD THE ALMIGHTY REIGNS
HALLELUJAH, HALLELUJAH
FOR THE LORD OUR GOD THE ALMIGHTY REIGNS
HALLELUJAH, HOSSANA HALLELUJAH x3

LINK: https://youtu.be/HRPtXuFpV9U

WATER YOU TURN INTO WINE

WATER YOU TURNED INTO WINE, OPENED THE EYES OF THE BLIND
THERE'S NO ONE LIKE YOU, NONE LIKE YOU
INTO THE DARKNESS YOU SHINE, OUT OF THE ASHES
WE RISE, THERE'S NO ONE LIKE YOU, NONE LIKE YOU
OUR GOD IS GREATER, OUR GOD IS STRONGER
GOD YOU ARE HIGHER THAN ANY OTHER
OUR GOD IS HEALER, AWESOME IN POWER OUR GOD, OUR GOD
LINK: https://youtu.be/NJpt1hSYf2o

GOD IS ABLE TO DO JUST WHAT HE SAYS HE WILL DO

GOD IS ABLE TO DO
JUST WHAT HE SAID HE WOULD DO
HE'S GONNA FLLFILL EVERY PROMISE TO YOU
DON'T GIVE UP ON GOD
CAUSE HE WON'T GIVE UP ON YOU
HE'S ABLE
HE'S ABLE
OH, OH, OH, OH, OH, OH,
HE'S ABLE
LINK: https://youtu.be/KLpO6ZndW2o

CREATOR OF THE UNIVERSE

CREATOR OF THE UNIVERSE WHAT CANT YOU DO
WHAT CAN'T YOU DO WHAT CAN'T YOU DO
WHAT CAN'T YOU DO JESUS, NAME ABOVE EVERY
NAME ABOVE EVERY OTHER NAME EVERY OTHER NAME
WHAT CAN'T YOU CHANGE, WHAT CAN'T YOU CHANGE JESUS
LIFT YOUR HANDS AND SAY YOU'RE ABLE
YOU ARE ABLE GREAT AND MIGHTY GREAT AND MIGHTY GOD
YOU'RE ABLE JESUS
LINK: https://youtu.be/HPqDaKajSnQ

OOO GLORY TO YOUR NAME (SHOUT IT LORD)

I WILL SING OF YOUR MERCY AND YOUR LOVE
OF GOODNESS AND TOUR GRACE
HALLELUJAH
OH, OH, OH, GLORY TO YOUR NAME
I SHOUT IT LOUD, GLORY TO YOUR NAME x2

LINK: https://youtu.be/69q_xxMfieQ

CONTEMPORARY: PRAISE AND WORSHIP – SET 17

WORSHIP-:

DAILY AS I LIVE

PRAISE-:

1. BLESSED BE THE NAME OF THE LORD
2. BLESSED JESUS, WE'VE COME TO GIVE YOU PRAISE
3. EVERY PRAISE TO OUR GOD
4. THE LORD REIGNS, LET THE EARTH REJOICE
5. CASTING CROWN

WORSHIP & PRAISE LYRICS

DAILY AS I LIVE

DAILY AS I LIVE, OFTEN AS I BREATHE
LET MY WHOLE LIFE BE EXPRESSIONS OF YOUR GRACE x3
WE CRY ABBA FATHER
HALLOWED BE YOUR NAME X3

LINK: https://youtu.be/dI5ruzWw-Hg

BLESSED BE THE NAME OF THE LORD

BLESSED BE THE NAME OF THE LORD x2
BLESSED BE THE NAME OF THE LORD, MOST HIGH
THE NAME OF THE LORD IS, A STRONG TOWER
THE RIGHTEOUS RUN INTO IT AND THEY ARE SAVED
THE NAME OF THE LORD IS, A STRONG TOWER
THE RIGHTEOUS RUN INTO IT AND THEY ARE SAVED

LINK: https://youtu.be/bYrcrP1ysjw

BLESSED JESUS WE'VE COME TO GIVE PRAISE

BLESSED JESUS
WE'VE COME TO GIVE PRAISE
YOU SRE WORTHY
AND BLESSED BE YOUR NAME
WE LOVE YOU LORD
WE LOVE YOU LORD

LINK: https://youtu.be/tHQxyREYj-c

EVERY PRAISE TO OUR GOD

DAILY AS I LIVE, OFTEN AS I BREATHE
LET MY WHOLE LIFE BE EXPRESSIONS OF YOUR GRACE x3
WE CRY ABBA FATHER
HALLOWED BE YOUR NAME X3

LINK: https://youtu.be/dI5ruzWw-Hg

THE LORD REIGNS, LET THE EARTH REJOICE

THE LORD REIGNS., THE LORD REIGNS.
THE LORD REIGNS.MLET THE EARTH REJOICE.
LET THE EARTH REJOICE., LET THE EARTH REJOICE.
LET THE PEOPLE BE GLAD, THAT OUR GOD REIGNS

LINK: https://youtu.be/aAgVvh2WgMM

CASTING CROWNS

CASTING CROWNS, LIFTING HANDS
BOWING HEARTS, IS ALL WE'VE COME TO DO
ADONAI, ADONAI, ADONAI, YOU REIGN ON HIGH
WE WILL RISE, IN YOUR NAME, ADONAI, YOU REIGN ON HIGH

LINK: https://youtu.be/2P-FIceZIDo

CONTEMPORRY: PRAISE AND WORSHIP - SET 18

WORSHIP-:

WAY MAKER, MIRACE WORKER, LIGHT IN THE DARKNESS

PRAISE-:

1. HOSANNA HOSANNA IN THE HIGHEST
2. JESUS YOUR MY FIRM FOUNDATION
3. WE WANNA SEE JESUS LIFTED HIGH
4. WATER HE TUNRNED INTO WINE
5. YES LORD YES LORD (AM TRADING)

WORSHIP & PRAISE LYRICS

WAY MAKER

WAY MAKER, MIRACE WORKER,
PROMISE KEEPER, LIGHT IN THE DARKNESS
MY GOD, THAT IS WHO YOU ARE
YOU ARE HERE, WORKING IN THIS PLACE
I WORSHIP YOU
YOU ARE HERE, MOVING IN OUR MIDST
I WORSHIP YOU

LINK: https://youtu.be/n4XWfwLHeLM

HOSSANA, HOSSANA IN THE HIGHEST

HOSSANA, HOSSANA, HOSSAN IN THE HIGHEST
HOSSANA, HOSSANA, HOSSAN IN THE HIGHEST
LORD WE LIGT UP YOUR NAME
WITH THE HEAT FULL OF PRAISE
BE EXALTED OH LORD MY GOD
HOSSANA IN THE HIGHEST

LINK: https://youtu.be/E1X-VDCMyAc

JESUS YOU ARE MY FIRM FOUNDATION

JESUS, YOU'RE MY FIRM FOUNDATION, I KNOW I CAN STAND SECURE;
JESUS, YOU'RE MY FIRM FOUNDATION, I PUT MY HOPE IN YOUR HOLY WORD,
I PUT MY HOPE IN YOUR HOLY WORD.
I HAVE A LIVING HOPE, I HAVE A FUTURE;
GOD HAS A PLAN FOR ME, OF THIS I'M SURE(2X)

LINK: https://youtu.be/KVPsW4csPs0

WE WANNA SEE JESUS LIFTED HIGH

WE WANNA SEE JESUS LIFTED HIGH
THE BANNER THAT FLIES ACROSS THE LAND
THAT ALL MEN MIGHT SEE THE TRUTH AND KNOW
HE IS THE WAYTO HEAVEN
WE WANT TO SEE, WE WANT TO SEE
WE WANT TO SEE JESIS LIFTED HIGH
STEP BY STEP WE ARE MOVING FORWARD
LITTLE BY LITTLE WE ARE TAKING GROUND
EVERY PRAYER A POWERFUL WEAPON
STRONGHOLDS COME TUMBLING DOWN AND
DOWN AND DOWN AND DOWN

LINK: https://youtu.be/Glqypn3a9XE

WATER YOU TURN INTO WINE

WATER YOU TURNED INTO WINE, OPENED THE EYES OF THE BLIND
THERE'S NO ONE LIKE YOU, NONE LIKE YOU
INTO THE DARKNESS YOU SHINE, OUT OF THE ASHES
WE RISE, THERE'S NO ONE LIKE YOU, NONE LIKE YOU
OUR GOD IS GREATER, OUR GOD IS STRONGER
GOD YOU ARE HIGHER THAN ANY OTHER
OUR GOD IS HEALER, AWESOME IN POWER OUR GOD, OUR GOD

LINK https://youtu.be/NJpt1hSYf2o

YES LORD, YES LORD, AMEN, (AM TRADING)

I'M TRADING MY SORROWS
I'M TRADING MY SHAME
I'M LAYING THEM DOWM
FOR THE JOY OF THE LORD
I'M TRADING MY SICKNESS
I'M TRADING MY PAIN
I'M LAYING THEM DOWM
FOR THE JOY OF THE LORD
YES LORD, YES LORD x3
YES, YES LORD

LINK: https://youtu.be/YYRc0JeQuC0

CONTEMPORARY PRAISE AND WORSHIP - SET 19

WORSHIP-:

WE BOW DOWN AND WORSHIP, YAHWEH

PRAISE-:

1. EVERY PRAISE IS TO OUR GOD
2. CREATOR OF THE UNIVERSE
3. OH, OH, OH, GLORY TO YOUR NAME, WE SHOUT IT LOUD
4. HOLY ARE YOU LORD; ALL CREATION CALLS YOU
5. LORD YOU ARE GOOD AND YOUR MERCY ENDURES FOREVER

WORSHIP & PRAISE LYRICS

WE BOW DOWN AND WORSHIP, YAHWEH

WE BOW DOWN AND WORSHIP, YAHWEH
YAHWEH, YAHWEH, YAHWEH
YAHWEH, YAHWEH, YAHWEH
WE BOW DOWN AND WORSHIP, YAHWEH
WE BOW DOWN AND WORSHIP, YAHWEH

LINK: https://youtu.be/oGQXKoZB5Bw

EVERY PRAISE TO OUR GOD

EVERY PRAISE IS TO OUR GOD
EVERY WORD OF WORSHIP, WITH ONE ACCORD
EVERY PRAISE, EVERY PRAISE
IS TO OUR GOD
SING HALLELUJAH TO OUR GOD
GLORY HALLELUJAH IS DUE OUR GOD
EVERY PRAISE, EVERY PRAISE, IS TO OUR GOD

LINK: https://youtu.be/X48B8AbkmbA

CREATOR OF THE UNIVERSE

CREATOR OF THE UNIVERSE WHAT CANT YOU DO
WHAT CAN'T YOU DO WHAT CAN'T YOU DO
WHAT CAN'T YOU DO JESUS, NAME ABOVE EVERY
NAME ABOVE EVERY OTHER NAME EVERY OTHER NAME
WHAT CAN'T YOU CHANGE, WHAT CAN'T YOU CHANGE JESUS
LIFT YOUR HANDS AND SAY YOU'RE ABLE
YOU ARE ABLE GREAT AND MIGHTY GREAT AND MIGHTY GOD
YOU'RE ABLE JESUS

LINK: https://youtu.be/HPqDaKajSnQ

OOO GLORY TO YOUR NAME (SHOUT IT LORD)

I WILL SING OF YOUR MERCY AND YOUR LOVE
OF GOODNESS AND TOUR GRACE
HALLELUJAH
OH, OH, OH, GLORY TO YOUR NAME
I SHOUT IT LOUD, GLORY TO YOUR NAME x2

LINK: https://youtu.be/69q_xxMfleQ

HOLY ARE YOU LORD (AWESOME GOD)

HOLY ARE YOU LORD
ALL CREATION CALL YOU GOD
WORTHY IS YOUR NAME, WE WORSHIP YOUR MAJESTY
AWESOME GOD, HOW GREAT THOU ART
YOU ARE GOD, MIGHTY ARE YOUR MIRACLES
WE STAND IN AWE OF YOUR HOLY NAME
LORD, WE BOW DOWN AND WORSHIP YOU

LINK: https://youtu.be/qnLvi392hhE

LORD YOU ARE GOOD AND YOUR MERCY

LORD YOU ARE GOOD AND YOUR MERCY
ENDURETH FOREVER x2
PEOPLE FROM EVERY NATION AND TONGUE
FROM GENERATION TO GENERATION
WE WORSHIP YOU, HALLELUJAH, HALLELUJAH
WE WORSHIP YOU FOR WHO YOU ARE

LINK: https://youtu.be/708opj5poOc

COMTEMPORARY: PRAISE AND WORSHIP - SET 20

WORSHIP-:

JEHOVAH IS YOUR NAME

PRAISE-:

1. WE WANNA SEE JESUS LIFTED HIGH
2. OPEN THE EYES OF MY HEART
3. GOD IS ABLE TO DO JUST WHAT HE SAYS HE WOULD DO
4. HOLY ARE YOU LORD, ALL CREATION CALL YOU LORD
5. OOO GLORY TO YOUR NAME (SHOUT IT LORD)

WORSHIP & PRAISE LYRICS

JEHOVAH IS YOUR NAME

JEHOVAH IS YOUR NAME
JEHOVAH IS YOUR NAME
MIGHTY WARROIR
GREAT IN BATTLE
JEHOVAH IS YOUR NAME

LINK: https://youtu.be/Ro9KtH6cSVU

WE WANNA SEE JESUS LIFTED HIGH

WE WANNA SEE JESUS LIFTED HIGH
THE BANNER THAT FLIES ACROSS THE LAND
THAT ALL MEN MIGHT SEE THE TRUTH AND KNOW
HE IS THE WAY TO HEAVEN
WE WANT TO SEE, WE WANT TO SEE
WE WANT TO SEE JESIS LIFTED HIGH
STEP BY STEP WE ARE MOVING FORWARD
LITTLE BY LITTLE WE ARE TAKING GROUND
EVERY PRAYER A POWERFUL WEAPON
STRONGHOLDS COME TUMBLING DOWN AND DOWN AND DOWN AND DOWN

LINK: https://youtu.be/Glqypn3a9XE

OPEN THE EYES OF MY HEART LORD

OPEN THE EYES OF MY HEART, LORD
OPEN THE EYES OF MY HEART, I WANT TO SEE YOU
TO SEE YOU HIGH AND LIFTED UP
SHININ' IN THE LIGHT OF YOUR GLORY
POUR OUT YOUR POWER AND LOVE
AS WE SING HOLY, HOLY, HOLY

LINK: https://youtu.be/fadU7b9aa78

GOD IS ABLE TO DO JUST WHAT HE SAYS

GOD IS ABLE TO DO
JUST WHAT HE SAID HE WOULD DO
HE'S GONNA FLLFILL EVERY PROMISE TO YOU
DON'T GIVE UP ON GOD
CAUSE HE WON'T GIVE UP ON YOU
HE'S ABLE
HE'S ABLE
OH, OH, OH, OH, OH, OH,
HE'S ABLE

LINK: https://youtu.be/KLpO6ZndW2o

HOLY ARE YOU LORD (AWESOME GOD)

HOLY ARE YOU LORD
ALL CREATION CALL YOU GOD
WORTHY IS YOUR NAME, WE WORSHIP YOUR MAJESTY
AWESOME GOD, HOW GREAT THOU ART
YOU ARE GOD, MIGHTY ARE YOUR MIRACLES
WE STAND IN AWE OF YOUR HOLY NAME
LORD, WE BOW DOWN AND WORSHIP YOU

LINK: https://youtu.be/qnLvi392hhE

OOO GLORY TO YOUR NAME (SHOUT IT LORD)

I WILL SING OF YOUR MERCY AND YOUR LOVE
OF GOODNESS AND TOUR GRACE
HALLELUJAH
OH, OH, OH, GLORY TO YOUR NAME
I SHOUT IT LOUD, GLORY TO YOUR NAME x2

LINK: https://youtu.be/69q_xxMfleQ

CONTEMPORARY: PRAISE AND WORSHIP - SET 21

WORSHIP-:

THE STEADFAST LOVE OF THE LORD NEVER CEASES

PRAISE-:

1. THE LORD REIGNS, LET THE EARTH REJOICE
2. PRAISE YE THE LORD OH MY SOUL
3. CASTING CROWN, LIFTING HAND
4. CREATOR OF THE UNIVERSE
5. OOO GLORY TO YOUR NAME (SHOUT IT LORD)

WORSHIP & PRAISE LYRICS

THE STEADFAST LOVE OF THE LORD NEVER CEASES

THE STEADFAST LOVE OF THE LORD NEVER CEASES
HIS MERCIES NEVER COME TO AN END
THEY ARE NEW EVERY MORNING
NEW EVERY MORNING
GREAT ISTHY FAITHFULNESS, OH LORD
GREAT IS THY FAITHFULNESS

LINK: https://youtu.be/G3zbp6BU1S0

THE LORD REIGNS, LET THE EARTH REJOICE

THE LORD REIGNS., THE LORD REIGNS.
THE LORD REIGNS.MLET THE EARTH REJOICE.
LET THE EARTH REJOICE., LET THE EARTH REJOICE.
LET THE PEOPLE BE GLAD, THAT OUR GOD REIGNS

LINK: https://youtu.be/aAgVvh2WgMM

PRAISE YE THE LORD OF MY SOUL

THIS IS THE DAY HE HAS MADE
HALLELUJAH
HALLELUJAJ
PRAISE YE THE LORD

LINK: https://youtu.be/n5bCj5VetwI

CASTING CROWNS

CASTING CROWNS, LIFTING HANDS
BOWING HEARTS, IS ALL WE'VE COME TO DO
ADONAI, ADONAI, ADONAI, YOU REIGN ON HIGH
WE WILL RISE, IN YOUR NAME, ADONAI, YOU REIGN ON HIGH

LINK: https://youtu.be/2P-FIceZlDo

CREATOR OF THE UNIVERSE

CREATOR OF THE UNIVERSE WHAT CANT YOU DO
WHAT CAN'T YOU DO WHAT CAN'T YOU DO
WHAT CAN'T YOU DO JESUS, NAME ABOVE EVERY
NAME ABOVE EVERY OTHER NAME EVERY OTHER NAME
WHAT CAN'T YOU CHANGE, WHAT CAN'T YOU CHANGE JESUS
LIFT YOUR HANDS AND SAY YOU'RE ABLE
YOU ARE ABLE GREAT AND MIGHTY GREAT AND MIGHTY GOD
YOU'RE ABLE JESUS
LINK: https://youtu.be/HPqDaKajSnQ

OOO GLORY TO YOUR NAME (SHOUT IT LORD)

I WILL SING OF YOUR MERCY AND YOUR LOVE
OF GOODNESS AND TOUR GRACE
HALLELUJAH
OH, OH, OH, GLORY TO YOUR NAME
I SHOUT IT LOUD, GLORY TO YOUR NAME x2

LINK: https://youtu.be/69q_xxMfIeQ

CONTEMPORARY: PRAISE AND WORSHIP - SET 22

WORSHIP-:

HOSANNA IN THE HIGHEST

PRAISE-:

1. CREATOR OF THE UNIVERSE
2. BLESSED JESUS, WE COME TO GIVE YOU PRAISE
3. BLESSED BE THE NAME OF THE LORD, BLESSED BE THE LORD
4. WE LIFT OUR HANDS IN THE SACTUARY
5. CELEBRATE JESUS, CELEBRATE

WORSHIP & PRAISE LYRICS

HOSANNA IN THE HIGHEST

HOSANNA IN THE HIGHEST
LET OUR GOD KING BE LIFTED HIGH HOSSANA
JESUS, YOU BE LIFTED HIGHER,
HIGHER, HIGHER, LET OUR KING BE LIFTED HIGH HOSSANA

LINK: https://youtu.be/sZ6utGRrsX4

CREATOR OF THE UNIVERSE

CREATOR OF THE UNIVERSE WHAT CANT YOU DO
WHAT CAN'T YOU DO WHAT CAN'T YOU DO
WHAT CAN'T YOU DO JESUS, NAME ABOVE EVERY
NAME ABOVE EVERY OTHER NAME EVERY OTHER NAME
WHAT CAN'T YOU CHANGE, WHAT CAN'T YOU CHANGE JESUS
LIFT YOUR HANDS AND SAY YOU'RE ABLE
YOU ARE ABLE GREAT AND MIGHTY GREAT AND MIGHTY GOD
YOU'RE ABLE JESUS

LINK: https://youtu.be/HPqDaKajSnQ

BLESSED JESUS WE'VE COME TO GIVE PRAISE

BLESSED JESUS
WE'VE COME TO GIVE PRAISE
YOU SRE WORTHY
AND BLESSED BE YOUR NAME
WE LOVE YOU LORD
WE LOVE YOU LORD

LINK: https://youtu.be/tHQxyREYj-c

BLESSED BE THE NAME OF THE LORD

BLESSED BE THE NAME OF THE LORD x2
BLESSED BE THE NAME OF THE LORD, MOST HIGH
THE NAME OF THE LORD IS, A STRONG TOWER
THE RIGHTEOUS RUN INTO IT AND THEY ARE SAVED
THE NAME OF THE LORD IS, A STRONG TOWER
THE RIGHTEOUS RUN INTO IT AND THEY ARE SAVED

LINK: https://youtu.be/bYrcrP1ysjw

WE LIFT OUR HANDS IN THE SANCTURARY

WE LIFT OUR HANDS IN THE SANCTURARY
WE LIFT OUR HANDS TO GIVE THE GLORY
WE LIFT OUR HANDS TO GIVE THE PRAISE
AND WE WILL PRAISE YOU FOR THE REST OF OUR DAYS
YES, WE WILL PRAISE YOU FOR THE REST OF OUR DAYS

LINK: https://youtu.be/iv68ruS6DVE

CELEBRATE JESUS, CELEBRATE

CELEBRATE JESUS, CELEBRATE x 3
HE IS RISEN, HE IS RISEN
AND HE LIVES FORVERMORE
HE IS RISEN, HE IS RISEN
COME ON AND CELEBRATE
THE RESURRECTION OF THE LORD

LINK: https://youtu.be/LQobUwL1aJ0

CONTEMPORARY: PRAISE AND WORSHIP - SET 23

WORSHIP-:

CASTING CROWN, LIFTING HANDS

PRAISE-:

1. HALLELUJAH FOR THE LORD OUR GOD, THE ALMIGHTY REIGNS
2. BLESSED JESUS, WE'VE COME TO GIVE PRAISE
3. OPEN THE EYES OF MY HEART LORD
4. WE WANNA SEE JESUS LIFTED HIGH
5. EVERY PRAISE TO OUR GOD

WORSHIP & PRAISE LYRICS

CASTING CROWNS

CASTING CROWNS, LIFTING HANDS
BOWING HEARTS, IS ALL WE'VE COME TO DO
ADONAI, ADONAI, ADONAI, YOU REIGN ON HIGH
WE WILL RISE, IN YOUR NAME, ADONAI, YOU REIGN ON HIGH

LINK: https://youtu.be/2P-FIceZIDo

HALLELUJAH FOR THE LORD OUR GOD THE ALMIGHTY REIGNS

HALLELUJAH, HALLELUJAH
FOR THE LORD OUR GOD THE ALMIGHTY REIGNS
HALLELUJAH, HALLELUJAH
FOR THE LORD OUR GOD THE ALMIGHTY REIGNS
HOSSANA HALLELUJAH x3

LINK: https://youtu.be/HRPtXuFpV9U

BLESSED JESUS WE'VE COME TO GIVE PRAISE

BLESSED JESUS
WE'VE COME TO GIVE PRAISE
YOU SRE WORTHY
AND BLESSED BE YOUR NAME
WE LOVE YOU LORD
WE LOVE YOU LORD

LINK: https://youtu.be/tHQxyREYj-c

OPEN THE EYES OF MY HEART LORD

OPEN THE EYES OF MY HEART, LORD
OPEN THE EYES OF MY HEART, I WANT TO SEE YOU
TO SEE YOU HIGH AND LIFTED UP
SHININ' IN THE LIGHT OF YOUR GLORY
POUR OUT YOUR POWER AND LOVE
AS WE SING HOLY, HOLY, HOLY

LINK: https://youtu.be/fadU7b9aa78

WE WANNA SEE JESUS LIFTED HIGH

WE WANNA SEE JESUS LIFTED HIGH
THE BANNER THAT FLIES ACROSS THE LAND
THAT ALL MEN MIGHT SEE THE TRUTH AND KNOW
HE IS THE WAY TO HEAVEN
WE WANT TO SEE, WE WANT TO SEE
WE WANT TO SEE JESIS LIFTED HIGH
STEP BY STEP WE ARE MOVING FORWARD
LITTLE BY LITTLE WE ARE TAKING GROUND
EVERY PRAYER A POWERFUL WEAPON
STRONGHOLDS COME TUMBLING DOWN AND DOWN AND DOWN AND DOWN
LINK: https://youtu.be/Glqypn3a9XE

EVERY PRAISE TO OUR GOD

EVERY PRAISE IS TO OUR GOD
EVERY WORD OF WORSHIP, WITH ONE ACCORD
EVERY PRAISE, EVERY PRAISE
IS TO OUR GOD
SING HALLELUJAH TO OUR GOD
GLORY HALLELUJAH IS DUE OUR GOD
EVERY PRAISE, EVERY PRAISE, IS TO OUR GOD

LINK: https://youtu.be/X48B8AbkmbA

COMTEMPORAY: PRAISE AND WORSHIP – SET 24

WORSHIP-:

YOU DESERVE THE GLORY AND THE HONOUR

PRAISE-:

1. ARISE, ARISE, ARISE
2. EVERY PRAISE TO OUR GOD
3. HOSSANA, HOSSANA IN THE HIGHEST
4. HE IS THE LORD AND HE REIGNS ON HIGH (SHOW YOUR POWER)
5. WATER HE TURNED INTO WINE

WORSHIP & PRAISE LYRICS

YOU DESERVE THE GLORY AND THE HONOUR

YOU DESERVE THE GLORY AND THE HONOUR
AND WE LIFT OUR HANDS IN WORSHIP
AS WE PRAISE YOUR HOLY NAME
YOU DESERVE THE GLORY AND THE HONOUR
AND WE LIFT OUR HANDS IN WORSHIP
AS WE PRAISE YOUR HOLY NAME

LINK: https://youtu.be/LLseRHq-dA0

ARISE, ARISE, ARISE

ONE THING WE ASK OF YOU, ONE THING THAT WE DESIRE
THAT AS WE WORSHIP YOU, LORD COME AND CHANGE
OUR LIVES
SO, ARISE, ARISE, ARISE, ARISE, TAKE YOUR
PLACEBE ENTHRONED ON OUR PRAISE, ARISE
KING OF KINGS, HOLY GOD, AS WE SING ARISE
ARISE, ARISE, ARISE

LINK: https://youtu.be/RFoe8ZgNZEI

EVERY PRAISE TO OUR GOD

EVERY PRAISE IS TO OUR GOD
EVERY WORD OF WORSHIP, WITH ONE ACCORD
EVERY PRAISE, EVERY PRAISE
IS TO OUR GOD
SING HALLELUJAH TO OUR GOD
GLORY HALLELUJAH IS DUE OUR GOD
EVERY PRAISE, EVERY PRAISE, IS TO OUR GOD

LINK: https://youtu.be/X48B8AbkmbA

HOSSANA, HOSSANA IN THE HIGHEST

HOSSANA, HOSSANA, HOSSAN IN THE HIGHEST
HOSSANA, HOSSANA, HOSSAN IN THE HIGHEST
LORD WE LIGT UP YOUR NAME
WITH THE HEAT FULL OF PRAISE
BE EXALTED OH LORD MY GOD
HOSSANA IN THE HIGHEST

LINK: https://youtu.be/E1X-VDCMyAc

HE IS THE LORD AND HE REIGNS ON HIGH

HE IS THE LORD AND HE REIGNS ON HIGH
HE IS THE LORD
SPOKE INTO THE DARKNESS, CREATED THE LIGHT
HE IS THE LORD
WHO IS LIKE UNTO HIM, NEVER ENDING IN DAYS
HE IS THE LORD
AND HE OME IN POWER WHEN WE CALL ON HIS NAME
HE IS THE LORD
SHOW YOU POWER, OH LORD OUR GOD
SHOW YOU POWER, OH LORD OUR GOD, OUR GOD

LINK: https://youtu.be/9EMHkcJWA6A

WATER YOU TURN INTO WINE

WATER YOU TURNED INTO WINE, OPENED THE EYES OF THE BLIND
THERE'S NO ONE LIKE YOU, NONE LIKE YOU
INTO THE DARKNESS YOU SHINE, OUT OF THE
ASHES WE RISE, THERE'S NO ONE LIKE YOU, NONE LIKE YOU
OUR GOD IS GREATER, OUR GOD IS STRONGER
GOD YOU ARE HIGHER THAN ANY OTHER
OUR GOD IS HEALER, AWESOME IN POWER OUR GOD, OUR GOD

LINK: https://youtu.be/NJpt1hSYf2o

COMTEMPORARY: PRAISE AND WORSHIP – SET 25

WORSHIP-:

YOU ALONE DESERVE MY WORSHIP, YAWEH

PRAISE-:

1. HE IS THE LORD AND HE REIGNS ON HIGH (SHOW YOUR POWER)
2. BLESSED JESUS WE'VE COME TO GIVE YOU PRAISE
3. BLESSED BE THE NAME OF THE LORD (THE NAME OF THE LORD IS A STRONG TOWER)
4. YES LORD, YES LORD AMEN (AM TRADING)
5. WHEN YOU CALL TO HIM (OH SING FOR JOY)

WORSHIP & PRAISE LYRICS

YOU ALONE DESERVE MY WORSHIP, YAWEH

YOU ALONE DESERVE MY WORSHIP
YOU ALONE DESERVE MY PRIASE
AND YOU ALONE DESERVE THE HONOUR
SO, WE LIFT YOU HIGH
YAHWEH, YAHWEH
WE LIFT YOU HIGH
YAHWEH, YAHWEH
WE LIFT YOU HIGH
YAHWEH, YAHWEH
LINK: https://youtu.be/akl3NbWHsdw

HE IS THE LORD AND HE REIGNS ON HIGH

HE IS THE LORD AND HE REIGNS ON HIGH
HE IS THE LORD
SPOKE INTO THE DARKNESS, CREATED THE LIGHT
HE IS THE LORD
WHO IS LIKE UNTO HIM, NEVER ENDING IN DAYS
HE IS THE LORD
AND HE OME IN POWER WHEN WE CALL ON HIS NAME
HE IS THE LORD
SHOW YOU POWER, OH LORD OUR GOD
SHOW YOU POWER, OH LORD OUR GOD, OUR GOD
LINK: https://youtu.be/9EMHkcJWA6A

BLESSED JESUS WE'VE COME TO GIVE PRAISE

BLESSED JESUS
WE'VE COME TO GIVE PRAISE
YOU SRE WORTHY
AND BLESSED BE YOUR NAME
WE LOVE YOU LORD
WE LOVE YOU LORD

LINK: https://youtu.be/tHQxyREYj-c

BLESSED BE THE NAME OF THE LORD

BLESSED BE THE NAME OF THE LORD x2
BLESSED BE THE NAME OF THE LORD, MOST HIGH
THE NAME OF THE LORD IS, A STRONG TOWER
THE RIGHTEOUS RUN INTO IT AND THEY ARE SAVED
THE NAME OF THE LORD IS, A STRONG TOWER
THE RIGHTEOUS RUN INTO IT AND THEY ARE SAVED

LINK: https://youtu.be/bYrcrP1ysjw

YES LORD, YES LORD, AMEN, (AM TRADING)

I'M TRADING MY SORROWS
I'M TRADING MY SHAME
I'M LAYING THEM DOWM
FOR THE JOY OF THE LORD
I'M TRADING MY SICKNESS
I'M TRADING MY PAIN
I'M LAYING THEM DOWM
FOR THE JOY OF THE LORD
YES LORD, YES LORD x3
YES, YES LORD
LINK: https://youtu.be/YYRc0JeQuC0

IF YOU CALL TO HIM (OH SING FOR JOY)

IF WE CALL TO HIM, HE WILL ANSWER US
IF WE RUN TO HIM, HE WILL RUN TO US
IF WE LIFT OUR HANDS, HE WILL LIFT US UP
COME NOW PRAISE HIS NAME, ALL YOU SAINTS OF GOD.
OH, SING FOR JOY TO GOD OUR STRENGTH (2X)

LINK: https://youtu.be/Dd6QploIXFc

COMTEMPORAY: PRAISE AND WORSHIP – SET 26

WORSHIP-:

HALLELUJAH, YOU HAVE WON THE VICTORY

PRAISE-:

1. I KNOW HE RESCUED MY SOUL.
2. I SEARCHED ALL OVER
3. PRAISE YE THE LORD OH MY SOUL
4. JESUS YOU ARE MY FIRM FOUNDATION
5. CREATOR OF THE UNIVERSE

WORSHIP & PRAISE LYRICS

HALLELUJAH, YOU HAVE WON THE VICTORY

HALLELUJAH, YOU HAVE WON THE VICTORY
HALLELUJAH, YOU HAVE WON IT ALL FOR ME
DEATH COULD NOT HOLD YOU DOWN
YOU ARE THE RISEN KING
SEATED IN MAJESTY
YOU ARE THE RISEN KING

LINK: https://youtu.be/w3wBpKVugqg

I KNOW YOU RESCUED MY SOUL

I KNOW HE RESCUED MY SOUL; HIS BLOOD HAS COVERED MY SIN
I BELIEVE, I BELIEVE, MY SHAME, HE'S TAKEN AWAY
MY PAIN IS HEALED IN HIS NAME, I BELIEVE, I BELIEVE,
I'LL RAISE A BANNER 'CAUSE MY LORD HAS CONQUERED THE GRAVE
MY REDEEMER LIVES (4X)

LINK: https://youtu.be/3glYEDzSyok

I SEARCHED ALL OVER

SEARCHED ALL OVER, COULDN'T FIND NOBODY
I LOOKED HIGH AND LOW, STILL COULDN'T FIND NOBODY
NOBODY GREATER, NOBODY GREATER
NOBODY GREATER THAN YOU
NOBODY GREATER, NOBODY GREATER JESUS
NOBODY GREATER THAN YOU
NOBODY GREATER, NOBODY GREATER NO
NOBODY GREATER THAN YOU

LINK: https://youtu.be/9QSbqSuwwx0

PRAISE YE THE LORD OF MY SOUL

THIS IS THE DAY HE HAS MADE
HALLELUJAH
HALLELUJAJ
PRAISE YE THE LORD

LINK: https://youtu.be/n5bCj5VetwI

JESUS YOU ARE MY FIRM FOUNDATION

JESUS, YOU'RE MY FIRM FOUNDATION, I KNOW I CAN STAND SECURE;
JESUS, YOU'RE MY FIRM FOUNDATION, I PUT MY HOPE IN YOUR HOLY WORD,
I PUT MY HOPE IN YOUR HOLY WORD.
I HAVE A LIVING HOPE, I HAVE A FUTURE;
GOD HAS A PLAN FOR ME, OF THIS I'M SURE(2X)

LINK: https://youtu.be/KVPsW4csPs0

CREATOR OF THE UNIVERSE

CREATOR OF THE UNIVERSE WHAT CANT YOU DO
WHAT CAN'T YOU DO WHAT CAN'T YOU DO
WHAT CAN'T YOU DO JESUS, NAME ABOVE EVERY
NAME ABOVE EVERY OTHER NAME EVERY OTHER NAME
WHAT CAN'T YOU CHANGE, WHAT CAN'T YOU CHANGE JESUS
LIFT YOUR HANDS AND SAY YOU'RE ABLE
YOU ARE ABLE GREAT AND MIGHTY GREAT AND MIGHTY GOD
YOU'RE ABLE JESUS

LINK: https://youtu.be/HPqDaKajSnQ

COMTEMPORAY: PRAISE AND WORSHIP – SET 27

WORSHIP-:

BOW DOWN AND WORSHIP HIM, COMSUMING FIRE SWEEAT PERFUME

PRAISE-:

1. YES LORD, YES LORD AMEN (I AM TRADING)
2. GOD IS ABLE TO DO JUST WHAT HE SAYS HE WILL DO
3. OOO GLORY TO YOUR NAME I SOUT IT LOUD
4. HALLELUJAH FOR THE LORD OUR GOD THE ALMIGHTY REIGN
5. ARISE, ARISE, ARISE

WORSHIP & PRAISE LYRICS

BOW DOWN AND WORSHIP HIM, CONSUMING

BOW DOWN AND WORSHIP HIM
WORSHIP HIM
OH, WORSHIP HIM
COMSUMING FIRE SWEEAT PERFUME
BOW DOWN AND WORSHIP HIM
ENTER IN
OH, ENTER IN x2
CONSUMING FIRE, SWEET PERFUME
HIS AWESOME PRESENCE FILLS THIS ROOM
THIS IS HOLY GROUND x3
SO COME AND BOW DOWN
LINK: https://youtu.be/sUFExff_7hk

YES LORD, YES LORD, AMEN, (AM TRADING)

I'M TRADING MY SORROWS
I'M TRADING MY SHAME
I'M LAYING THEM DOWM
FOR THE JOY OF THE LORD
I'M TRADING MY SICKNESS
I'M TRADING MY PAIN
I'M LAYING THEM DOWM
FOR THE JOY OF THE LORD
YES LORD, YES LORD x3
YES, YES LORD
LINK: https://youtu.be/YYRc0JeQuC0

GOD IS ABLE TO DO JUST WHAT HE SAYS HE WILL

GOD IS ABLE TO DO
JUST WHAT HE SAID HE WOULD DO
HE'S GONNA FLLFILL EVERY PROMISE TO YOU
DON'T GIVE UP ON GOD
CAUSE HE WON'T GIVE UP ON YOU
HE'S ABLE
HE'S ABLE
OH, OH, OH, OH, OH, OH,
HE'S ABLE
LINK: https://youtu.be/KLpO6ZndW2o

OOO GLORY TO YOUR NAME (SHOUT IT LORD)

I WILL SING OF YOUR MERCY AND YOUR LOVE
OF GOODNESS AND TOUR GRACE
HALLELUJAH
OH, OH, OH, GLORY TO YOUR NAME
I SHOUT IT LOUD, GLORY TO YOUR NAME x2

LINK: https://youtu.be/69q_xxMfleQ

HALLELUJAH FOR THE LORD OUR GOD THE ALMIGHTY REIGNS

HALLELUJAH, HALLELUJAH
FOR THE LORD OUR GOD THE ALMIGHTY REIGNS
HALLELUJAH, HALLELUJAH
FOR THE LORD OUR GOD THE ALMIGHTY REIGNS
HOSSANA HALLELUJAH x3

LINK: https://youtu.be/HRPtXuFpV9U

ARISE, ARISE, ARISE

ONE THING WE ASK OF YOU, ONE THING THAT WE DESIRE
THAT AS WE WORSHIP YOU, LORD COME AND CHANGE OUR LIVES
SO, ARISE, ARISE, ARISE, ARISE, TAKE YOUR PLACEBE ENTHRONED ON OUR PRAISE, ARISE
KING OF KINGS, HOLY GOD, AS WE SING ARISE
ARISE, ARISE, ARISE

LINK: https://youtu.be/RFoe8ZgNZEI

COMTEMPORARY: PRAISE AND WORSHIP – SET 28

WORSHIP-:

YOU ALONE DESERVE MY WORSHIP, YAWEH

PRAISE-:

1. EVERY PRAISE TO OUR GOD
2. CREATOR OF THE UNIVERSE
3. HE IS THE LORD AND HE REIGNS ON HIGH, HE IS THE LORD
4. TAKE ALL THE PRAISE, I HAVE COME TO SAY THANK
5. OOO GLORY TO YOUR NAME, I SHOUT IT LORD GLORY TO YOUR NAME

WORSHIP & PRAISE LYRICS

YOU ALONE DESERVE MY WORSHIP, YAWEH

YOU ALONE DESERVE MY WORSHIP
YOU ALONE DESERVE MY PRIASE
AND YOU ALONE DESERVE THE HONOUR
SO, WE LIGT YOU HIGH
YAHWEH, YAHWEH
WE LIFT YOU HIGH
YAHWEH, YAHWEH
WE LIFT YOU HIGH
YAHWEH, YAHWEH

LINK: https://youtu.be/akl3NbWHsdw

EVERY PRAISE TO OUR GOD

EVERY PRAISE IS TO OUR GOD
EVERY WORD OF WORSHIP, WITH ONE ACCORD
EVERY PRAISE, EVERY PRAISE
IS TO OUR GOD
SING HALLELUJAH TO OUR GOD
GLORY HALLELUJAH IS DUE OUR GOD
EVERY PRAISE, EVERY PRAISE, IS TO OUR GOD

LINK: https://youtu.be/X48B8AbkmbA

CREATOR OF THE UNIVERSE

CREATOR OF THE UNIVERSE WHAT CANT YOU DO
WHAT CAN'T YOU DO WHAT CAN'T YOU DO
WHAT CAN'T YOU DO JESUS, NAME ABOVE EVERY
NAME ABOVE EVERY OTHER NAME EVERY OTHER NAME
WHAT CAN'T YOU CHANGE, WHAT CAN'T YOU CHANGE JESUS
LIFT YOUR HANDS AND SAY YOU'RE ABLE
YOU ARE ABLE GREAT AND MIGHTY GREAT AND MIGHTY GOD
YOU'RE ABLE JESUS

LINK: https://youtu.be/HPqDaKajSnQ

HE IS THE LORD AND HE REIGNS ON HIGH

HE IS THE LORD AND HE REIGNS ON HIGH
HE IS THE LORD
SPOKE INTO THE DARKNESS, CREATED THE LIGHT
HE IS THE LORD
WHO IS LIKE UNTO HIM, NEVER ENDING IN DAYS
HE IS THE LORD
AND HE OME IN POWER WHEN WE CALL ON HIS NAME
HE IS THE LORD
SHOW YOU POWER, OH LORD OUR GOD
SHOW YOU POWER, OH LORD OUR GOD, OUR GOD

LINK: https://youtu.be/9EMHkcJWA6A

TAKE ALL THE PRAISE

I HAVE COME, TO SAY THANK YOU LORD
I HAVE COME, TO GIVE BACK TO YOU
I HAVE COME, TO SAY THANK YOU LORD
TAKE ALL THE PRAISE x3
TAKE ALL THE PRAISE, YOU DESERVE

LINK: https://youtu.be/07dgTV33pTA

OOO GLORY TO YOUR NAME (SHOUT IT LORD)

I WILL SING OF YOUR MERCY AND YOUR LOVE
OF GOODNESS AND TOUR GRACE
HALLELUJAH
OH, OH, OH, GLORY TO YOUR NAME
I SHOUT IT LOUD, GLORY TO YOUR NAME x2

LINK: https://youtu.be/69q_xxMfleQ

COMTEMPORARY: PRAISE AND WORSHIP – SET 29

WORSHIP-:

HOSANNA IN THE HIGHEST

PRAISE-:

1. THE LORD REIGNS, LET THE EARTH REJOICE
2. BLESSED BE THE NAME OF LORD, (A STRONG TOWER)
3. WE LIFT OUR HANDS IN THE SANCTUARY
4. WE HAVE COME TO YOU THE PRAISE, (TAKE ALL THE PRAISE)
5. EVERY PRAISE TO OUR GOD

WORSHIP & PRAISE LYRICS

HOSANNA IN THE HIGHEST

HOSANNA IN THE HIGHEST
LET OUR GOD KING BE LIFTED HIGH
HOSSANA
JESUS, YOU BE LIFTED HIGHER,
HIGHER, HIGHER, LET OUR KING BE LIFTED HIGH
HOSSANA

LINK: https://youtu.be/sZ6utGRrsX4

THE LORD REIGNS, LET THE EARTH REJOICE

THE LORD REIGNS., THE LORD REIGNS.
THE LORD REIGNS.MLET THE FARTH REJOICE.
LET THE EARTH REJOICE., LET THE EARTH REJOICE.
LET THE PEOPLE BE GLAD, THAT OUR GOD REIGNS

LINK: https://youtu.be/aAgVvh2WgMM

BLESSED BE THE NAME OF THE LORD

BLESSED BE THE NAME OF THE LORD x2
BLESSED BE THE NAME OF THE LORD, MOST HIGH
THE NAME OF THE LORD IS, A STRONG TOWER
THE RIGHTEOUS RUN INTO IT AND THEY ARE SAVED
THE NAME OF THE LORD IS, A STRONG TOWER
THE RIGHTEOUS RUN INTO IT AND THEY ARE SAVED

LINK: https://youtu.be/bYrcrP1ysjw

WE LIFT OUR HANDS IN THE SANCTURARY

WE LIFT OUR HANDS IN THE SANCTUARY
WE LIFT OUR HANDS TO GIVE THE GLORY
WE LIFT OUR HANDS TO GIVE THE PRAISE
AND WE WILL PRAISEYOU FOR THE REST OF OUR DAYS
YES, WE WILL PRAISE YOU FOR THE REST OF OUR DAYS

LINK: https://youtu.be/iv68ruS6DVE

TAKE ALL THE PRAISE

I HAVE COME, TO SAY THANK YOU LORD
I HAVE COME, TO GIVE BACK TO YOU
I HAVE COME, TO SAY THANK YOU LORD
TAKE ALL THE PRAISE x3
TAKE ALL THE PRAISE, YOU DESERVE

LINK: https://youtu.be/07dgTV33pTA

EVERY PRAISE TO OUR GOD

EVERY PRAISE IS TO OUR GOD
EVERY WORD OF WORSHIP, WITH ONE ACCORD
EVERY PRAISE, EVERY PRAISE
IS TO OUR GOD
SING HALLELUJAH TO OUR GOD
GLORY HALLELUJAH IS DUE OUR GOD
EVERY PRAISE, EVERY PRAISE, IS TO OUR GOD

LINK: https://youtu.be/X48B8AbkmbA

COMTEMPORAY: PRAISE AND WORSHIP – SET 30

WORSHIP-:

HOW GREAT IS OUR GOD, SING WITH ME HOW GREAT IS OUR GOD

PRAISE-:

1. EVERY PRAISE TO OUR GOD
2. WATER HE TURNED INTO WINE
3. YES LORD, YES LORD (AM TRADING)
4. WE LIFT OUR HANDS IN THE SANCTURAY
5. HOLY ARE YOU LORD, ALL CREATION CALL YOU LORD

WORSHIP & PRAISE LYRICS

HOW GREAT IS OUR GOD,

HOW GREAT IS OUR GOD, SING WITH ME HOW GREAT IS OUR GOD
ALL WE SEE, HOW GREAT, HOW GREAT IS OUR GOD.
NAME ABOVE ALL NAMES
YOU ARE WORTHY OF OUR PRAISE
MY HEART WILL SING
HOW GREAT IS OU GOD

LINK: https://youtu.be/KBD18rsVJHk

EVERY PRAISE TO OUR GOD

EVERY PRAISE IS TO OUR GOD
EVERY WORD OF WORSHIP, WITH ONE ACCORD
EVERY PRAISE, EVERY PRAISE
IS TO OUR GOD
SING HALLELUJAH TO OUR GOD
GLORY HALLELUJAH IS DUE OUR GOD
EVERY PRAISE, EVERY PRAISE, IS TO OUR GOD

LINK: https://youtu.be/X48B8AbkmbA

WATER YOU TURN INTO WINE

WATER YOU TURNED INTO WINE, OPENED THE EYES OF THE BLIND
THERE'S NO ONE LIKE YOU, NONE LIKE YOU
INTO THE DARKNESS YOU SHINE, OUT OF THE ASHES WE RISE, THERE'S NO ONE LIKE YOU, NONE LIKE YOU
OUR GOD IS GREATER, OUR GOD IS STRONGER
GOD YOU ARE HIGHER THAN ANY OTHER
OUR GOD IS HEALER, AWESOME IN POWER OUR GOD, OUR GOD

LINK: https://youtu.be/NJpt1hSYf2o

YES LORD, YES LORD, AMEN, (AM TRADING)

I'M TRADING MY SORROWS
I'M TRADING MY SHAME
I'M LAYING THEM DOWM
FOR THE JOY OF THE LORD
I'M TRADING MY SICKNESS
I'M TRADING MY PAIN
I'M LAYING THEM DOWM
FOR THE JOY OF THE LORD
YES LORD, YES LORD x3
YES, YES LORD

LINK: https://youtu.be/YYRc0JeQuC0

WE LIFT OUR HANDS IN THE SANCTUARY

WE LIFT OUR HANDS IN THE SANCTUARY
WE LIFT OUR HANDS TO GIVE THE GLORY
WE LIFT OUR HANDS TO GIVE THE PRAISE
AND WE WILL PRAISEYOU FOR THE REST OF OUR DAYS
YES, WE WILL PRAISE YOU FOR THE REST OF OUR DAYS

LINK: https://youtu.be/iv68ruS6DVE

HOLY ARE YOU LORD (AWESOME GOD)

HOLY ARE YOU LORD
ALL CREATION CALL YOU GOD
WORTHY IS YOUR NAME, WE WORSHIP YOUR MAJESTY
AWESOME GOD, HOW GREAT THOU ART
YOU ARE GOD, MIGHTY ARE YOUR MIRACLES
WE STAND IN AWE OF YOUR HOLY NAME
LORD, WE BOW DOWN AND WORSHIP YOU

LINK: https://youtu.be/qnLvi392hhE

CONTEMPORAY: PRAISE AND WORSHIP- SET 31

WORSHIP-:

JEHOVAH, WE PRAISE YOU, JEHOVAH WE PRAISE YOU, WE PRAISE YOUR NAME

PRAISE-:

1. ARISE, ARISE, ARISE
2. YOU ARE MY STRENGTH
3. WATER HE TURNED INTO WINE
4. EVERY PRAISE TO OUR GOD
5. JESUS YOU ARE MY FIRM FOUNDATION

WORSHIP & PRAISE LYRICS

JEHOVAH, WE PRAISE YOU, JEHOVAH WE PRAISE

PRAISE JEHOVAH
LORD GOD ALMIGHTY
PRAISE JEHOVAH
EVERLASTING KING
WE PRAISE YOUR NAME x2
JEHOVAH, WE PRAISE YOU x2
WE PRAISE YOUR NAME x2
JEHOVAH, WE PRAISE YOU
LINK: https://youtu.be/tFnSdhMSeE4

ARISE, ARISE, ARISE

ONE THING WE ASK OF YOU, ONE THING THAT WE DESIRE
THAT AS WE WORSHIP YOU, LORD COME AND CHANGE OUR LIVES
SO, ARISE, ARISE, ARISE, ARISE, ARISE, TAKE YOUR PLACEBE ENTHRONED ON OUR PRAISE, ARISE
KING OF KINGS, HOLY GOD, AS WE SING ARISE
ARISE, ARISE, ARISE

LINK: https://youtu.be/RFoe8ZgNZEI

YOU ARE MY STRENGTH

YOU ARE MY STRENGTH, STRENGTH LIKE NO OTHER, STRENGTH LIKE NO OTHER
REACHES TO ME
YOU ARE MY HOPE, HOPE LIKE NO OTHER
HOPE LIKE NO OTHER, REACHES TO ME
IN THE FULLNESS OF YOUR GRACE
IN THE POWER OF YOUR GRACE
YOU LIFT ME UP, YOU LIFT UP
LINK: https://youtu.be/LA4eKhj-2ic

WATER HE TURNED INTO WINE

WATER HE TURNED INTO WINE , OPENED THE EYES OF THE BLIND
THERE'S NO ONE LIKE YOU, NONE LIKE YOU
INTO THE DARKNESS YOU SHINE, OUT OF THE ASHES WE RISE, THERE'S NO ONE LIKE YOU, NONE LIKE YOU
OUR GOD IS GREATER, OUR GOD IS STRONGER
GOD YOU ARE HIGHER THAN ANY OTHER
OUR GOD IS HEALER, AWESOME IN POWER OUR GOD, OUR GOD
LINK: https://youtu.be/NJpt1hSYf2o

EVERY PRAISE TO OUR GOD

EVERY PRAISE IS TO OUR GOD
EVERY WORD OF WORSHIP, WITH ONE ACCORD
EVERY PRAISE, EVERY PRAISE
IS TO OUR GOD
SING HALLELUJAH TO OUR GOD
GLORY HALLELUJAH IS DUE OUR GOD
EVERY PRAISE, EVERY PRAISE, IS TO OUR GOD

LINK: https://youtu.be/X48B8AbkmbA

JESUS YOU ARE MY FIRM FOUNDATION

JESUS, YOU'RE MY FIRM FOUNDATION, I KNOW I CAN STAND SECURE;
JESUS, YOU'RE MY FIRM FOUNDATION, I PUT MY HOPE IN YOUR HOLY WORD,
I PUT MY HOPE IN YOUR HOLY WORD.
I HAVE A LIVING HOPE, I HAVE A FUTURE;
GOD HAS A PLAN FOR ME, OF THIS I'M SURE(2X)

LINK: https://youtu.be/KVPsW4csPs0

COMTEMPORAY: PRAISE AND WORSHIP – SET 32

WORSHIP-:

BLESS THE LORD OH MY SOUL, WORSHIP HIS HOLY NAME

PRAISE-:

1. YOU ARE MY STRENGTH
2. CREATOR OF UNIVERSE
3. BLESSED JESUS WE'VE COME TO GIVE YOU PRAISE
4. WATER YOU TURNED IN THE WINE
5. I KNOW HE RESCUED MY SOUL

WORSHIP & PRAISE LYRICS

BLESS THE LORD OH MY SOUL

THE SUN COMES UP, IT'S A NEW DAY DAWNING
IS TIME TO SIMG YOUR SONG AGAIN, WHATEVER MAY PASS, AND WHATEVER LIES BEFORE ME, LET ME BE SINGING WHEN THE EVENING COMES
BLESS THE LORD OH MY SOUL
WORSHIP HIS HOLY NAME
SING LIKE NEVER BEFORE, OH MY SOUL
I WORSHIP HIS HOLY NAME
LINK: https://youtu.be/vSxocnIaN0A

YOU ARE MY STRENGTH

YOU ARE MY STREGTH, STRENGTH LIKE NO OTHER
STRENGTH LIKE NO OTHER REACHES TO ME
YOU ARE MY HOPE, HOPE LIKE NO OTHER
HOPE LIKE NO OTHER, REACHES TO ME
IN THE FULLNESS OF YOUR GRACE
IN THE POWER OF YOUR GRACE
YOU LIFT ME UP, YOU LIFT UP
LINK: https://youtu.be/LA4eKhj-2ic

CREATOR OF THE UNIVERSE

CREATOR OF THE UNIVERSE WHAT CANT YOU DO
WHAT CAN'T YOU DO WHAT CAN'T YOU DO
WHAT CAN'T YOU DO JESUS, NAME ABOVE EVERY NAME ABOVE EVERY OTHER NAME EVERY OTHER NAME
WHAT CAN'T YOU CHANGE, WHAT CAN'T YOU CHANGE JESUS
LIFT YOUR HANDS AND SAY YOU'RE ABLE
YOU ARE ABLE GREAT AND MIGHTY GREAT AND MIGHTY GOD
YOU'RE ABLE JESUS
LINK: https://youtu.be/HPqDaKajSnQ

BLESSED JESUS WE'VE COME TO GIVE PRAISE

BLESSED JESUS
WE'VE COME TO GIVE PRAISE
YOU ARE WORTHY
AND BLESSED BE YOUR NAME
WE LOVE YOU LORD
WE LOVE YOU LORD

LINK: https://youtu.be/tHQxyREYj-c

WATER YOU TURN INTO WINE

WATER YOU TURNED INTO WINE, OPENED THE EYES OF THE BLIND
THERE'S NO ONE LIKE YOU, NONE LIKE YOU
INTO THE DARKNESS YOU SHINE, OUT OF THE ASHES WE RISE, THERE'S NO ONE LIKE YOU, NONE LIKE YOU
OUR GOD IS GREATER, OUR GOD IS STRONGER
GOD YOU ARE HIGHER THAN ANY OTHER
OUR GOD IS HEALER, AWESOME IN POWER OUR GOD, OUR GOD
LINK: https://youtu.be/NJpt1hSYf2o

I KNOW YOU RESCUED MY SOUL

I KNOW HE RESCUED MY SOUL; HIS BLOOD HAS COVERED MY SIN
I BELIEVE, I BELIEVE, MY SHAME, HE'S TAKEN AWAY
MY PAIN IS HEALED IN HIS NAME, I BELIEVE, I BELIEVE, I'LL RAISE A BANNER 'CAUSE MY LORD HAS CONQUERED THE GRAVE
MY REDEEMER LIVES (4X)

LINK: https://youtu.be/3gIYEDzSyok

COMTEMPORAY: PRAISE AND WORSHIP – SET 33

WORSHIP-:

MY HEART SINGS

PRAISE-:

1. WE WANNA SEE JESUS LIFTED HIGH
2. OPEN THE EYES OF HEART LORD
3. BLESSED JESUS, WE'VE COME TO GIVE YOU PRAISE
4. HALLELUJAH FOR THE LORD OUR GOD, THE ALMIGHTY REIGNS
5. EVERY PRAISE TO OUR GOD

WORSHIP & PRAISE LYRICS

MY HEART SINGS

HOW COULD I DESCRIBE
A GOD THAT'S INDESCRIBABLE
HOW COULD I EXPLAIN
A LOVE THAT'S UNEXPLAINABLE
I'M AT A LOSS FOR WORDS
OH, OH, OH
MY HEART SINGS
OH, OH, OH

LINK: https://youtu.be/3aAmvXmbX4w

WE WANNA SEE JESUS LIFTED HIGH

WE WANNA SEE JESUS LIFTED HIGH
THE BANNER THAT FLIES ACROSS THE LAND
THAT ALL MEN MIGHT SEE THE TRUTH AND KNOW
HE IS THE WAY TO HEAVEN
WE WANT TO SEE, WE WANT TO SEE
WE WANT TO SEE JESIS LIFTED HIGH
STEP BY STEP WE ARE MOVING FORWARD
LITTLE BY LITTLE WE ARE TAKING GROUND
EVERY PRAYER A POWERFUL WEAPON
STRONGHOLDS COME TUMBLING DOWN AND DOWN AND DOWN AND DOWN

LINK: https://youtu.be/Glqypn3a9XE

OPEN THE EYES OF MY HEART LORD

OPEN THE EYES OF MY HEART, LORD
OPEN THE EYES OF MY HEART, I WANT TO SEE YOU
TO SEE YOU HIGH AND LIFTED UP
SHININ' IN THE LIGHT OF YOUR GLORY
POUR OUT YOUR POWER AND LOVE
AS WE SING HOLY, HOLY, HOLY

LINK: https://youtu.be/fadU7b9aa78

BLESSED JESUS WE'VE COME TO GIVE PRAISE

BLESSED JESUS
WE'VE COME TO GIVE PRAISE
YOU SRE WORTHY
AND BLESSED BE YOUR NAME
WE LOVE YOU LORD
WE LOVE YOU LORD

LINK: https://youtu.be/tHQxyREYj-c

HALLELUJAH FOR THE LORD OUR GOD THE ALMIGHTY REIGNS

HALLELUJAH, HALLELUJAH
FOR THE LORD OUR GOD THE ALMIGHTY REIGNS
HALLELUJAH, HALLELUJAH
FOR THE LORD OUR GOD THE ALMIGHTY REIGNS
HOSSANA HALLELUJAH x3

LINK: https://youtu.be/HRPtXuFpV9U

EVERY PRAISE TO OUR GOD

EVERY PRAISE IS TO OUR GOD
EVERY WORD OF WORSHIP, WITH ONE ACCORD
EVERY PRAISE, EVERY PRAISE
IS TO OUR GOD
SING HALLELUJAH TO OUR GOD
GLORY HALLELUJAH IS DUE OUR GOD
EVERY PRAISE, EVERY PRAISE, IS TO OUR GOD

LINK: https://youtu.be/X48B8AbkmbA

COMTEMPORARY: PRAISE AND WOSHIP – SET 34

WORSHIP-:

JEHOVAH IS YOUR NAME MIGHTY WARRIOR GREAT IN BATTLE

PRAISE-:

1. CREATOR OF THE UNIVERSE
2. HE IS THE LORD AND HE REIGNS ON HIGH
3. ARISE, ARISE, ARISE
4. EVERY PRAISE TO OUR GOD
5. WATER HE TURNED INTO WINE

WORSHIP & PRAISE LYRICS

JEHOVAH IS YOUR NAME

JEHOVAH IS YOUR NAME
JEHOVAH IS YOUR NAME
MIGHTY WARRIOR GREAT IN BATTLE
JEHOVAH IS YOUR NAME
MIGHTY WARRIOR GREAT IN BATTLE
JEHOVAH IS YOUR NAME

LINK: https://youtu.be/Ro9KtH6cSVU

CREATOR OF THE UNIVERSE

CREATOR OF THE UNIVERSE WHAT CANT YOU DO
WHAT CAN'T YOU DO WHAT CAN'T YOU DO
WHAT CAN'T YOU DO JESUS, NAME ABOVE EVERY
NAME ABOVE EVERY OTHER NAME EVERY OTHER NAME
WHAT CAN'T YOU CHANGE, WHAT CAN'T YOU CHANGE JESUS
LIFT YOUR HANDS AND SAY YOU'RE ABLE
YOU ARE ABLE GREAT AND MIGHTY GREAT AND MIGHTY GOD
YOU'RE ABLE JESUS

LINK: https://youtu.be/HPqDaKajSnQ

HE IS THE LORD AND HE REIGNS ON HIGH

HE IS THE LORD AND HE REIGNS ON HIGH
HE IS THE LORD
SPOKE INTO THE DARKNESS, CREATED THE LIGHT
HE IS THE LORD
WHO IS LIKE UNTO HIM, NEVER ENDING IN DAYS
HE IS THE LORD
AND HE OME IN POWER WHEN WE CALL ON HIS NAME
HE IS THE LORD
SHOW YOU POWER, OH LORD OUR GOD
SHOW YOU POWER, OH LORD OUR GOD, OUR GOD

LINK: https://youtu.be/9EMHkcJWA6A

ARISE, ARISE, ARISE

ONE THING WE ASK OF YOU, ONE THING THAT WE DESIRE
THAT AS WE WORSHIP YOU, LORD COME AND
CHANGE OUR LIVES
SO, ARISE, ARISE, ARISE, ARISE, ARISE, TAKE YOUR
PLACEBE ENTHRONED ON OUR PRAISE, ARISE
KING OF KINGS, HOLY GOD, AS WE SING ARISE
ARISE, ARISE, ARISE

LINK: https://youtu.be/RFoe8ZgNZEI

EVERY PRAISE TO OUR GOD

EVERY PRAISE IS TO OUR GOD
EVERY WORD OF WORSHIP, WITH ONE ACCORD
EVERY PRAISE, EVERY PRAISE
IS TO OUR GOD
SING HALLELUJAH TO OUR GOD
GLORY HALLELUJAH IS DUE OUR GOD
EVERY PRAISE, EVERY PRAISE, IS TO OUR GOD

LINK: https://youtu.be/X48B8AbkmbA

WATER YOU TURN INTO WINE

WATER YOU TURNED INTO WINE, OPENED THE EYES OF THE BLIND
THERE'S NO ONE LIKE YOU, NONE LIKE YOU
INTO THE DARKNESS YOU SHINE, OUT OF THE
ASHES WE RISE, THERE'S NO ONE LIKE YOU, NONE LIKE YOU
OUR GOD IS GREATER, OUR GOD IS STRONGER
GOD YOU ARE HIGHER THAN ANY OTHER
OUR GOD IS HEALER, AWESOME IN POWER OUR GOD, OUR GOD

LINK: https://youtu.be/NJpt1hSYf2o

CONTEMPORARY: PRAISE AND WORSHIP - SET 35

WORSHIP-:

YOU REIGN, YOU ANCIENT ZION'S KING, KADOSH, KADOSH

PRAISE-:

1. GOD IS ABLE TO DO JUST WHAT HE SAYS HE WILL DO
2. OPEN THE EYES OF HEART LORD
3. WE WANNA SEE JESUS LIFTED HIGH
4. HOLY ARE LORD ALL CREATION CALL YOU LORD
5. EVERY PAISE TO OUR GOD

WORSHIP & PRAISE LYRICS

YOU REIGN, YOU ANCIENT ZION'S KING

YOU REIGN, YOU ANCIENT ZION'S KING
KADOSH, KADOSH, YOU ARE MIGHTY ON YOUR THRONE
OH SING, OH FOUNTAIN OF THE HILL, I AM
KADOSH, YOU ARE MIGHTY ON YOUR THRONE
REIGN FORTH, OH SPIRIT OF THE HILL, THAT IS
KADOSH, YOU ARE MIGHTY ON YOUR THRONE

LINK: https://youtu.be/lj-S6xk-Q4M

GOD IS ABLE TO DO JUST WHAT HE SAYS HE WILL DO

GOD IS ABLE TO DO
JUST WHAT HE SAID HE WOULD DO
HE'S GONNA FLLFILL EVERY PROMISE TO YOU
DON'T GIVE UP ON GOD
CAUSE HE WON'T GIVE UP ON YOU
HE'S ABLE
HE'S ABLE
OH, OH, OH, OH, OH, OH,
HE'S ABLE

LINK: https://youtu.be/KLpO6ZndW2o

OPEN THE EYES OF MY HEART LORD

OPEN THE EYES OF MY HEART, LORD
OPEN THE EYES OF MY HEART, I WANT TO SEE YOU
TO SEE YOU HIGH AND LIFTED UP
SHININ' IN THE LIGHT OF YOUR GLORY
POUR OUT YOUR POWER AND LOVE
AS WE SING HOLY, HOLY, HOLY

LINK: https://youtu.be/fadU7b9aa78

WE WANNA SEE JESUS LIFTED HIGH

WE WANNA SEE JESUS LIFTED HIGH
THE BANNER THAT FLIES ACROSS THE LAND
THAT ALL MEN MIGHT SEE THE TRUTH AND KNOW
HE IS THE WAY TO HEAVEN
WE WANT TO SEE, WE WANT TO SEE
WE WANT TO SEE JESIS LIFTED HIGH
STEP BY STEP WE ARE MOVING FORWARD
LITTLE BY LITTLE WE ARE TAKING GROUND
EVERY PRAYER A POWERFUL WEAPON
STRONGHOLDS COME TUMBLING DOWN AND
DOWN AND DOWN AND DOWN

LINK: https://youtu.be/Glqypn3a9XE

HOLY ARE YOU LORD (AWESOME GOD)

HOLY ARE YOU LORD
ALL CREATION CALL YOU GOD
WORTHY IS YOUR NAME, WE WORSHIP YOUR MAJESTY
AWESOME GOD, HOW GREAT THOU ART
YOU ARE GOD, MIGHTY ARE YOUR MIRACLES
WE STAND IN AWE OF YOUR HOLY NAME
LORD, WE BOW DOWN AND WORSHIP YOU

LINK: https://youtu.be/qnLvi392hhE

EVERY PRAISE TO OUR GOD

EVERY PRAISE IS TO OUR GOD
EVERY WORD OF WORSHIP, WITH ONE ACCORD
EVERY PRAISE, EVERY PRAISE
IS TO OUR GOD
SING HALLELUJAH TO OUR GOD
GLORY HALLELUJAH IS DUE OUR GOD
EVERY PRAISE, EVERY PRAISE, IS TO OUR GOD

LINK: https://youtu.be/X48B8AbkmbA

CONTEMPORAY: PRAISE AND WORSHIP – SET 36

WORSHIP-:

NOBODY LIKE YOU LORD

PRAISE-:

1. EVERY PRAISE IS TO OUR GOD
2. WATER YOU TURN INTO WINE
3. BLESSED BE THE NAME OF THE LORD (YOU GIVE AND GIVE AGAIN)
4. TAKE ALL THE PRAISE (I HAVE COME)
5. HALLELUJAH FOR THE LORD OUR GOD, THE ALMIGHTY REIGN

WORSHIP & PRAISE LYRICS

NOBODY LIKE YOU LORD

OH, LORD OUR LORD
HOW EXCELLENT IS YOUR NAME
YOUR IS STRENGTH
YOUR NAME IS POWER
A STRONG TOWER, MAKES ME SAFE
OH, OH, OH
NOBODY LIKE LORD
NOBODY LIKE LORD
LINK: https://youtu.be/RqrsMVzjcil

EVERY PRAISE TO OUR GOD

EVERY PRAISE IS TO OUR GOD
EVERY WORD OF WORSHIP, WITH ONE ACCORD
EVERY PRAISE, EVERY PRAISE
IS TO OUR GOD
SING HALLELUJAH TO OUR GOD
GLORY HALLELUJAH IS DUE OUR GOD
EVERY PRAISE, EVERY PRAISE, IS TO OUR GOD
LINK: https://youtu.be/X48B8AbkmbA

WATER YOU TURN INTO WINE

WATER YOU TURNED INTO WINE, OPENED THE EYES
OF THE BLIND
THERE'S NO ONE LIKE YOU, NONE LIKE YOU
INTO THE DARKNESS YOU SHINE, OUT OF THE ASHES
WE RISE, THERE'S NO ONE LIKE YOU, NONE LIKE YOU
OUR GOD IS GREATER, OUR GOD IS STRONGER
GOD YOU ARE HIGHER THAN ANY OTHER
OUR GOD IS HEALER, AWESOME IN POWER OUR GOD, OUR GOD
LINK: https://youtu.be/NJpt1hSYf2o

BLESSED BE THE NAME OF THE LORD

BLESSED BE THE NAME OF THE LORD x2
BLESSED BE THE NAME OF THE LORD, MOST HIGH
THE NAME OF THE LORD IS, A STRONG TOWER
THE RIGHTEOUS RUN INTO IT AND THEY ARE SAVED
THE NAME OF THE LORD IS, A STRONG TOWER
THE RIGHTEOUS RUN INTO IT AND THEY ARE SAVED
LINK: https://youtu.be/bYrcrP1ysjw

TAKE ALL THE PRAISE

I HAVE COME, TO SAY THANK YOU LORD
I HAVE COME, TO GIVE BACK TO YOU
I HAVE COME, TO SAY THANK YOU LORD
TAKE ALL THE PRAISE x3
TAKE ALL THE PRAISE, YOU DESERVE

LINK: https://youtu.be/07dgTV33pTA

HALLELUJAH FOR THE LORD OUR GOD THE ALMIGHTY REIGNS

HALLELUJAH, HALLELUJAH
FOR THE LORD OUR GOD THE ALMIGHTY REIGNS
HALLELUJAH, HALLELUJAH
FOR THE LORD OUR GOD THE ALMIGHTY REIGNS
HOSSANA HALLELUJAH x3

LINK: https://youtu.be/HRPtXuFpV9U

PART B

AFRICAN: PRAISE AND WORSHIP - SET 1

WORSHIP-:

OPEN THE FLOODGATES IN ABUNDANCE

PRAISE-:

1. MY GOD IS A GOOD GOD, YES, HE IS
2. AT THE MENTION OF YOUR NAME
3. LORD YOU ARE SO GOOD, BLESSED BE YOUR NAME
4. THERE IS SOMETHING THAT MAKES ME COME INTO YOUR PRESENCE
5. JEHOVAH, YOU ARE THE MOST HIGH

WORSHIP & PRAISE LYRICS

WE ARE IN YOUR PRESENCE, LET IT RAIN

WE ARE IN YOUR PRESENCE, LET IT RAIN
OHH YOUR RAIN (JESUS), LET IT FALL ON ME
WE ARE IN YOUR PRESENCE, LET IT RAIN
OPEN THE FLOOD GATES IN ABUNDANCE
AND CAUSE YOUR RAIN TO FALL ON ME
BABA OH... OH, BABA OH... OH-OH-OH-OH

LINK: https://youtu.be/63nyGawcJbQ

MY GOD IS A GOOD GOD, YES, HE IS

MY GOD IS A GOOD GOD YES, HE IS
HE LIFTS ME UP (HE LIFTS ME UP)
HE TURNS ME AROUND (HE TURNS ME AROUND)
HE SETS ME FEET, UPON THE SOLID ROCK
I FEEL LIKE DANCING, I FEEL LIKE CLAPPING

LINK: https://youtu.be/5RcwYmVRttA

AT THE MENTION OF YOUR NAME

AT THE MENTION OF YOUR NAME
EVERY KNEE MUST BOW
AT THE MENTION OF YOUR NAME
EVERY TONGUE CONFESS
THAT YOU ARE LORD
YOU ARE LORD, YOU ARE LORD of LORDS
YOU ARE KING, YOU ARE KING OF KINGS

LINK: https://youtu.be/SpIL4YBBHfY

LORD YOU ARE SO GOOD, BLESSED BE YOUR NAME

LORD YOU ARE SO GOOD, BLESSED BE YOUR NAME
LORD YOU ARE SO GOOD, BLESSED BE YOUR NAME
IN HEAVEN YOU ARE THE LORD
ON EARTH YOU REIGN FOREVER
OH LORD HOW GREAT THOU ART
BLESSSED BE YOUR NAME

LINK: https://youtu.be/QhxObPYSWS8

THERE IS SOMETHING THAT MAKES ME COME INTO

THERE IS SOMETHING THAT MAKES ME COME INTO YOUR PRESENCE - MY HELPER
THERE IS SOMETHING THAT MAKES ME COME INTO YOUR PRESENCE - MY HELPER
MY HELPER O MY HELPER (2X)
THERE IS SOMETHING THAT MAKES ME COME INTO YOUR PRESENCE - MY HELPER
LINK: https://youtu.be/mT6B6eoAIug

JEHOVAH, YOU ARE THE MOST HIGH

JEHOVAH, YOU ARE THE MOST HIGH
JEHOVAH, YOU ARE THE MOST HIGH GOD
JEHOVAH, YOU ARE THE MOST HIGH
JEHOVAH, YOU ARE THE MOST HIGH GOD

LINK: https://youtu.be/QPNIsEy7n5M

AFRICAN: PRAISE AND WORSHIP - SET 2

WORSHIP-:

WAY MAKER, MIRACLE WORKER

PRAISE-:

1. HOSANNA, HOSANNA, HOSSANA IN THE HIGHEST
2. MY GOD WHO BEGAN IT
3. HALLELUJAH EH, HALLELUYAH OHH
4. HALLE, HALLE, HALLELUJAH, GLORY, GLORY WE PRAISE YOUR NAME
5. AWESOME GOD, MIGHTY GOD

WORSHIP & PRAISE LYRICS

WAY MAKER

WAY MAKER, MIRACE WORKER,
PROMISE KEEPER, LIGHT IN THE DARKNESS
MY GOD, THAT IS WHO YOU ARE
YOU ARE HERE, WORKING IN THIS PLACE
I WORSHIP YOU
YOU ARE HERE, MOVING IN OUR MIDST
I WORSHIP YOU

LINK: https://youtu.be/n4XWfwLHeLM

HOSANNA, HOSANNA, HOSSANA IN THE HIGHEST

HOSANNA, HOSANNA
HOSANNA, IN THE HIGHEST
LORD, WE LIFT UP YOUR NAME
WE A HEART FULL OF PRAISE,
BE EXALTED, OH LORD MY GOD
HOSANNA IN THE HIGHEST

LINK: https://youtu.be/E1X-VDCMyAc

MY GOD WHO BEGAN IT

MY LORD WHO BEGAN IT, HE WILL ACCOMPLISH IT (2X)
HE'S THE ALPHA AND OMEGA, THE BEGINNING
AND THE END
HE WILL ACCOMPLISH IT, HE WILL ACCOMPLISH IT
MY GOD WHO BEGAN IT, MY GOD WHO BEGAN IT,
HE WILL ACCOMPLISH IT

LINK: https://youtu.be/8aaCWX_f_B0

HALLELUJAH EH HALLELUJAH O OH!

HALLELUJAH EH! HALLELUJAH O OH!
HALLELUJAH EH! IT'S THE SOUND OF VICTORY
HALLELUJAH EH! HALLELUJAH O OH!
LET THE SOUND OF REJOICING FILL THIS HOUSE

LINK: https://youtu.be/BgGkljd7qe4

HALLE, HALLE HALLELUYAH

HALLE HALLE HALLUYAH,
GLORY, GLORY, WE PRAISE YOUR NAME
YOU ARE THE KING OF KINGS AND THE LORD OF LORD,
WE PRAISE YOUR NAME

LINK: https://youtu.be/2NszJzqbNIE

AWESOME GOD, MIGHTY GOD

AWESOME GOD, MIGHTY GOD
AWESOME GOD, MIGHTY GOD
WE GIVE YOU PRAISE, AWESOME GOD
WE GIVE YOU PRAISE, MIGHTY GOD
YOU ARE HIGHLY LIFTED UP, AWESOME GOD
YOU ARE HIGHLY LIFTED UP, MIGHTY GOD

LINK: https://youtu.be/V5dcczS2GsE

AFRICAN: PRAISE AND WORSHIP - SET 3

WORSHIP-:

GLORIOUS GOD, BEAUTIFUL KING, EXCELLENT GOD, WE BOW BEFORE YOUR THRONE

PRAISE-:

1. I WILL PRAISE YOU FOR THE REST OF MY DAYS.
2. WHO HAS THE FINAL SAY
3. YOU ARE GOOD AND YOUR MERCIES ARE FOREVER, HALLELUJAH
4. YOU ARE GOD YOU ARE NOT JUST BIG OHH
5. JEHOVAH, YOU THE MOST HIGH

WORSHIP & PRAISE LYRICS

GLORIOUS GOD, BEAUTIFUL KING

GLORIOUS GOD, BEAUTIFUL KING
EXCELLENT GOD, WE BOW BEFORE YOUR THRONE
BOW BEFORE YOUR THRONE
WORSHIP AT YOUR FEET
BOW BEFORE YOUR THRONE
YOU'RE THE GLORIOUS GOD
YOU NAME IS ALPHA, OMEGA, AGESLESS,
CHANGELESS, AMIGHTY, JEHOVAH
GLORIOUS GOD, WE BOW BEFORE YOUR THRONE
LINK: https://youtu.be/xYCI11VD4dQ

I'LL PRAISE YOU FOR THE REST OF THE DAYS

I'LL PRAISE YOU FOR THE REST OF THE DAYS
I WILL PRAISE YOU
I'LL PRAISE YOU FOR THE REST OF THE DAYS
I WILL PRAISE YOU

I WILL PRAISE YOU; I WILL PRAISE YOU x3

WHO HAS THE FINAL SAY, JEHOHAH, WE LIFT YOU

WHO HAS THE FINAL SAY
JEHOVAH, HAS THE FINAL SAY
WHO HAS THE FINAL SAY
JEHOVAH, HAS THE FINAL SAY
JEHOVAH, TURNED MY LIFE AROUND x2
HE MAKES A WAY, WHERE THERE IS NO WAY
JEHOVAH, HAS THE FINAL SAY
WE LIFT YOU UP
LINK: https://youtu.be/Bx2T8aunyvs

YOU ARE GOOD AND YOUR MERCY IS FOREVER

YOU ARE GOOD AND YOUR MERCY IS FOREVER,
HALLELUJAH!
YOU ARE GOOD AND YOUR MERCY IS FOREVER,
HALLELUJAH!

LINK: https://youtu.be/Wyo3kqNgcYQ

YOU ARE GOD

YOU ARE GOD, YOU ARE NOT JUST BIG OH
YOU ARE NOT JUST LARGE OH
YOU ARE A GREAT GOD
YOU ARE BIG, BIG, BIG, BIG, BIG, BIG
LARGE, LARGE, LARGE, LARGE, LARGE
GREAT, GREAT, GREAT, GREAT, GREAT
YOU ARE A GREAT GOD

LINK: https://youtu.be/VZd2fQS8yLI

JEHOVAH, YOU ARE THE MOST HIGH

JEHOVAH, YOU ARE THE MOST HIGH
JEHOVAH, YOU ARE THE MOST HIGH GOD
JEHOVAH, YOU ARE THE MOST HIGH
JEHOVAH, YOU ARE THE MOST HIGH GOD

LINK: https://youtu.be/QPNIsEy7n5M

AFRICAN: PRAISE AND WORSHIP - SET 4

WORSHIP-:

LORD YOU REIGN, KADOSH, KADOSH

PRAISE-:

1. WHAT SHALL WE SAY UNTO THE LORD, ALL WE HAVE TO SAY IS THANK YOU LORD
2. YOU ARE GOOD AND YOUR MERCIES ARE FOREVER, HALLELUJAH
3. AT THE MENTION OF YOUR NAME
4. WE CALL YOU MIGHTY WARRIOR
5. YOU ARE GOD, YOU ARE NOT JUST BIG...

WORSHIP & PRAISE LYRICS

YOU REIGN, YOU ANCIENT ZION'S KING

YOU REIGN, YOU ANCIENT ZION'S KING
KADOSH, KADOSH, YOU ARE MIGHTY ON YOUR THRONE
OH SING, OH FOUNTAIN OF THE HILL, I AM
KADOSH, YOU ARE MIGHTY ON YOUR THRONE
REIGN FORTH, OH SPIRIT OF THE HILL, THAT IS
KADOSH, YOU ARE MIGHTY ON YOUR THRONE

LINK: https://youtu.be/Jj-S6xk-Q4M

WHAT SHALL WE SAY UNTO THE LORD

WHAT SHALL WE SAY UNTO THE LORD
ALL WE HAVE TO SAY IS THANK YOU LORD
WHAT SHALL WE SAY UNTO THE LORD
ALL WE HAVE TO SAY IS THANK YOU LORD
THANK YOU, LORD
THANK YOU, LORD
ALL WE HAVE TO SAY IS THANK YOU LORD

LINK: https://youtu.be/bJlogO_rmeo

YOU ARE GOOD AND YOUR MERCY IS FOREVER

YOU ARE GOOD AND YOUR MERCY IS FOREVER, HALLELUJAH!
YOU ARE GOOD AND YOUR MERCY IS FOREVER, HALLELUJAH!

LINK: https://youtu.be/Wyo3kqNgcYQ

AT THE MENTION OF YOUR NAME

AT THE MENTION OF YOUR NAME
EVERY KNEE MUST BOW
AT THE MENTION OF YOUR NAME
EVERY TONGUE CONFESS
THAT YOU ARE LORD
YOU ARE LORD, YOU ARE LORD of LORDS
YOU ARE KING, YOU ARE KING OF KINGS

LINK: https://youtu.be/SplL4YBBHfY

THEY CALL YOU MIGHTY WARRIOR JEHOVAH JIREH

THEY CALL YOU MIGHTY WARRIOR JEHOVAH JIREH, MIGHTY WARRIOR
AHE HEE, JEHOVA, MIGHTY WARRIOR
THEY CALL YOU MIGHTY WARRIOR JEHOVAH JIREH, MIGHTY WARRIOR
AHE HEE, JEHOVA, MIGHTY WARRIOR

SOMEBODY, CALL HIM MIGHTY WARRIOR x 3

YOU ARE GOD

YOU ARE GOD, YOU ARE NOT JUST BIG OH
YOU ARE NOT JUST LARGE OH
YOU ARE A GREAT GOD
YOU ARE BIG, BIG, BIG, BIG, BIG, BIG, BIG
LARGE, LARGE, LARGE, LARGE, LARGE, LARGE
GREAT, GREAT, GREAT, GREAT, GREAT
YOU ARE A GREAT GOD

LINK: https://youtu.be/VZd2fQS8yLI

AFRICAN: PRAISE AND WORSHIP – SET 5

WORSHIP-:

THAT IS WHY YOU ARE CALLED JEHOVAH

PRAISE-:

1. AWESOME GOD, MIGHTY GOD
2. HE'S A MIGHTY GOD
3. YOU ARE GREAT, YES YOU ARE
4. YOU ARE GOD, YOU ARE NOT JUST BIG
5. PRAISE JEHOVAH, YOU TUNRNED MY LIFE AROUND

WORSHIP & PRAISE LYRICS

THAT IS WHY YOU ARE CALLED JEHOVAH

THAT IS WHY YOU ARE CALLED JEHOVAH
THAT IS WHY YOU ARE CALLED JEHOVAH
WHAT YOU SAY YOU WILL DO
THAT IS WHAT YOU WILL DO
THAT IS WHY YOU ARE CALLED JEHOVAH

LINK: https://youtu.be/NH1OojwkWtk

AWESOME GOD, MIGHTY GOD

AWESOME GOD, MIGHTY GOD
AWESOME GOD, MIGHTY GOD
WE GIVE YOU PRAISE, AWESOME GOD
WE GIVE YOU PRAISE, MIGHTY GOD
YOU ARE HIGHLY LIFTED UP, AWESOME GOD
YOU ARE HIGHLY LIFTED UP, MIGHTY GOD

LINK: https://youtu.be/V5dcczS2GsE

HE'S A MIGHTY GOD

HE'S A MIGHTY GOD
HE'S A MIGHTY GOD
JESUS, IS A MIGHTY GOD
EVERY POWER BOW BEFORE HIM
HE'S A MIGHTY GOD

LINK: https://youtu.be/OIUH6Sd_yCo

YOU ARE GREAT, YES YOU ARE

YOU ARE GREAT YES YOU ARE HOLY ONE
WALKED UPON THE SEA RISE THE DEAD
YOU REIGN IN MAJESTY MIGHTY GOD
EVERYTHING WRITTEN ABOUT YOU IS GREAT
YOU ARE GREAT YOU ARE GREAT 4X
EVERYTHING WRITTEN ABOUT YOU IS GREAT

LINK: https://youtu.be/q2KiwKlG85s

YOU ARE GOD

YOU ARE GOD, YOU ARE NOT JUST BIG OH
YOU ARE NOT JUST LARGE OH
YOU ARE A GREAT GOD
YOU ARE BIG, BIG, BIG, BIG, BIG, BIG
LARGE, LARGE, LARGE, LARGE, LARGE
GREAT, GREAT, GREAT, GREAT, GREAT
YOU ARE A GREAT GOD

LINK: https://youtu.be/VZd2fQS8yLI

JEHOVAH, HE TURNED MY LIFE AROUND

JEHOVAH TURNED MY LIFE AROUND (2X)
HE MAKES A WAY WHERE THERE SEEMS NO WAY, JEHOVAH
JEHOVAH TURNED MY LIFE AROUND
JEHOVAH TURNED MY LIFE AROUND OOOHH...
HE MAKES A WAY WHERE THERE SEEMS NO WAY

LINK: https://youtu.be/PYnt_KhKodA

AFRICAN: PRAISE AND WORSHIP - SET 6

WORSHIP-:

WAY MAKER, MIRACE WORKER

PRAISE-:

1. HALE, HALE, HALLELUJAH, GLORY, GLORY, WE PRAISE YOUR NAME
2. RECEIVE OUR PRAISE OH LORD
3. YOU ARE GOD, YOU ARE NOT JUST BIG
4. HOSSANA, HOSSANA, HOSSANA IN THE HIGHEST
5. HIGHER, HIGHER EVERYDAY

WORSHIP & PRAISE LYRICS

WAY MAKER, MIRACLE WORKER

WAY MAKER, MIRACE WORKER,
PROMISE KEEPER, LIGHT IN THE DARKNESS
MY GOD, THAT IS WHO YOU ARE
YOU ARE HERE, WORKING IN THIS PLACE
I WORSHIP YOU
YOU ARE HERE, MOVING IN OUR MIDST
I WORSHIP YOU

LINK: https://youtu.be/n4XWfwLHeLM

HALLE, HALLE HALLELUYAH

HALLE HALLE HALLUYAH,
GLORY, GLORY, WE PRAISE YOUR NAME
YOU ARE THE KING OF KINGS AND THE LORD OF LORD,
WE PRAISE YOUR NAME

LINK: https://youtu.be/2NszJzqbNIE

RECEIVE OUR PRAISE OH LORD

RECEIVE OUR PRAISE OH LORD
RECEIVE OUR PRAISE OH LORD
GLORY AND HONOUR
WE GIVE UNTO YOU
RECEIVE OUR PRAISE OH LORD

LINK: https://youtu.be/spJip_MHGDo

YOU ARE GOD

YOU ARE GOD, YOU ARE NOT JUST BIG OH
YOU ARE NOT JUST LARGE OH
YOU ARE A GREAT GOD
YOU ARE BIG, BIG, BIG, BIG, BIG, BIG, BIG
LARGE, LARGE, LARGE, LARGE, LARGE, LARGE
GREAT, GREAT, GREAT, GREAT, GREAT
YOU ARE A GREAT GOD

LINK: https://youtu.be/VZd2fQS8yLI

HOSSANA, HOSSANA IN THE HIGHEST

HOSSANA, HOSSANA, HOSSAN IN THE HIGHEST
HOSSANA, HOSSANA, HOSSAN IN THE HIGHEST
LORD WE LIGT UP YOUR NAME
WITH THE HEAT FULL OF PRAISE
BE EXALTED OH LORD MY GOD
HOSSANA IN THE HIGHEST

LINK: https://youtu.be/E1X-VDCMyAc

HIGHER, HIGHER EVERYDAY

HIGHER, HIGHER EVERYDAY
I LIFT MY JESUS HIGHER EVERYDAY
WE SING, HIGHER, HIGHER EVERYDAY
I LIFT MY JESUS HIGHER EVERYDAY
WE SING, HIGHER, HIGHER EVERYDAY
I LIFT MY JESUS HIGHER EVERYDAY

LINK: https://youtu.be/Hq9Mq0WMuSc

AFRICAN: PRAISE AND WORSHIP - SET 7

WORSHIP-:

WE GIVE GLORY LORD AS WE HONOUR YOU

PRAISE-:

1. HALLELUJAH EE, HALLELUJAH OO, IT'S A SOUND OF VICTORY
2. HALLE, HALLE, HALLELUJAH, GLORY, GLORY, WE PRAISE YOUR NAME
3. HE'S A MIGHTY GOD
4. WHO HAS THE FINAL SAY
5. GLORY BE TO THE LORD IN THE HIGHEST, HALLELUJAH

WORSHIP & PRAISE LYRICS

WE GIVE GLORY LORD AS WE HONOUR YOU

WE GIVE GLORY LORD AS WE HONOUR YOU
WE GIVE GLORY LORD AS WE HONOUR YOU
YOU ARE WONDERFUL, YOU ARE WORTHY
OH LORD
YOU ARE WONDERFUL, YOU ARE WORTHY
OH LORD

LINK: https://youtu.be/vHxBleOPX_M

HALLELUJAH EH HALLELUJAH O OH!

HALLELUJAH EH! HALLELUJAH O OH!
HALLELUJAH EH! IT'S THE SOUND OF VICTORY
HALLELUJAH EH! HALLELUJAH O OH!
LET THE SOUND OF REJOICING FILL THIS HOUSE

LINK: https://youtu.be/BgGkIjd7qe4

HALLE, HALLE, HALLUYAH

HALLE, HALLE, HALLUYAH,
GLORY, GLORY, WE PRAISE YOUR NAME
YOU ARE THE KING OF KINGS AND THE LORD OF LORD, WE PRAISE YOUR NAME

LINK: https://youtu.be/2NszJzqbNIE

HE'S A MIGHTY GOD

HE'S A MIGHTY GOD
HE'S A MIGHTY GOD
JESUS, IS A MIGHTY GOD
EVERY POWER BOW BEFORE HIM
HE'S A MIGHTY GOD

LINK: https://youtu.be/OIUH6Sd_yCo

WHO HAS THE FINAL SAY, JEHOHAH, WE LIFT YOU UP

WHO HAS THE FINAL SAY
JEHOVAH, HAS THE FINAL SAY
WHO HAS THE FINAL SAY
JEHOVAH, HAS THE FINAL SAY
JEHOVAH, TURNED MY LIFE AROUND x2
HE MAKES A WAY, WHERE THERE IS NO WAY
JEHOVAH, HAS THE FINAL SAY
WE LIFT YOU UP
LINK: https://youtu.be/Bx2T8aunyvs

GLORY BE TO THE LORD IN THE HIGHEST

GLORY BE TO THE LORD IN THE HIGHEST,
HALLELUJAH
GLORY BE TO THE LORD IN THE HIGHEST,
HALLELUJAH
EVERYBODY SHOUT, HALLELU, HALLELUJAH
HALLELUJAH, HALLELUJAH

LINK: https://youtu.be/drmL-zAfdtg

AFRICAN: PRAISE AND WORSHIP – SET 8

WORSHIP-:

BLESS THE LORD OH MY SOUL

PRAISE-:

1. JOY OVERFLOW IN MY HEART
2. HALLE, HALLE, HALLELUJAH, GLORY, GLORY, WE PRAISE YOUR NAME
3. AWESOME GOD, MIGHTY GOD
4. HOSSANA, HOSSANA, HOSSSANA IN THE HIGHEST
5. LORD YOU ARE GOOD AND YOUR MERCY IS FOREVER, HALLELUJAH

WORSHIP & PRAISE LYRICS

BLESS THE LORD OH MY SOUL

BLESS THE LORD OH MY SOUL
AND ALL THAT IS WITHIN ME
BLESS HIS HOLY NAME
HE HAS DONE GREAT THINGS
HE HAS DONE GREAT THINGS
HE HAS DONE GREAT THINGS
BLESS HIS HOLY NAME

LINK: https://youtu.be/vSxocnIaN0A

JOY OVERFLOW IN MY HEART

JOY OVERFLOWS IN MY HEART
SING A NEW SONG TO THE LORD
I WILL PRAISE YOUR NAME
I WILL WORSHIP YOU
GLORY HALLELUYAH SING A NEW SONG TO THE LORD (2X)

LINK: https://youtu.be/Aq4UDCRRdJc

HALLE, HALLE, HALLELUJAH, GLORY, GLORY,

HALLE, HALLE, HALLELUJAH
GLORY, GLORY, WE PRAISE YOUR NAME
YOU ARE THE KING OF KINGS
AND THE LORD OF LORD, WE PRAISE YOUR NAME
HALLE, HALLE, HALLELUJAH

LINK: https://youtu.be/2NszJzqbNIE

AWESOME GOD, MIGHTY GOD

AWESOME GOD, MIGHTY GOD
AWESOME GOD, MIGHTY GOD
WE GIVE YOU PRAISE, AWESOME GOD
WE GIVE YOU PRAISE, MIGHTY GOD
YOU ARE HIGHLY LIFTED UP, AWESOME GOD
YOU ARE HIGHLY LIFTED UP, MIGHTY GOD

LINK: https://youtu.be/V5dcczS2GsE

HOSSANA, HOSSANA IN THE HIGHEST

HOSSANA, HOSSANA, HOSSAN IN THE HIGHEST
HOSSANA, HOSSANA, HOSSAN IN THE HIGHEST
LORD WE LIGT UP YOUR NAME
WITH THE HEAT FULL OF PRAISE
BE EXALTED OH LORD MY GOD
HOSSANA IN THE HIGHEST

LINK: https://youtu.be/E1X-VDCMyAc

LORD YOU ARE GOOD AND YOUR MERCY

LORD YOU ARE GOOD AND YOUR MERCY IS
FOREVER HALLELUJAH
LORD YOU ARE GOOD AND YOUR MERCY IS
FOREVER HALLELUJAH

LINK: https://youtu.be/Wyo3kqNgcYQ

AFRICAN: PRAISE AND WORSHIP – SET 9

WORSHIP-:

WE LIFT YOUR NAME HIGHER

PRAISE-:

1. WE ARE SAYING THANK YOU, JESUS THANK YOU
2. YOU ARE GOOD AND YOUR MERCY IS FOREVER, HALLELUJAH
3. OH LORD, WE PRAISE YOU
4. WE WILL HAIL YOUR NAME
5. HAIL MY JESUS, POWERFUL WARRIOR

WORSHIP & PRAISE LYRICS

WE LIFT YOUR NAME HIGHER

WE LIFT YOUR NAME HIGHER
WE LIFT YOUR NAME HIGHER
WE LIFT YOUR NAME HIGHER
WE LIFT YOUR NAME HIGHER
YES, WE LIFT YOUR NAME HIGHER
JESUS, WE LIFT YOUR NAME HIGHER

LINK: https://youtu.be/qNuPtFFPoLs

WE ARE SAYING THANK YOU, JESUS THANK YOU

WE ARE SAYING THANK YOU, JESUS THANK YOU
JEHOVAH, THANK YOU
EVERYBODY IS SAYING THANK YOU
JESEUS THNAK YOU
THANK YOU, LORD

LINK: https://youtu.be/Oy1SMGMB7Rw

YOU ARE GOOD AND YOUR MERCY IS FOREVER

YOU ARE GOOD AND YOUR MERCY IS FOREVER, HALLELUJAH!
YOU ARE GOOD AND YOUR MERCY IS FOREVER, HALLELUJAH!

LINK: https://youtu.be/Wyo3kqNgcYQ

OH LORD, WE PRAISE YOU

OH LORD, WE PRAISE YOU
OH LORD, WE PRAISE YOU
WE EXALT YOUR NAME x2
OH LORD, WE YOUR'RE WONDERFUL GOD AMEN
OH LORD, WE YOUR'RE WONDERFUL GOD AMEN

LINK: https://youtu.be/MPSnWLd3yR4

WE WILL HAIL YOUR NAME

WE WILL HAIL,
HAIL YOUR NAME
DAY BY DAY
ALL THE WAY x2
WE WILL HAIL, HAIL, HAIL, HAIL
HAIL YOUR NAME, NAME, NAME
DAY BY DAY, DAY, DAY
ALL THE WAY, ALL WAY
LINK: https://youtu.be/1HgZNm1bjSI

HAIL MY JESUS, POWERFUL WARRIOR

HAIL MY JESUS
POWERFUL, POWERFUL WARRIOR
HAIL MY JESUS
POWERFUL, POWERFUL WARRIOR
HAIL MY JESUS,
POWERFUL, POWERFUL WARRIOR

LINK: https://youtu.be/xh3yQKrjBls

AFRICAN: PRAISE AND WORSHIP – SET 10

WORSHIP-:

WE BOW DOWN AND WORSHIP YAHWEH

PRAISE-:

1. THANK YOU LORD ALL WE HAVE TO SAY IS THANK YOU LORD
2. JEHOVAH YOU ARE THE MOST HIGH
3. HAIL MY JESUS, POWERFUL WARRIOR
4. MY GOD IS A GOOD, YES, HE IS
5. HEY, HEY, MY GOD IS GOOD OH

WORSHIP & PRAISE LYRICS

WE BOW DOWN AND WORSHIP YAHWEH

WE BOW DOWN AND WORSHIP YAHWEH
WE BOW DOWN AND WORSHIP YAHWEH
YAHWEH, YAHWEH, YAHWEH
YAHWEH, YAHWEH, YAHWEH
WE BOW DOWN AND WORSHIP YAHWEH
WE BOW DOWN AND WORSHIP YAHWEH

LINK: https://youtu.be/oGQXKoZB5Bw

THANK YOU, LORD, THANK YOU LORD

THANK YOU, LORD
THANK YOU, LORD
ALL WE HAVE TO SAY IS THANK YOU LORD
THANK YOU, LORD,
THANK YOU, LORD
ALL WE HAVE TO SAY IS THANK YOU LORD

LINK: https://youtu.be/bJIogO_rmeo

JEHOVAH, YOU ARE THE MOST HIGH

JEHOVAH, YOU ARE THE MOST HIGH
JEHOVAH, YOU ARE THE MOST HIGH GOD
JEHOVAH, YOU ARE THE MOST HIGH
JEHOVAH, YOU ARE THE MOST HIGH GOD

LINK: https://youtu.be/QPNIsEy7n5M

HAIL MY JESUS, POWERFUL WARRIOR

HAIL MY JESUS
POWERFUL POWER WARROIR
HAIL MY JESUS
POWERFUL POWER WARROIR

LINK: https://youtu.be/xh3yQKrjBls

MY GOD IS A GOOD GOD, YES HE IS

MY GOD IS A GOOD GOD, YES HE IS
HE LIFTS ME UP (HE LIFTS ME UP)
HE TURNS ME AROUND (HE TURNS ME AROUND)
HE SETS ME FEET, UPON THE SOLID ROCK
I FEEL LIKE DANCING, I FEEL LIKE CLAPPING

LINK: https://youtu.be/5RcwYmVRttA

HEY, HEY, MY GOD IS GOOD OH

HEY, HEY, MY GOD IS GOOD OH
HEY, HEY, MY GOD IS GOOD OH
EVERYTHING IS DOUBLE, DOUBLE OOO
MY BLESSINGS ARE DOUBLE, DOUBLE

LINK: https://youtu.be/d4J1ueG98lw

AFRICAN: PRAISE AND WOSHIP – SET 11

WORSHIP-:

JEHOVAH IS YOUR NAME MIGHTY WARRIOR GREAT IN BATTLE

PRAISE-:

1. MASTER OF THE UNIVERSE, CONQUEROR AND KING
2. ALMIGHTY FATHER, WE GIVE YOU GLORY
3. WE CALL HIM MIGHTY WARRIOR JEHOVAH JIREH
4. YOU ARE GOD, YOU ARE NOT JUST BIG OHH
5. WHO HAS THE FINAL SAY, JEHOVAH HAS THE FINAL SAY

WORSHIP & PRAISE LYRICS

JEHOVAH IS YOUR NAME

JEHOVAH IS YOUR NAME
JEHOVAH IS YOUR NAME
MIGHTY WARRIOR
GREAT IN BATTLE
JEHOVAH IS YOUR NAME

LINK: https://youtu.be/Ro9KtH6cSVU

MASTER OF THE UNIVERSE

YOU ARE THE MASTER, MASTER OF THE UNIVERSE
CONQUEROR AND KING, LORD! MASTER OF THE UNIVERSE
YOU ARE THE EMPEROR ALWAYS, YOU ARE THE HEIR
OVER PRINCIPALITIES, YOU ARE THE HEIR, OVER
POWERS, YOU ARE THE HEIR, OVER RULERS, YOU ARE
THE MASTER
MASTER OF THE UNIVERSE

LINK: https://youtu.be/kJ48XEDMBoY

ALMIGHTY FATHER, WE GIVE YOU GLORY

ALMIGHTY FATHER
WE GIVE YOU GLORY
MY GOD, YOU ARE GOOD
ALMIGHTY FATHER, WE GIVE YOU GLORY
MY GOD, YOU ARE GOOD
MY GOD YOU GOOD, MY GOD YOU ARE GOOD x3

THEY CALL YOU MIGHTY WARRIOR JEHOVAH JIREH

THEY CALL YOU MIGHTY WARRIOR JEHOVAH JIREH,
MIGHTY WARRIOR
AHE HEE, JEHOVA, MIGHTY WARRIOR
THEY CALL YOU MIGHTY WARRIOR JEHOVAH JIREH,
MIGHTY WARRIOR
AHE HEE, JEHOVA, MIGHTY WARRIOR

SOMEBODY, CALL HIM MIGHTY WARRIOR x 3

YOU ARE GOD

YOU ARE GOD, YOU ARE NOT JUST BIG OH
YOU ARE NOT JUST LARGE OH
YOU ARE A GREAT GOD
YOU ARE BIG, BIG, BIG, BIG, BIG, BIG
LARGE, LARGE, LARGE, LARGE, LARGE
GREAT, GREAT, GREAT, GREAT, GREAT
YOU ARE A GREAT GOD

LINK: https://youtu.be/VZd2fQS8yLI

WHO HAS THE FINAL SAY, JEHOHAH,

WHO HAS THE FINAL SAY
JEHOVAH, HAS THE FINAL SAY
WHO HAS THE FINAL SAY
JEHOVAH, HAS THE FINAL SAY
JEHOVAH, TURNED MY LIFE AROUND x2
HE MAKES A WAY, WHERE THERE IS NO WAY
JEHOVAH, HAS THE FINAL SAY
WE LIFT YOU UP

LINK: https://youtu.be/Bx2T8aunyvs

AFRICAN: PRAISE AND WORSHIP - SET 12

WORSHIP-:

COVENANT KEEPING GOD, THERE IS NO ONE LIKE YOU

PRAISE-:

1. OH LORD, WE PRAISE YOU
2. THERE'S NO ONE, THERE'S NO ONE LIKE JESUS
3. SHOUT HALLELUJAH TO THE LORD
4. HE'S A MIGHYTY GOD
5. PRAISE JEHOVAH, HE'S TURNED MY LIFR AROUND

WORSHIP & PRAISE LYRICS

COVENANT KEEPING GOD

COVENANT KEEPING GOD
THERE IS NO ONE LIKE YOU
ALPHA, OMEGA
THERE IS NO ONE LIKE YOU
YOU ARE THE COVENANT, KEEPING GOD

LINK: https://youtu.be/Xyqqrb3wZQw

OH LORD, WE PRAISE YOU

OH LORD, WE PRAISE YOU
OH LORD, WE PRAISE YOU
WE EXALT YOUR NAME x2
OH LORD, WE YOUR'RE WONDERFUL GOD AMEN
OH LORD, WE YOUR'RE WONDERFUL GOD AMEN

LINK: https://youtu.be/MPSnWLd3yR4

THERE'S NO ONE, THERE'S NO ONE LIKE JESUS

THERE'S NO ONE
THERE'S NO ONE LIKE JESUS
THERE'S NO ONE
THERE'S NO ONE LIKE HIM
THERE'S NO ONE
THERE'S NO ONE LIKE JESUS
THERE'S NO ONE, THERE'S NO ONE LIKE HIM

LINK: https://youtu.be/ziwMQGKtkHo

SHOUT HALLELLUJAH TO THE LORD

SHOUT HALLELLUJAH TO THE LORD
SHOUT HALLELLUJAH TO THE LORD
SHOUT HOSSANA TO THE LORD
SHOUT HALLELLUJAH TO THE LORD
SHOUT HALLELLUJAH TO THE LORD
SHOUT HOSSANA TO THE LORD

LINK: https://youtu.be/S9iNGlWAUok

HE'S A MIGHTY GOD

HE'S A MIGHTY GOD
HE'S A MIGHTY GOD
JESUS, IS A MIGHTY GOD
EVERY POWER BOW BEFORE HIM
HE'S A MIGHTY GOD

LINK: https://youtu.be/OIUH6Sd_yCo

PRAISE JEHOVAH, HE TURNED MY LIFE AROUND

PRAISE JEHOVAH TURNED MY LIFE AROUND
PRAISE JEHOVAH TURNED MY LIFE AROUND
JEHOVAH TURNED MY LIFE AROUND
JEHOVAH TURNED MY LIFE AROUND OOOHH...
HE MAKES A WAY WHERE THERE SEEMS NO WAY
JEHOVAH HAS THE FINAL SAY

LINK: https://youtu.be/PYnt_KhKodA

AFRICAN: PRAISE AND WORSHIP - SET 13

WORSHIP-:

WE BOW DOWN AND WORSHIP, YAHWEH

PRAISE-:

1. WE ARE SAYING THANK YOU JESUS THANK YOU
2. THANK YOU LORD ALL WE HAVE TO SAY IS THANK YOU
3. OH LORD, WE PRAISE YOU
4. AWESOME GOD MIGHTY GOD
5. SOME PEOPLE SAY YOU SO GOOD

WORSHIP & PRAISE LYRICS

WE BOW DOWN AND WORSHIP, YAHWEH

WE BOW DOWN AND WORSHIP, YAHWEH
YAHWEH, YAHWEH, YAHWEH
YAHWEH, YAHWEH, YAHWEH
WE BOW DOWN AND WORSHIP, YAHWEH
WE BOW DOWN AND WORSHIP, YAHWEH

LINK: https://youtu.be/q0A6nHOspkc

WE ARE SAYING THANK, JESUS THANK

WE ARE SAYING THANK
JESUS THANK YOU
JEHOVAH THAN YOU
EVERYBODY IS SAYING THANK YOU
JESUS THANK YOU
THANK YOU, LORD,

LINK: https://youtu.be/Oy1SMGMB7Rw

THANK YOU, LORD, ALL WE HAVE TO SAY

THANK YOU, LORD
THANK YOU, LORD
ALL WE HAVE TO SAY IS THANK YOU LORD
THANK YOU, LORD
THANK YOU, LORD
ALL WE HAVE TO SAY IS THANK YOU LORD

LINK: https://youtu.be/bJlogO_rmeo

OH LORD, WE PRAISE YOU

OH LORD, WE PRAISE YOU
OH LORD, WE PRAISE YOU
WE EXALT YOUR NAME x2
OH LORD, WE YOUR'RE WONDERFUL GOD AMEN
OH LORD, WE YOUR'RE WONDERFUL GOD AMEN

LINK: https://youtu.be/MPSnWLd3yR4

AWESOME GOD, MIGHTY GOD

AWESOME GOD, MIGHTY GOD
AWESOME GOD, MIGHTY GOD
WE GIVE YOU PRAISE, AWESOME GOD
WE GIVE YOU PRAISE, MIGHTY GOD
YOU ARE HIGHLY LIFTED UP, AWESOME GOD
YOU ARE HIGHLY LIFTED UP, MIGHTY GOD

LINK: https://youtu.be/V5dcczS2GsE

YOU ARE BIGGER THAN WHAT PEOPLE SAY

YOU ARE BIGGER THAN WHAT PEOPLE SAY
JEHOVAH YOU ARE BIGGER THAN WHAT PEOPLE SAY
YOU ARE BIGGER THAN WHAT PEOPLE SAY
JEHOVAH YOU ARE BIGGER THAN WHAT PEOPLE SAY
JEHOVAH, YOU ARE GOOD, YOU ARE KIND
YOU ARE BIGGER THAN WHAT PEOPLE SAY

LINK: https://youtu.be/is_9GAbT0lI

AFRICAN: PRAISE AND WORSHIP – SET 14

WORSHIP-:

GLORY, GLORY, GLORY TO THE LAMB

PRAISE-:

1. COME AND SEE THE LORD IS GOD
2. E E E MY GOD IS GOOD OOO
3. I WILL LIFT UP MY VOICE, I WILL JOYFULLY SING
4. THERE IS SOMETHING THAT MAKES ME COME INTO YOUR PRESENCE
5. JEHOVAH REIGNS, JEHOVAH REIGNS

WORSHIP & PRAISE LYRICS

GLORY, GLORY, GLORY TO THE LAMB

GLORY, GLORY, GLORY TO THE LAMB
GLORY, GLORY, GLORY TO THE LAMB
FOR YOU ARE GLORIOUS
AND WORTHY TO BE PAISED
YOU ARE THE LAMB UPON THE THRONE
YOU ARE THE LAMB UPON THE THRONE

LINK: https://youtu.be/wtR_vNTP61k

COME AND SEE THE LORD IS GOD

COME AND SEE THE LORD IS GOD, OOO
COME AND SEE THE LORD IS GOD
THERE IS NOTHING HE CANNOT DO
COME AND SEE THE LORD IS GOOD
HE GAVE ME VOCTORY
HE GAVE PEACE OF MIND
THERE IS NOTHING HE CANNOT DO
COME AND SEE THE LORD ID GODD

LINK: https://youtu.be/w1dZGX0kGGs

E E E, MY GOD IS GOOD OH

HEY, HEY, MY GOD IS GOOD OH
HEY, HEY, MY GOD IS GOOD OH
EVERYTHING IS DOUBLE, DOUBLE OOO
MY BLESSINGS ARE DOUBLE, DOUBLE

LINK: https://youtu.be/d4J1ueG98lw

I WILL LIFT UP MY VOICE, I WILL JOYFULLY SING

I WILL LIFT UP MY VOICE, I WILL JOYFULLY SING
NOT FOR WHAT YOU HAVE DONE,
BUT FOR WHO ARE
YOU ARE THE REASON I SING, MELODY IN MY HEART
YOU ARE THE SONG THAT I SING
I WILL PRAISE YOU LORD
HE REIGNS, HE REIGNS, HE REIGNS
FORVERMORE

LINK: https://fb.watch/hOCoHjyvzY/

THERE IS SOMETHING THAT MAKES ME COME INTO YOUR PRESENCE

THERE IS SOMETHING THAT MAKES ME COME INTO YOUR PRESENCE - MY HELPER
THERE IS SOMETHING THAT MAKES ME COME INTO YOUR PRESENCE - MY HELPER
MY HELPER O MY HELPER (2X)
THERE IS SOMETHING THAT MAKES ME COME INTO YOUR PRESENCE - MY HELPER

LINK: https://youtu.be/mT6B6eoAlug

JEHOVAH REIGNS, JEHOVAH REIGNS

JEHOVAH REIGNS, JEHOVAH REIGNS
JEHOVAH REIGNS, JEHOVAH REIGNS
YOU ARE LIFTED UP ABOVE OTHER GOD
YOU ARE LIFTED UP ABOVE OTHER GOD
YOU ARE LIFTED UP ABOVE OTHER GOD
YOU ARE LIFTED UP ABOVE OTHER GOD

LINK: https://youtu.be/SK9Qh_EV-b0

AFRICAN: PRAISE AND WORSHIP - SET 15

WORSHIP-:

OH, BE LIFTED, ABOVE ALL OTHER GOD'S

PRAISE-:

1. ALMIGHTY GOD, ALL POWERFUL GOD
2. YOU ARE MARVELOUS LORD
3. TO YOU LORD, BE ALL THE GLORY
4. WHAT A MARVELOUS GOD
5. FATHER WE OFFER PRAISE

WORSHIP & PRAISE LYRICS

OH, BE LIFTED, ABOVE ALL OTHER GOD'S

OH, BE LIFTED
ABOVE ALL OTHER GOD'S
WE LAY OUR CROWN
AND WORSHIP YOU
OH, GLORIOUS GOD
WE PRAISE YOUR NAME
WE LAY OUR CROWN
AND WORSHIP YOU
LINK: https://youtu.be/yH1FJEQBzss

ALMIGHTY GOD, ALL POWERFUL GOD

ALMIGHTY GOD
ALL POWERFUL GOD
ALMIGHTY GOD
ALL POWERFUL GOD
YOU ARE WORTHY TO RECEIVE ALL OUR PRAISE
YOU REIGN FOREVERMORE x2

YOU ARE MARVELOUS LORD

YOU ARE MARVELOUS LORD
YOU ARE MARVELOUS LORD
YOU ARE MARVELOUS LORD x 3
YOU ARE POWERFUL LORD
YOU WONDERFUL LORD
YOU ARE GLORIOUS LORD

LINK: https://youtu.be/OCadihcZYXc

TO YOU LORD, BE ALL THE GLORY

TO YOU LORD,
BE ALL THE GLORY
TO YOU LORD,
BE ALL THE HONOUR
TO YOU LORD,
BE ALL THE GLORY
AND ADORTION FORVERMORE

LINK: https://youtu.be/y97kFpm9wNM

WHAT A MARVELOUS GOD

WHAT A MARVELOUS GOD
WHAT A MARVELOUS GOD
HE HAS DONE MARVELOUS THINGSS FOR ME
WHAT A MARVELOUS GOD
WHAT A MARVELOUS GOD
HE HAS DONE MARVELOUS THINGS FOR ME
HALLELUJAH

LINK: https://youtu.be/DmVWMZjeyEU

FATHER, WE OFFER PRAISE, WE OFFER PRAISE

FATHER, WE OFFER PRAISE,
WE OFFER PRAISE
WE GLORIFY, YOUR HOLY
FATHER, WE OFFER PRAISE,
WE OFFER PRAISE
WE GLORIFY, YOUR HOLY

AFRICAN: PRAISE AND WORSHIP – SET 16

WORSHIP-:

WAY MAKER

PRAISE-:

1. HE'S A MIGHTY GOD
2. MY GOD IS A GOOD GOD, YES, HE IS.
3. E E E MY GOD IS GOOD OOO
4. THERE IS SOMETHING THAT MAKES ME COME INTO YOUR PRESENCE
5. WHAT A MIGHTY GOD, WE SAERVE

WORSHIP & PRAISE LYRICS

WAY MAKER

WAY MAKER, MIRACE WORKER,
PROMISE KEEPER, LIGHT IN THE DARKNESS
MY GOD, THAT IS WHO YOU ARE
YOU ARE HERE, WORKING IN THIS PLACE
I WORSHIP YOU
YOU ARE HERE, MOVING IN OUR MIDST
I WORSHIP YOU

LINK: https://youtu.be/n4XWfwLHeLM

HE'S A MIGHTY GOD

HE'S A MIGHTY GOD, HE'S A MIGHTY GOD
JESUS, HE'S A MIGHTY GOD
HE'S A MIGHTY GOD
EVERY POWER BOW BEFORE HIM
HE'S A MIGHTY GOD

LINK: https://youtu.be/OIUH6Sd_yCo

MY GOD IS A GOOD GOD, YES HE IS

MY GOD IS A GOOD GOD, YES HE IS
HE LIFTS ME UP (HE LIFTS ME UP)
HE TURNS ME AROUND (HE TURNS ME AROUND)
HE SETS ME FEET, UPON THE SOLID ROCK
I FEEL LIKE DANCING, I FEEL LIKE CLAPPING

LINK: https://youtu.be/5RcwYmVRttA

E E E, MY GOD IS GOOD OH

HEY, HEY, MY GOD IS GOOD OH
HEY, HEY, MY GOD IS GOOD OH
EVERYTHING IS DOUBLE, DOUBLE OOO
MY BLESSINGS ARE DOUBLE, DOUBLE

LINK: https://youtu.be/d4J1ueG98lw

THERE IS SOMETHING THAT MAKES ME COME INTO YOUR PRESENCE

THERE IS SOMETHING THAT MAKES ME COME INTO YOUR PRESENCE - MY HELPER
THERE IS SOMETHING THAT MAKES ME COME INTO YOUR PRESENCE - MY HELPER
MY HELPER O MY HELPER (2X)
THERE IS SOMETHING THAT MAKES ME COME INTO YOUR PRESENCE - MY HELPER

LINK: https://youtu.be/mT6B6eoAlug

WHAT A MIGHTY GOD, WE SAERVE

WHAT A MIGHTY GOD, WE SAERVE
WHAT A MIGHTY GOD, WE SAERVE
WHAT A MIGHTY GOD, WE SAERVE
HEAVEN AND EARTH ADORE HIM
ANGELS BOW BEFORE, WHAT A MIGHYY GOD WE SERVE
HALLELUJAH

LINK: https://youtu.be/Wt2ujhek2IE

AFRICAN: PRAISE AND WORSHIP – SET 17

WORSHIP-:

JEHOVAH, WE PRAISE YOU, WE PRAISE YOUR NAME

PRAISE-:

1. OH, THAT MEN WILL PRAISE THE LORD
2. I WILL EXALT YOU LORD, FOR THOU HAS LIFTED ME
3. TO YOU LORD BE ALL THE GLORY
4. YOU ARE MARVELOUS LORD
5. AWESOME GOD, MIGHTY GOD

WORSHIP & PRAISE LYRICS

JEHOVAH, WE PRAISE YOU

JEHOVAH, WE PRAISE YOU
JEHOVAH, WE PRAISE YOU
WE PRAISE YOUR NAME,
WE PRAISE YOUR NAME
JEHOVAH, WE PRAISE YOU

LINK: https://youtu.be/tFnSdhMSeE4

OH, THAT MEN WILL PRAISE THE LORD

OH, THAT MEN WILL PRAISE THE LORD
OH, THAT MEN WILL PRAISE THE LORD
FOR HIS GOODNESS
AND FOR HIS WONDERFUL WORKS
TO THE CHILDREN OF MEN x2
HE HAS BROKEN THE GATES OF BRASS
AND SAWN THE BARS OF IRON ASUNDER x2

LINK: https://youtu.be/xXH-pwZEqNs

I WILL EXALT YOU LORD, FOR THOU HAS LIFTED ME

I WILL EXALT YOU LORD, FOR THOU HAS LIFTED ME
ABOVE MY ENEMIES
YOUR BANNER OVER ME IS LOVE
I WILL EXALT YOU LORD, FOR THOU HAS LIFTED ME
ABOVE MY ENEMIES
YOUR BANNER OVER ME IS LOVE

LINK: https://youtu.be/S9cPBYE9qWQ

TO YOU LORD BE ALL THE GLORY

TO YOU LORD BE ALL THE GLORY
TO YOU LORD BE ALL THE HONOUR
TO YOU LORD BE ALL THE GLORY
AND ADORATION FORVERMORE

LINK: https://youtu.be/y97kFpm9wNM

YOU ARE MARVELOUS LORD

YOU ARE MARVELOUS LORD
YOU ARE MARVELOUS LORD
YOU ARE MARVELOUS LORD x 3
YOU ARE POWERFUL LORD
YOU WONDERFUL LORD
YOU ARE GLORIOUS LORD

LINK: https://youtu.be/OCadihcZYXc

AWESOME GOD, MIGHTY GOD

AWESOME GOD, MIGHTY GOD
AWESOME GOD, MIGHTY GOD
WE GIVE YOU PRAISE, AWESOME GOD
WE GIVE YOU PRAISE, MIGHTY GOD
YOU ARE HIGHLY LIFTED UP, AWESOME GOD
YOU ARE HIGHLY LIFTED UP, MIGHTY GOD

LINK: https://youtu.be/V5dcczS2GsE

AFRICAN: PRAISE AND WORSHIP - SET 18

WORSHIP-:

YOU ARE A COVENANT KEEPING GOD

PRAISE-:

1. ALMIGHTY FATHER, WE GIVE YOU GLORY
2. GIVE HIM PRAISE, GIVE HIM PRAISE
3. JEHOVAH REIGNS, JEHOVAH REIGNS
4. YOU ARE GOD YOU ARE NOT JUST BIG OHH
5. WE LIFT YOUR NAME HIGHER

WORSHIP & PRAISE LYRICS

YOU ARE A COVENANT KEEPING GOD

YOU ARE A COVENANT KEEPING GOD
YAHWEH, THE COVENANT KEEPING GOD
YOU ARE A CONVENANT KEEPING GOD
YAHWEH, THE COVENANT KEEPING GOD
YOU ARE A CONVENANT KEEPING GOD

LINK: https://youtu.be/wRmVBIpnIAk

ALMIGHTY FATHER, WE GIVE YOU GLORY

ALMIGHTY FATHER
WE GIVE YOU GLORY
MY GOD, YOU ARE GOOD

ALMIGHTY FATHER
WE GIVE YOU GLORY
MY GOD, YOU ARE GOOD

MY GOD, YOU ARE GOOD x3

GIVE HIM PRAISE, GIVE HIM PRAISE

GIVE HIM PRAISE, GIVE HIM PRAISE
GIVE HIM PRAISE, GIVE HIM PRAISE
WE ARE HERE TO GIVE ALL THE PRAISE TO LORD

GIVE HIM PRAISE, GIVE HIM PRAISE
GIVE HIM PRAISE, GIVE HIM PRAISE
WE ARE HERE TO GIVE ALL THE PRAISE TO LORD

JEHOVAH REIGNS, JEHOVAH REIGNS

JEHOVAH REIGNS, JEHOVAH REIGNS
JEHOVAH REIGNS, JEHOVAH REIGNS

YOU ARE LIFTED UP ABOVE OTHER GOD
YOU ARE LIFTED UP ABOVE OTHER GOD
YOU ARE LIFTED UP ABOVE OTHER GOD
YOU ARE LIFTED UP ABOVE OTHER GOD

LINK: https://youtu.be/SK9Qh_EV-b0

YOU ARE GOD

YOU ARE GOD, YOU ARE NOT JUST BIG OH
YOU ARE NOT JUST LARGE OH
YOU ARE A GREAT GOD
YOU ARE BIG, BIG, BIG, BIG, BIG, BIG
LARGE, LARGE, LARGE, LARGE, LARGE, LARGE
GREAT, GREAT, GREAT, GREAT, GREAT
YOU ARE A GREAT GOD

LINK: https://youtu.be/VZd2fQS8yLI

WE LIFT YOUR NAME HIGHER

WE LIFT YOUR NAME HIGHER
WE LIFT YOUR NAME HIGHER
WE LIFT YOUR NAME HIGHER
JESUS, WE LIFT YOUR NAME HIGHER
WE LIFT YOUR NAME HIGHER

LINK: https://youtu.be/c5gOT8HzqnI

AFRICAN: PRAISE AND WORSHIP – SET 19

WORSHIP-:

DAILY AS I LIVE

PRAISE-:

1. MASTER OF THE UNIVERSE
2. YOU ARE GREAT, YES YOU ARE
3. JOY OVERFLOWS IN MY HEART
4. I'LL PRAISE YOU FOR THE REST OF MY DAYS, I WILL PRAISE YOU
5. WHO HAS THE FINAL SAY

WORSHIP & PRAISE LYRICS

DAILY AS I LIVE

DAILY AS I LIVE
OFTEN, AS I BREATH
LIKE MY WHOLE LIFE
BE EXPRESSIONS OF YOUR GRACE
WE CRY ABBA FATHER
HALLOWED BE YOUR NAME x3

LINK: https://youtu.be/dl5ruzWw-Hg

MASTER OF THE UNIVERSE

YOU ARE THE MASTER, MASTER OF THE UNIVERSE
CONQUEROR AND KING, LORD, MASTER OF THE UNIVERSE
YOU ARE THE EMPEROR ALWAYS, YOU ARE THE HEIR
OVER PRINCIPALITIES, YOU ARE THE HEIR,
OVERPOWERS, YOU ARE THE HEIR, OVER RULERS, YOU ARE THE MASTER
MASTER OF THE UNIVERSE

LINK: https://youtu.be/kJ48XEDMBoY

YOU ARE GREAT, YES YOU ARE

YOU ARE GREAT YES YOU ARE HOLY ONE
WALKED UPON THE SEA RISE THE DEAD
YOU REIGN IN MAJESTY MIGHTY GOD
EVERYTHING WRITTEN ABOUT YOU IS GREAT
YOU ARE GREAT YOU ARE GREAT 4X
EVERYTHING WRITTEN ABOUT YOU IS GREAT

LINK: https://youtu.be/q2KiwKIG85s

JOY OVERFLOW IN MY HEART

JOY OVERFLOWS IN MY HEART
SING A NEW SONG TO THE LORD
I WILL PRAISE YOUR NAME
I WILL WORSHIP YOU
GLORY HALLELUYAH SING A NEW SONG TO THE LORD (2X)

LINK: https://youtu.be/Aq4UDCRRdJc

I'LL PRAISE YOU FOR THE REST OF THE DAY

I'LL PRAISE YOU FOR THE REST OF THE DAYS
I WILL PRAISE YOU
I'LL PRAISE YOU FOR THE REST OF THE DAYS
I WILL PRAISE YOU
I WILL PRAISE YOU
I WILL PRAISE YOU x3

WHO HAS THE FINAL SAY, JEHOHAH, WE LIFT YOU U

WHO HAS THE FINAL SAY
JEHOVAH, HAS THE FINAL SAY
WHO HAS THE FINAL SAY
JEHOVAH, HAS THE FINAL SAY
JEHOVAH, TURNED MY LIFE AROUND x2
HE MAKES A WAY, WHERE THERE IS NO WAY
JEHOVAH, HAS THE FINAL SAY
WE LIFT YOU UP
LINK: https://youtu.be/Bx2T8aunyvs

ARICAN PRAISE AND WORSHIP - SET 20

WORSHIP-:

YES, YOU ARE THE LORD MOST HIGH

PRAISE-:

1. OH LORD, WE PRAISE YOU
2. WHO HAS THE FINAL SAY
3. YOU ARE GREAT YES YOU ARE
4. I WILL PRAISE YOU FOR THE REST OF MY LIFE
5. JEHOVAH REIGNS, JEHOVAH REIGNS

WORSHIP & PRAISE LYRICS

YES, YOU ARE THE LORD MOST HIGH

YES, YOU ARE THE LORD MOST HIGH
YES, YOU ARE THE LORD MOST HIGH
YES, YOU ARE THE LORD MOST HIGH
YES, YOU ARE THE LORD MOST HIGH
YES, YOU ARE THE LORD MOST HIGH

LINK: https://youtu.be/MpCKY9WfaA8

OH LORD, WE PRAISE YOU

OH LORD, WE PRAISE YOU
OH LORD, WE PRAISE YOU
WE EXALT YOUR NAME x2
OH LORD, WE YOUR'RE WONDERFUL GOD AMEN
OH LORD, WE YOUR'RE WONDERFUL GOD AMEN

LINK: https://youtu.be/MPSnWLd3yR4

WHO HAS THE FINAL SAY, JEHOHAH, WE LIFT YOU

WHO HAS THE FINAL SAY
JEHOVAH, HAS THE FINAL SAY
WHO HAS THE FINAL SAY
JEHOVAH, HAS THE FINAL SAY
JEHOVAH, TURNED MY LIFE AROUND x2
HE MAKES A WAY, WHERE THERE IS NO WAY
JEHOVAH, HAS THE FINAL SAY
WE LIFT YOU UP
LINK: https://youtu.be/Bx2T8aunyvs

YOU ARE GREAT, YES YOU ARE

YOU ARE GREAT YES YOU ARE HOLY ONE
WALKED UPON THE SEA RISE THE DEAD
YOU REIGN IN MAJESTY MIGHTY GOD
EVERYTHING WRITTEN ABOUT YOU IS GREAT
YOU ARE GREAT YOU ARE GREAT 4X
EVERYTHING WRITTEN ABOUT YOU IS GREAT

LINK: https://youtu.be/q2KiwKlG85s

I'LL PRAISE YOU FOR THE REST OF THE DAYS

I'LL PRAISE YOU FOR THE REST OF THE DAYS
I WILL PRAISE YOU
I'LL PRAISE YOU FOR THE REST OF THE DAYS
I WILL PRAISE YOU
I WILL PRAISE YOU
I WILL PRAISE YOU x3

JEHOVAH REIGNS, JEHOVAH REIGNS

JEHOVAH REIGNS, JEHOVAH REIGNS
JEHOVAH REIGNS, JEHOVAH REIGNS
YOU ARE LIFTED UP ABOVE OTHER GOD
YOU ARE LIFTED UP ABOVE OTHER GOD
YOU ARE LIFTED UP ABOVE OTHER GOD
YOU ARE LIFTED UP ABOVE OTHER GOD

LINK: https://youtu.be/SK9Qh_EV-b0

AFRICAN: PRAISE AND WORSHIP – SET 21

WORSHIP-:

HOLY ARE YOU LORD, ALL CREATION CALL YOU GOD

PRAISE-:

1. LORD YOU ARE SO GOOD, BLESSED BE YOUR NAME
2. THERE IS SOMETHING THAT MAKES ME RUN INTO YOUR PRESENCE
3. HAIL MY JESUS, POWERFUL WARROIR
4. WE WILL HAIL, HAIL YOUR NAME
5. WE LIFT YOUR NAME HIGHER

WORSHIP & PRAISE LYRICS

HOLY ARE YOU LORD

HOLY ARE YOU LORD
ALL CREATION CALL YOU GOD
WORTHY IS YOUR NAME
WE WORSHIP YOUR MAJESTY
AWESOME GOD, HOW GREAT THOU ART
YOU ARE GOD, MIGHTY ARE YOUR MIRACLES
WE STAND IN AWE OF YOUR HOLY NAME
LORD, WE BOW DOWN AND WORSHIP YOU

LINK: https://youtu.be/qnLvi392hhE

LORD YOU ARE SO GOOD, BLESSED BE YOUR NAME

LORD YOU ARE SO GOOD, BLESSED BE YOUR NAME
LORD YOU ARE SO GOOD, BLESSED BE YOUR NAME
IN HEAVEN YOU ARE THE LORD
ON EARTH YOU REIGN FOREVER
OH LORD HOW GREAT THOU ART
BLESSSED BE YOUR NAME

LINK: https://youtu.be/QhxObPYSWS8

THERE IS SOMETHING THAT MAKES ME COME

THERE IS SOMETHING THAT MAKES ME COME
INTO YOUR PRESENCE - MY HELPER
THERE IS SOMETHING THAT MAKES ME COME
INTO YOUR PRESENCE - MY HELPER
MY HELPER O MY HELPER (2X)
THERE IS SOMETHING THAT MAKES ME COME
INTO YOUR PRESENCE - MY HELPER

LINK: https://youtu.be/mT6B6eoAlug

HAIL MY JESUS, POWERFUL WARRIOR

HAIL MY JESUS
POWERFUL POWER WARROIR
HAIL MY JESUS
POWERFUL POWER WARROIR

LINK: https://youtu.be/xh3yQKrjBls

WE WILL HAIL, HAIL YOUR NAME

WE WILL HAIL
HAIL YOUR NAME
DAY BY DAY, ALL THE WAY
ALL THE WAY
WE WILL HAIL, HAIL, HAIL, HAIL
HAIL YOUR NAME, NAME, NAME
DAY BY DAY, DAY, DAY, DAY

LINK: https://youtu.be/1HgZNm1bjSl

WE LIFT YOUR NAME HIGHER

WE LIFT YOUR NAME HIGHER
WE LIFT YOUR NAME HIGHER
WE LIFT YOUR NAME HIGHER
JESUS, WE LIFT YOUR NAME HIGHER
WE LIFT YOUR NAME HIGHER

LINK: https://youtu.be/c5gOT8Hzqnl

AFRICAN: PRAISE AND WORSHIP - SET 22

WORSHIP-:

YOU ARE WORTHY TO BE GLORIFIED, YOU ARE WORTHY JEHOVAH

PRAISE-:

1. JOY OVERFLOWS IN MY HEART
2. WHAT WILL I GIVE TO YOU, MY PRAISE
3. YOU ARE GOD, YOU ARE JUST BIG
4. OH LORD, WE PRAISE YOU
5. THERE IS SOMETHING THAT MAKE COME INTO YOUR PRESENCE

WORSHIP & PRAISE LYRICS

YOU ARE WORTHY TO BE GLORIFIED

YOU ARE WORTHY TO BE GLORIFIED
YOU ARE WORTHY JEHOVAH
YOU ARE WORTHY TO BE GLORIFIED
YOU ARE WORTHY JEHOVAH

LINK: https://youtu.be/nFpU1BlG-hA

JOY OVERFLOW IN MY HEART

JOY OVERFLOWS IN MY HEART
SING A NEW SONG TO THE LORD
I WILL PRAISE YOUR NAME
I WILL WORSHIP YOU
GLORY HALLELUYAH SING A NEW SONG TO THE LORD (2X)

LINK: https://youtu.be/Aq4UDCRRdJc

WHAT WILL I GIVE TO YOU, MY PRAISE

WHAT WILL I GIVE TO YOU
MY PRAISE
WHAT WILL I GIVE TO YOU
MY PRAISE
I DON'T HAVE MONEY
MY PRAISE
WHAT WILL I GIVE TO YOU
MY PRAISE
LINK: https://youtu.be/ZAjhMlnXN1c

YOU ARE GOD

YOU ARE GOD, YOU ARE NOT JUST BIG OH
YOU ARE NOT JUST LARGE OH
YOU ARE A GREAT GOD
YOU ARE BIG, BIG, BIG, BIG, BIG, BIG, BIG
LARGE, LARGE, LARGE, LARGE, LARGE, LARGE
GREAT, GREAT, GREAT, GREAT, GREAT
YOU ARE A GREAT GOD

LINK: https://youtu.be/VZd2fQS8yLI

OH LORD, WE PRAISE YOU

OH LORD, WE PRAISE YOU
OH LORD, WE PRAISE YOU
WE EXALT YOUR NAME x2
OH LORD, WE YOUR'RE WONDERFUL GOD AMEN
OH LORD, WE YOUR'RE WONDERFUL GOD AMEN

LINK: https://youtu.be/MPSnWLd3yR4

THERE IS SOMETHING THAT MAKES ME COME INTO YOUR PRESENCE

THERE IS SOMETHING THAT MAKES ME COME INTO YOUR PRESENCE - MY HELPER
THERE IS SOMETHING THAT MAKES ME COME INTO YOUR PRESENCE - MY HELPER
MY HELPER O MY HELPER (2X)
THERE IS SOMETHING THAT MAKES ME COME INTO YOUR PRESENCE - MY HELPER
LINK: https://youtu.be/mT6B6eoAlug

AFRICAN: PRAISE AND WORSHIP – SET 23

WORSHIP-:

GREAT ARE YOU LORD

PRAISE-:

1. LORD YOU ARE SO GOOD, LORD YOU ARE KIND, MY GOD YOU ARE EXCELLENT
2. HE'S A MIGHTY GOD
3. WE CALL YOU MIGHTY WARRIOR JEHOVAH SHAMMAH MIGHTY WARRIOR
4. AWESOME GOD, MIGHYTY GOD
5. OH LORD, WE PRAISE YOU, YOU ARE A WONDERFUL GOD AMEN.

WORSHIP & PRAISE LYRICS

GREAT ARE YOU LORD

GREAT ARE YOU LORD
GREATLY TO BE PRAISED
GREATLY TO BE PRAISED
FATHER, YOU REIGN
GREAT ARE YOU LORD
GREATLY TO BE PRAISED
FATHER, YOU REIGN

LINK: https://youtu.be/0ORTihWykSA

LORD YOU ARE SO GOOD, LORD YOU ARE KIND

LORD YOU ARE SO GOOD
LORD YOU ARE KIND
LORD YOU ARE WONDERFUL
MY GOD YOU ARE EXCELLENT
EXCELLENT, IS YOUR NAME
EXCELLENT, IS YOUR POWER
LORD YOU ARE WONDERFUL
MY GOD, YOU ARE EXCELLENT

LINK: https://youtu.be/JWkcjVPoUY4

HE'S A MIGHTY GOD

HE IS A MIGHTY GOD
YOU ARE A MIGHTY GOD
EVERY POWER BOW BEFORE YOU
YOU ARE A MIGHTY GOD
EVERY POWER BOW BEFORE YOU
YOU ARE A MIGHTY GOD

LINK: https://youtu.be/OIUH6Sd_yCo

AWESOME GOD, MIGHTY GOD

AWESOME GOD, MIGHTY GOD
AWESOME GOD, MIGHTY GOD
WE GIVE YOU PRAISE, AWESOME GOD
WE GIVE YOU PRAISE, MIGHTY GOD
YOU ARE HIGHLY LIFTED UP, AWESOME GOD
YOU ARE HIGHLY LIFTED UP, MIGHTY GOD

LINK: https://youtu.be/V5dcczS2GsE

THEY CALL YOU MIGHTY WARRIOR JEHOVAH JIREH

THEY CALL YOU MIGHTY WARRIOR JEHOVAH JIREH, MIGHTY WARRIOR
AHE HEE, JEHOVA, MIGHTY WARRIOR
THEY CALL YOU MIGHTY WARRIOR JEHOVAH JIREH, MIGHTY WARRIOR
AHE HEE, JEHOVA, MIGHTY WARRIOR
SOMEBODY, CALL HIM MIGHTY WARRIOR x 3

OH LORD, WE PRAISE YOU

OH LORD, WE PRAISE YOU
OH LORD, WE PRAISE YOU
WE EXALT YOUR NAME x2
OH LORD, WE YOUR'RE WONDERFUL GOD AMEN
OH LORD, WE YOUR'RE WONDERFUL GOD AMEN

LINK: https://youtu.be/MPSnWLd3yR4

AFRICAN: PRAISE AND WORSHIP – SET 24

WORSHIP -:

HOW GREAT IS OUR GOD, SING WITH HOW GREAT IS OUR GOD

PRAISE -:

1. COME LET'S PRAISE THE LORD
2. I CALL YOU MIGHTY WARRIORS, JEHOHAH JIREH
3. HE'S A MIGHTY GOD
4. PRAISE JEHOVAH, HE'S TURNED MY LIFE AROUND
5. ALL THE GLORY MUST BE UNTO THE LORD IN THE HIGHEST, HALLELUJAH

WORSHIP & PRAISE LYRICS

HOW GREAT IS OUR GOD

HOW GREAT IS OUR GOD
SING WITH HOW GREAT IS OUR GOD
ALL WE HOW GREAT
HOW GREAT IS OUR GOD
NAME ABOVE ALL NAMES
YOU ARE WORTHY OF ALL PRAISE
MY HEART WILL SING
HOW GREAT, IS OUR GOD
LINK: https://youtu.be/KBD18rsVJHk

COME LET'S PRAISE THE LORD

COME LET'S PRAISE THE LORD
HE IS JEHOVAH (TALK ABOUT HIS FAITHFULNESS)
HE IS EL-SHADDAI (TELL THE WORLD OF HIS SALVALTION)
SPREAD THE NEWS AROUND (TELL THEOF HIS PRAISE
LET US PRAISE THE LORD (PRAISE THE LORD)
FOREVER AND EVER MY GOD HE IS THE SAME
HE'LL NEVER CHANGE, FROM ETERNITY TO ETERNITY
HE'LL BE MY GOD, OOH
PRAISE HIM, PRAISE HIM x 4

WE CALL YOU MIGHTY WARRIOR JEHOVAH JIREH

THEY CALL YOU MIGHTY WARRIOR JEHOVAH
JIREH, MIGHTY WARRIOR
AHE HEE, JEHOVA, MIGHTY WARRIOR
THEY CALL YOU MIGHTY WARRIOR JEHOVAH
JIREH, MIGHTY WARRIOR
AHE HEE, JEHOVA, MIGHTY WARRIOR
SOMEBODY, CALL HIM MIGHTY WARRIOR x 3
LINK:

HE'S A MIGHTY GOD

YOU ARE A MIGHTY GOD
YOU ARE A MIGHTY GOD
EVERY POWER BOW BEFORE YOU
YOU ARE A MIGHTY GOD
EVERY POWER BOW BEFORE YOU
YOU ARE A MIGHTY GOD

LINK: https://youtu.be/OIUH6Sd_yCo

PRAISE JEHOVAH, HE'S TURNED MY LIFE AROUND

PRAISE JEHOVAH
HE HAS TURNED MY LIFE AROUND
PRAISE JEHOVAH
HE HAS TURNED MY LIFE AROUND
HE'S TURNED MY AROUND
HE'S TUENED MY AROUND x2

ALL THE GLORY MUST BE TO THE LORD IN THE HIGHEST

ALL THE GLORY MUST BE
UNTO THE LORD IN THE HIGHEST, HALLELUJAH x2
EVERYBODY SHOUT HALLELU
HALLELUJAH
HALLELUJAH, HALLELUJAH x2

LINK: https://youtu.be/drmL-zAfdtg

AFRICAN: PRAISE AND WORSHIP – SET 25

WORSHIP-:

HOSANNA IN THE HIGHEST

PRAISE-:

1. TO YOU LORD BE ALL THE GLORY
2. EXCELLENT OH GOD
3. YOU ARE MARVELOUS LORD
4. YOU'VE BEEN FAITHFUL LORD, FROM THE AGES PAST
5. ALPHA, OMEGA, YOU ARE WORTHY OF OUR PRAISES TODAY

WORSHIP & PRAISE LYRICS

HOSANNA IN THE HIGHEST

HOSANNA IN THE HIGHEST
LET OUR KING BE LIFTED HIGH
HOSSANA
JESUS, YOU BE LIFTED HIGHER, HIGHER, HIGHER
JESUS, YOU BE LIFTED HIGHER, HIGHER, HIGHER
LET OUR KING BE LIFTED HIGH
HOSSANA

LINK: https://youtu.be/sZ6utGRrsX4

TO YOU LORD BE ALL THE GLORY

TO YOU LORD BE ALL THE GLORY
TO YOU LORD BE ALL THE HONOUR
TO YOU LORD BE ALL THE GLORY
AND ADORATION FORVERMORE

LINK: https://youtu.be/y97kFpm9wNM

EXCELLENT OH GOD

EXCELLENT OH GOD
EXCELLENT OH GOD
YOUR NAME IS EXCELLENT
EXCELLENT OH GOD
POWERFUL OH GOD
YOUR NAME IS POWERFUL
POWERFUL OH GOD

YOU ARE MARVELOUS LORD

YOU ARE MARVELOUS LORD
YOU ARE MARVELOUS LORD
YOU ARE MARVELOUS LORD x 3
YOU ARE POWERFUL LORD
YOU WONDERFUL LORD
YOU ARE GLORIOUS LORD

LINK: https://youtu.be/OCadihcZYXc

YOU'VE BEEN FAITHFUL LORD FROM THE AGES PAST

YOU'VE BEEN FAITHFUL LORD
FROM THE AGES PAST
THAT IS WHY YOUR NAME IS FOREVERMORE
YOU ALONE ARE WORTHY LORD
TO BE PRAISED AND ADORE
YOU ALONE ARE WORTHY LORD
TO BE PRAISED AND ADORE

LINK: https://youtu.be/uUicRWWcfig

ALPHA, OMEGA, YOU ARE WORTHY

ALPHA, OMEGA
ALPHA, OMEGA
YOU ARE WORTHY OF OUR PRAISES TODAY
YOU ARE WORTHY OF OUR PRAISES TODAY
ALPHA, OMEGA
ALPHA, OMEGA
YOU ARE WORTHY OF OUR PRAISES TODAY x 3

AFRICAN: PRAISE AND WORSHIP – SET 26

WORSHIP-:

OPEN THE FLOOD GATES IN ABUNDANCE

PRAISE-:

1. YOU ARE GOOD AND YOUR MERCIES FOR EVER HALLELUIA
2. WE CALL MIGHTY WARRIOR JEHOVAH SHAMMAH
3. YOU ARE GOD, YOU ARE NOT JUST BIG OOO
4. HE'S A MIGHTY GOD
5. YOU ARE GREAT, YES YOU ARE

WORSHIP & PRAISE LYRICS

WE ARE IN YOUR PRESENCE, LET IT RAIN

WE ARE IN YOUR PRESENCE, LET IT RAIN
OHH YOUR RAIN (JESUS), LET IT FALL ON ME
WE ARE IN YOUR PRESENCE, LET IT RAIN
OPEN THE FLOOD GATES IN ABUNDANCE
AND CAUSE YOUR RAIN TO FALL ON ME
BABA OH… OH , BABA OH… OH-OH-OH-OH

LINK: https://youtu.be/63nyGawcJbQ

YOU ARE GOOD AND YOUR MERCY IS FOREVER

YOU ARE GOOD AND YOUR MERCY IS FOREVER, HALLELUJAH!
YOU ARE GOOD AND YOUR MERCY IS FOREVER, HALLELUJAH!

LINK: https://youtu.be/Wyo3kqNgcYQ

WE CALL YOU MIGHTY WARRIOR JEHOVAH JIREH

THEY CALL YOU MIGHTY WARRIOR JEHOVAH JIREH, MIGHTY WARRIOR
AHE HEE, JEHOVA, MIGHTY WARRIOR
THEY CALL YOU MIGHTY WARRIOR JEHOVAH JIREH, MIGHTY WARRIOR
AHE HEE, JEHOVA, MIGHTY WARRIOR
SOMEBODY, CALL HIM MIGHTY WARRIOR x 3

YOU ARE GOD

YOU ARE GOD, YOU ARE NOT JUST BIG OH
YOU ARE NOT JUST LARGE OH
YOU ARE A GREAT GOD
YOU ARE BIG, BIG, BIG, BIG, BIG, BIG, BIG
LARGE, LARGE, LARGE, LARGE, LARGE, LARGE
GREAT, GREAT, GREAT, GREAT, GREAT
YOU ARE A GREAT GOD

LINK: https://youtu.be/VZd2fQS8yLI

HE'S A MIGHTY GOD

YOU ARE A MIGHTY GOD
YOU ARE A MIGHTY GOD
EVERY POWER BOW BEFORE YOU
YOU ARE A MIGHTY GOD
EVERY POWER BOW BEFORE YOU
YOU ARE A MIGHTY GOD

LINK: https://youtu.be/OIUH6Sd_yCo

YOU ARE GREAT, YES YOU ARE

YOU ARE GREAT YES YOU ARE HOLY ONE
WALKED UPON THE SEA RISE THE DEAD
YOU REIGN IN MAJESTY MIGHTY GOD
EVERYTHING WRITTEN ABOUT YOU IS GREAT
YOU ARE GREAT YOU ARE GREAT 4X
EVERYTHING WRITTEN ABOUT YOU IS GREAT

LINK: https://youtu.be/q2KiwKlG85s

AFRICAN: PRAISE AND WORSHIP - SET 27

WORSHIP-:

YOU ARE YAHWEH, ALPHA, AND OMEGA

PRAISE-:

1. HOSANNA, HOSANNA, HOSANNA IN THE HIGHEST
2. MASTER OF THE UNIVERSE
3. JEHOVAH REIGNS, JEHOVAH REIGNS
4. JEHOVAH, YOU ARE THE MOST HIGH
5. JEHOVAH EE EEH, JOHOVAH AAH

WORSHIP & PRAISE LYRICS

YOU ARE YAHWEH

YOU ARE YAHWEH EEE
YOU ARE YAHWEH EEE
YOU ARE YAHWEH
ALPHA AND OMEGA
YOU ARE YAHWEH
ALPHA AND OMEGA

LINK: https://youtu.be/mCyN3Ty6_BE

HOSSANA, HOSSANA IN THE HIGHEST

HOSSANA, HOSSANA, HOSSAN IN THE HIGHEST
HOSSANA, HOSSANA, HOSSAN IN THE HIGHEST
LORD WE LIGT UP YOUR NAME
WITH THE HEAT FULL OF PRAISE
BE EXALTED OH LORD MY GOD
HOSSANA IN THE HIGHEST

LINK: https://youtu.be/E1X-VDCMyAc

MASTER OF THE UNIVERSE

YOU ARE THE MASTER, MASTER OF THE UNIVERSE
CONQUEROR AND KING, LORD, MASTER OF THE UNIVERSE
YOU ARE THE EMPEROR ALWAYS, YOU ARE THE HEIR
OVER PRINCIPALITIES, YOU ARE THE HEIR,
OVERPOWERS, YOU ARE THE HEIR, OVER RULERS,
YOU ARE THE MASTER
MASTER OF THE UNIVERSE

LINK: https://youtu.be/kJ48XEDMBoY

JEHOVAH REIGNS, JEHOVAH REIGNS

JEHOVAH REIGNS, JEHOVAH REIGNS
JEHOVAH REIGNS, JEHOVAH REIGNS
YOU ARE LIFTED UP ABOVE OTHER GOD
YOU ARE LIFTED UP ABOVE OTHER GOD
YOU ARE LIFTED UP ABOVE OTHER GOD
YOU ARE LIFTED UP ABOVE OTHER GOD

LINK: https://youtu.be/SK9Qh_EV-b0

JEHOVAH, YOU ARE THE MOST HIGH

JEHOVAH, YOU ARE THE MOST HIGH
JEHOVAH, YOU ARE THE MOST HIGH GOD
JEHOVAH, YOU ARE THE MOST HIGH
JEHOVAH, YOU ARE THE MOST HIGH GOD

LINK: https://youtu.be/QPNlsEy7n5M

JEHOVAH EE EEH, JEHOVAH AAH

JEHOVAH EE EEH (LORD)
JEHOVAH AAH
MY GOD
JEHOVAH EE EEH (LORD)
JEHOVAH AAH

LINK: https://youtu.be/o8pGIMRqKMM

AFRICAN: PRAISE AND WORSHIP – SET 28

WORSHIP-:

WE BOW DOWN AND WORSHIP, YAHWEH

PRAISE-:

1. WE LIFT YOUR NAME HIGHER
2. YOU ARE GOD, YOU RE NOT JUST BIG OH
3. HALLE, HALLE, HALLELUJAH, GLORY, GLORY, WE PRAISE YOUR NAME
4. ALMIGHTY FATHER, WE GIVE YOU GLORY
5. ALL THE GLORY MUST UNTO THE LORD IN THE HIGHEST, HALLELUJAH

WORSHIP & PRAISE LYRICS

WE BOW DOWN AND WORSHIP, YAHWEH

WE BOW DOWN AND WORSHIP, YAHWEH
WE BOW DOWN AND WORSHIP, YAHWEH
YAHWEH, YAHWEH, YAHWEH
YAHWEH, YAHWEH, YAHWEH
WE BOW DOWN AND WORSHIP, YAHWEH
WE BOW DOWN AND WORSHIP, YAHWEH

LINK: https://youtu.be/oGQXKoZB5Bw

WE LIFT YOUR NAME HIGHER

WE LIFT YOUR NAME HIGHER
WE LIFT YOUR NAME HIGHER
WE LIFT YOUR NAME HIGHER
JESUS, WE LIFT YOUR NAME HIGHER
WE LIFT YOUR NAME HIGHER

LINK: https://youtu.be/c5gOT8Hzqnl

YOU ARE GOD

YOU ARE GOD, YOU ARE NOT JUST BIG OH
YOU ARE NOT JUST LARGE OH
YOU ARE A GREAT GOD
YOU ARE BIG, BIG, BIG, BIG, BIG, BIG
LARGE, LARGE, LARGE, LARGE, LARGE
GREAT, GREAT, GREAT, GREAT, GREAT
YOU ARE A GREAT GOD

LINK: https://youtu.be/VZd2fQS8yLl

HALLE, HALLE HALLUYAH

HALLE HALLE HALLUYAH,
GLORY, GLORY, WE PRAISE YOUR NAME
YOU ARE THE KING OF KINGS AND THE LORD OF LORD, WE PRAISE YOUR NAME

LINK: https://youtu.be/2NszJzqbNIE

ALMIGHTY FATHER, WE GIVE YOU GLORY

ALMIGHTY FATHE, WE GIVE YOU GLORY
MY GOD, YOU ARE GOOD
MY GOD, YOU ARE GOOD
MY GOD, YOU ARE GOOD
ALMIGHTY FATHER,
WE GIVE YOU GLORY, MY GOD, YOU ARE GOOD
MY GOD YOU ARE GOOD x3

ALL THE GLORY MUST BE TO THE LORD IN THE HIGHEST

ALL THE GLORY MUST BE
UNTO THE LORD IN THE HIGHEST, HALLELUJAH x2
EVERYBODY SHOUT HALLELU
HALLELUJAH
HALLELUJAH, HALLELUJAH x2

LINK: https://youtu.be/drmL-zAfdtg

AFRICAN: PRAISE AND WORSHIP – SET 29

WORSHIP-:

YOU ARE WORTHY TO BE GLORIFIED, YOU ARE WORTHY LORD

PRAISE-:

1. AT THE MENTION OF NAME
2. YOU ARE GOOD AND YOUR MERCY IS FOREVER, HALLELUJAH
3. JEHOVAH, YOU ARE THE MOST HIGH
4. GIVE HIM PRAISE, GIVE HIM PRAISE
5. EH, EH, EH THE GOD IS GOOD OH

WORSHIP & PRAISE LYRICS

YOU ARE WORTHY TO BE GLORIFIED

YOU ARE WORTHY TO BE GLORIFIED
YOU ARE WORTHY, JEHOVAH
YOU ARE WORTHY TO BE GLORIFIED
YOU ARE WORTHY LORD

LINK: https://youtu.be/nFpU1BIG-hA

AT THE MENTION OF YOUR NAME

AT THE MENTION OF YOUR NAME
EVERY KNEE MUST BOW
AT THE MENTION OF YOUR NAME
EVERY TONGUE CONFESS
THAT YOU ARE LORD
YOU ARE LORD, YOU ARE LORD of LORDS
YOU ARE KING, YOU ARE KING OF KINGS

LINK: https://youtu.be/SpIL4YBBHfY

YOU ARE GOOD AND YOUR MERCY IS FOREVER

YOU ARE GOOD AND YOUR MERCY IS FOREVER, HALLELUJAH!
YOU ARE GOOD AND YOUR MERCY IS FOREVER, HALLELUJAH!

LINK: https://youtu.be/Wyo3kqNgcYQ

JEHOVAH, YOU ARE THE MOST HIGH

JEHOVAH, YOU ARE THE MOST HIGH
JEHOVAH, YOU ARE THE MOST HIGH GOD
JEHOVAH, YOU ARE THE MOST HIGH
JEHOVAH, YOU ARE THE MOST HIGH GOD

LINK: https://youtu.be/QPNIsEy7n5M

GIVE HIM PRAISE, GIVE HIM PRAISE

GIVE HIM PRAISE, GIVE HIM PRAISE
WE ARE HERE TO GIVE
ALL THE PRAISE TO THE LORD
GIVE HIM PRAISE, GIVE HIM PRAISE
WE ARE HERE TO GIVE
ALL THE PRAISE TO THE LORD

HEY, HEY, MY GOD IS GOOD OH

HEY, HEY, MY GOD IS GOOD OH
HEY, HEY, MY GOD IS GOOD OH
EVERYTHING IS DOUBLE, DOUBLE OOO
MY BLESSINGS ARE DOUBLE, DOUBLE

LINK: https://youtu.be/d4J1ueG98Iw

AFRICAN: PRAISE AND WORSHIP - SET 30

WORSHIP-:

ANCIENT OF DAYS, AS OLD AS YOU ARE

PRAISE-:

1. COME AND SEE THE LORD IS GOOD
2. WHAT SHALL WE DO TODAY, TODAY OO, I WILL LIFT UP
3. MASTER OF THE UNIVERSE
4. WHO HAS THE FINAL SAY
5. JEHOVAH REIGNS

WORSHIP & PRAISE LYRICS

ANCIENT OF DAYS

ANCIENT OF DAYS
AS OLD AS YOU ARE
AS OLD AS YOU ARE
YOU WILL NEVER CHANGE
ANCIENT OF DAYS
AS OLD AS YOU ARE
AS OLD AS YOU ARE
YOU WILL NEVER CHANGE
LINK: https://youtu.be/kkazyTusx_A

COME AND SEE THE LORD IS GOOD

COME AND SEE THE LORD IS GOOD
COME AND SEE THE LORD IS GOOD
THERE IS NOTHING HE CANNOT DO
COME AND SEE THE LORD IS GOOD
HE GAVE ME VICTORY
HE GAVE ME PEACE OF MIND
THERE IS NOTHING HE CANNOT DO
COME AND SEE THE LORD IS GOOD
LINK: https://youtu.be/2Cy-6YnG-8w

WHAT SHALL WE DO TODAY

WHAT SHALL WE DO TODAY
TODAY, OO, I WILL LIFT UP IN PRAISE
FOR ALL I KNOW, YOU ARE ALWAYS THERE FOR ME
ALMIGHTY GOD, YOU'RE MY ALL IN ALL
NO MATTER WHAT THEY SAY
WHEN TROUBLE COMES MY WAY
I WILL PRAISE YOUR NAME

LINK: https://youtu.be/wtvnEGNVKGE

MASTER OF THE UNIVERSE

YOU ARE THE MASTER, MASTER OF THE UNIVERSE
CONQUEROR AND KING, LORD, MASTER OF THE UNIVERSE
YOU ARE THE EMPEROR ALWAYS, YOU ARE THE HEIR
OVER PRINCIPALITIES, YOU ARE THE HEIR,
OVERPOWERS, YOU ARE THE HEIR, OVER RULERS, YOU
ARE THE MASTER
MASTER OF THE UNIVERSE

LINK: https://youtu.be/kJ48XEDMBoY

WHO HAS THE FINAL SAY, JEHOVAH, WE LIFT YOU UP

WHO HAS THE FINAL SAY
JEHOVAH, HAS THE FINAL SAY
WHO HAS THE FINAL SAY
JEHOVAH, HAS THE FINAL SAY
JEHOVAH, TURNED MY LIFE AROUND x2
HE MAKES A WAY, WHERE THERE IS NO WAY
JEHOVAH, HAS THE FINAL SAY
WE LIFT YOU UP
LINK: https://youtu.be/Bx2T8aunyvs

JEHOVAH REIGNS, JEHOVAH REIGNS

JEHOVAH REIGNS, JEHOVAH REIGNS
JEHOVAH REIGNS, JEHOVAH REIGNS
YOU ARE LIFTED UP ABOVE OTHER GOD
YOU ARE LIFTED UP ABOVE OTHER GOD
YOU ARE LIFTED UP ABOVE OTHER GOD
YOU ARE LIFTED UP ABOVE OTHER GOD

LINK: https://youtu.be/SK9Qh_EV-b0

AFRICAN: PRAISE AND WORSHIP – SET 31

WORSHIP-:

WE LIFT YOUR NAME HIGHER; WE LIFT YOUR NAME HIGHER

PRAISE-:

1. HALLE, HALLE, HALLELUJAH, GLORY, GLORY WE PRAISE YOUR NAME
2. GLORY, GLORY, HALLELUJAH, PRAISE YOUR NAME
3. JEHOVAH, YOU ARE THE MOST HIGH
4. WE WILL HAIL., HAIL YOUR NAME
5. HAIL MY JESUS, POWERFUL WARROIR

WORSHIP & PRAISE LYRICS

WE LIFT YOUR NAME HIGHER

WE LIFT YOUR NAME HIGHER
WE LIFT YOUR NAME HIGHER
WE LIFT YOUR NAME HIGHER
JESUS, WE LIFT YOUR NAME HIGHER
WE LIFT YOUR NAME HIGHER

LINK: https://youtu.be/zZkmtJo9GgY

HALLE, HALLE HALLELUYAH

HALLE, HALLE, HALLELUYAH,
GLORY, GLORY, WE PRAISE YOUR NAME
YOU ARE THE KING OF KINGS AND THE LORD OF LORD,
WE PRAISE YOUR NAME

LINK: https://youtu.be/2NszJzqbNIE

GLORY, GLORY, HALLELUJAH, PRAISE YOUR NAME

GLORY, GLORY, HALLELUJAH
GLORY, GLORY, PRAISE YOUR NAME

GLORY, GLORY, HALLELUJAH
GLORY, GLORY, PRAISE YOUR NAME
GLORY, GLORY, HALLELUJAH
GLORY, GLORY, PRAISE YOUR NAME

JEHOVAH, YOU ARE THE MOST HIGH

JEHOVAH, YOU ARE THE MOST HIGH
JEHOVAH, YOU ARE THE MOST HIGH GOD
JEHOVAH, YOU ARE THE MOST HIGH
JEHOVAH, YOU ARE THE MOST HIGH GOD

LINK: https://youtu.be/QPNIsEy7n5M

WE WILL HAIL YOUR NAME

WE WILL HAIL,
HAIL YOUR NAME
DAY BY DAY
ALL THE WAY x2
WE WILL HAIL, HAIL, HAIL, HAIL
HAIL YOUR NAME, NAME, NAME
DAY BY DAY, DAY, DAY
ALL THE WAY, ALL WAY
LINK: https://youtu.be/1HgZNm1bjSI

HAIL MY JESUS, POWERFUL WARRIOR

HAIL MY JESUS
POWERFUL POWER WARROIR
HAIL MY JESUS
POWERFUL POWER WARROIR

LINK: https://youtu.be/xh3yQKrjBls

AFRICAN: PRAISE AND WORSHIP - SET 32

WORSHIP-:

JEHOVAH IS YOUR NAME, MIGHTY WARRIOR

PRAISE-:

1. JESUS, WE LIFT YOUR NAME ON HIGH, YOUR NAME ON HIGH BE LIFTED UP
2. WE GIVE YOU ALL THE PRAISE
3. JEHOVAH, HE TURNED MY LIFE AROUND
4. COME LET'S PRAISE THE LORD
5. JEHOVAH REIGNS, JEHOVAH REIGNS

WORSHIP & PRAISE LYRICS

JEHOVAH IS YOUR NAME

JEHOVAH IS YOUR NAME,
MIGHTY WARRIOR
GREAT IN BATTLE
JEHOVAH IS YOUR NAME
MIGHTY WARRIOR
GREAT IN BATTLE
JEHOVAH IS YOUR NAME

LINK: https://youtu.be/Ro9KtH6cSVU

JEHOVAH REIGNS, JEHOVAH REIGNS

JEHOVAH REIGNS, JEHOVAH REIGNS
JEHOVAH REIGNS, JEHOVAH REIGNS
YOU ARE LIFTED UP ABOVE OTHER GOD
YOU ARE LIFTED UP ABOVE OTHER GOD
YOU ARE LIFTED UP ABOVE OTHER GOD
YOU ARE LIFTED UP ABOVE OTHER GOD

LINK: https://youtu.be/SK9Qh_EV-b0

JEHOVAH, HE TURNED MY LIFE AROUND

JEHOVAH TURNED MY LIFE AROUND (2X)
HE MAKES A WAY WHERE THERE SEEMS NO WAY, JEHOVAH
JEHOVAH TURNED MY LIFE AROUND
JEHOVAH TURNED MY LIFE AROUND OOOHH...
HE MAKES A WAY WHERE THERE SEEMS NO WAY

LINK: https://youtu.be/PYnt_KhKodA

COME LET'S PRAISE THE LORD

COME LET'S PRAISE THE LORD
HE IS JEHOVAH (TALK ABOUT HIS FAITHFULNESS)
HE IS EL-SHADDAI (TELL THE WORLD OF HIS SALVALTION)
SPREAD THE NEWS AROUND (TELL THEOF HIS PRAISE
LET US PRAISE THE LORD (PRAISE THE LORD)
FOREVER AND EVER MY GOD HE IS THE SAME
HE'LL NEVER CHANGE, FROM ETERNITY TO ETERNITY
HE'LL BE MY GOD, OOH
PRAISE HIM, PRAISE HIM x 4

LINK: https://youtu.be/YEXJ9N-qHSM

YOU ARE GREAT, YES YOU ARE

YOU ARE GREAT YES YOU ARE HOLY ONE
WALKED UPON THE SEA RISE THE DEAD
YOU REIGN IN MAJESTY MIGHTY GOD
EVERYTHING WRITTEN ABOUT YOU IS GREAT
YOU ARE GREAT YOU ARE GREAT 4X
EVERYTHING WRITTEN ABOUT YOU IS GREAT

LINK: https://youtu.be/q2KiwKIG85s

HE'S A MIGHTY GOD

YOU ARE A MIGHTY GOD
YOU ARE A MIGHTY GOD
EVERY POWER BOW BEFORE YOU
YOU ARE A MIGHTY GOD
EVERY POWER BOW BEFORE YOU
YOU ARE A MIGHTY GOD

LINK: https://youtu.be/OIUH6Sd_yCo

AFRICAN: PRAISE AND WORSHIP - SET 33

WORSHIP-:

WORTHY YOU ARE WORTHY, KING OF KINGS, LORD OF LORD YOU ARE WORTHY

PRAISE-:

1. I WILL LIFT UP MY VOICE AND JOYFUL SING
2. YOU ARE YAHWEH AH AH YOU ARE YAHWEH ALPHA AND OMEGA
3. MY GOD IS A GOOD GOD
4. WE LIFT YOUR NAME HIGHER
5. HALLELUJAH THAT'S WHAT OUR SONG WILL BE

WORSHIP & PRAISE LYRICS

WORTHY YOU ARE WORTHY, KING OF KINGS

WORTHY YOU ARE WORTHY
KING OF KINGS
LORD OF LORDS YOU ARE WORTHY
WORTHY YOU ARE WORTHY
KING OF KINGS
LORD OF LORDS
I WORSHIP YOU

LINK: https://youtu.be/xZpmwquJgBo

I WILL LIFT UP MY VOICE AND JOYFUL SING

I WILL LIFT UP MY VOICE AND JOYFUL SING
NOT FOR WHAT YOU HAVE FOR ME
BUT WHO YOU ARE
YOU ARE THE SONG THAT I SING
YOU ARE THE REASON I SING
MELODY IN MY HEART
YOU ARE THE SONG THAT I SING
I WILL PRAISE YOU LORD
YOU REIGN x3, FOREVERMORE

LINK: https://fb.watch/hOCoHjyvzY/

YOU ARE YAHWEH AH AH, YOU ARE YAHWEH

YOU ARE YAHWEH AH AH
YOU ARE YAHWEH
YOU ARE YAHWEH AH AH
YOU ARE YAHWEH
YOU ARE YAHWEH, ALPHA AND OMEGA
YOU ARE YAHWEH, ALPHA AND OMEGA

LINK: https://youtu.be/gDQAr3gmSqY

MY GOD IS A GOOD GOD, YES HE IS

MY GOD IS A GOOD GOD, YES HE IS
HE LIFTS ME UP (HE LIFTS ME UP)
HE TURNS ME AROUND (HE TURNS ME AROUND)
HE SETS ME FEET, UPON THE SOLID ROCK
I FEEL LIKE DANCING, I FEEL LIKE CLAPPING

LINK: https://youtu.be/5RcwYmVRttA

WE LIFT YOUR NAME HIGHER

WE LIFT YOUR NAME HIGHER
WE LIFT YOUR NAME HIGHER
WE LIFT YOUR NAME HIGHER
JESUS, WE LIFT YOUR NAME HIGHER
WE LIFT YOUR NAME HIGHER
WE LIFT YOUR NAME HIGHER

LINK: https://youtu.be/c5gOT8HzqnI

HALLELUJAH THAT'S WHAT OUR SONG WILL BE

HALLELUJAH,
THAT'S WHAT OUR SONG WILL BE
THAT'S WHAT OUR SONG WILL BE
THAT'S WHAT OUR SONG WILL BE

LINK: https://youtu.be/eYJpUgTXOUk

AFRICAN: PRAISE AND WORSHIP – SET 34

WORSHIP-:

GLORY BE TO GOD IN THE HIGHEST AMEN

PRAISE-:

1. LORD YOU ARE SO GOOD, BLESSED BE YOUR NAME, IN HEAVEN
2. YOU ARE GOOD AND YOUR MERCIES FOREVER, HALLELUJAH
3. JEHOVAH EEH JEHOVAH AAH (LORD, SAVOIUR)
4. I WILL PRAISE THE LORD IN THE SANCTURAY
5. AWESOME GOD, MIGHTY GOD

WORSHIP & PRAISE LYRICS

GLORY BE TO GOD IN THE HIGHEST AMEN

GLORY BE TO GOD IN THE HIGHEST AMEN
GLORY BE TO GOD IN THE HIGHEST AMEN
FOR HIS MERCIES ENDRETH FOREVER AMEN
FOR HIS MERCIES ENDRETH FOREVER AMEN
FOR HIS MERCIES ENDRETH FOREVER AMEN
FOR HIS MERCIES ENDRETH FOREVER AMEN

LINK: https://youtu.be/p9LfTYZmOVE

LORD YOU ARE SO GOOD, BLESSED BE YOUR NAME,

LORD YOU ARE SO GOOD, BLESSED BE YOUR NAME
LORD YOU ARE SO GOOD, BLESSED BE YOUR NAME
IN HEAVEN YOU ARE THE LORD
ON EARTH YOU REIGN FOREVER
OH LORD HOW GREAT THOU ART
BLESSDED BE YOUR NAME

LINK: https://youtu.be/QhxObPYSWS8

YOU ARE GOOD AND YOUR MERCY IS FOREVER

YOU ARE GOOD AND YOUR MERCY IS FOREVER, HALLELUJAH!
YOU ARE GOOD AND YOUR MERCY IS FOREVER, HALLELUJAH!

LINK: https://youtu.be/Wyo3kqNgcYQ

JEHOVAH EEH JEHOVAH AAH (LORD, SAVOIUR)

JEHOVAH LORD, JEHOVAH AA
JEHOVAH EEH JEHOVAH AAH
JEHOVAH LORD, JEHOVAH AA
JEHOVAH EEH JEHOVAH AAH

LINK: https://youtu.be/o8pGlMRqKMM

I WILL PRAISE THE LORD IN THE SANCTURAY

I WILL PRAISE THE LORD IN THE SANCTURAY
I WILL PRAISE THE LORD IN THE SANCTURAY
YOU ARE WORTHY OF MY PRAISE, I WILL DANCE AND CELEBRATE
I WILL PRAISE THE LORD IN THE SANCTURAY
LET THE PEOPLE NOW REJOICE FOR LORD IS GOOD
I WILL PRAISE THE LORD IN THE SANCTURAY

LINK: https://youtu.be/dDl1hWPCbTE

AWESOME GOD, MIGHTY GOD

AWESOME GOD, MIGHTY GOD
AWESOME GOD, MIGHTY GOD
WE GIVE YOU PRAISE, AWESOME GOD
WE GIVE YOU PRAISE, MIGHTY GOD
YOU ARE HIGHLY LIFTED UP, AWESOME GOD
YOU ARE HIGHLY LIFTED UP, MIGHTY GOD

LINK; https://youtu.be/V5dcczS2GsE

AFRICAN: PRAISE AND WORSHIP – SET 35

WORSHIP-:

YOU DO MIGHTY THINGS; YOU DO GLORIOUS THINGS

PRAISE-:

1. I WILL LIFT UP MY VOICE I WILL JOYFULLY SING
2. JEHOVAH SHAMMAH, JEHOVAH NISSI, YOU ARE MY EBENEZER
3. HE'S A MIGHTY GOD
4. THERE IS SOMETHING THAT MAKES ME COME IN TO YOUR PRESENCE
5. JOY OVERFLOWS IN MY HEART

WORSHIP & PRAISE LYRICS

YOU DO MIGHTY THINGS

I STAND AMAZED IN YOUR PRESENCE
THERE IS NOTHING YOU CANNOT DO
I STAND AMAZED IN YOUR PRESENCE
THERE IS JOY, PEACE, AND HOPE
THERE'S NO ONE LIKE YOU, JESUS
THERE'S NO ONE LIKE YOU, IN ALL THE EARTH
THERE'S NO ONE LIKE YOU, JESUS
THERE'S NO ONE LIKE YOU
YOU DO MIGHTY THINHGS, YOU DO GLORIOUS THINGS, YOU'RE A FAITHFUL GOD, AWESOME IS YOUR NAME

LINK: https://youtu.be/aZBAegRpREY

I WILL LIFT UP MY VOICE AND JOYFUL SING

I WILL LIFT UP MY VOICE AND JOYFUL SING
NOT FOR WHAT YOU HAVE FOR ME
BUT WHO YOU ARE
YOU ARE THE SONG THAT I SING
YOU ARE THE REASON I SING
MELODY IN MY HEART
YOU ARE THE SONG THAT I SING
I WILL PRAISE YOU LORD

LINK: https://fb.watch/hOCoHjyvzY/

JEHOVAH SHAMMAH, JEHOVAH NISSI, YOU ARE MY

JEHOVAH JIREH
JEHOVAH NISSI
YOU ARE MY EBENEZAR
YOU ARE MY ADONAI
I GIVE YOU GLORY HONOUR POWER MAJESTY
YOU ARE MY LORD, FOREVER

LINK: https://youtu.be/0EByR980ypQ

HE'S A MIGHTY GOD

HE'S A MIGHTY GOD
HE'S A MIGHTY GOD
JESUS, IS A MIGHTY GOD
EVERY POWER BOW BEFORE HIM
HE'S A MIGHTY GOD

LINK: https://youtu.be/OIUH6Sd_yCo

AT THE MENTION OF YOUR NAME

AT THE MENTION OF YOUR NAME
EVERY KNEE MUST BOW
AT THE MENTION OF YOUR NAME
EVERY TONGUE CONFESS
THAT YOU ARE LORD
YOU ARE LORD, YOU ARE LORD OF LORDS
YOU ARE KING, YOU ARE KING OF KINGS
AT THE MENTION OF YOUR NAME, EVERY KNEE MUST BOW

LINK: https://youtu.be/SpIL4YBBHfY

JOY OVERFLOW IN MY HEART

JOY OVERFLOWS IN MY HEART
SING A NEW SONG TO THE LORD
I WILL PRAISE YOUR NAME
I WILL WORSHIP YOU
GLORY HALLELUYAH SING A NEW SONG TO THE LORD (2X)

LINK: https://youtu.be/Aq4UDCRRdJc

AFRICAN: PRAISE AND WORSHIP – SET 36

WORSHIP-:

YOUR NAME IS YAHWEH

PRAISE-:

1. YOU ARE GOOD AND YOUR MERCY IS FOREVER, HALLELUJAH
2. I WILL LIFT UP MY VOICE, I WILL JOYFULLY SING
3. WHAT WILL I GIVE TO YOU, MY PRAISE
4. YOU ARE GREAT YES YOU ARE
5. HAIL MY JESUS, POWERFUL WARRIOR

WORSHIP & PRAISE LYRICS

YOUR NAME IS YAHWEH

YOUR NAME IS YAHWEH
YOUR NAME IS YAHWEH
YOUR NAME IS YAHWEH
ALPHA AND OMEGA
YOU ARE YAHWEH
ALPHA AND OMEGA

LINK: https://youtu.be/mCyN3Ty6_BE

YOU ARE GOOD AND YOUR MERCY IS FOREVER

YOU ARE GOOD AND YOUR MERCY IS FOREVER, HALLELUJAH!
YOU ARE GOOD AND YOUR MERCY IS FOREVER, HALLELUJAH!

LINK: https://youtu.be/Wyo3kqNgcYQ

I WILL LIFT UP MY VOICE AND JOYFUL SING

I WILL LIFT UP MY VOICE AND JOYFUL SING
NOT FOR WHAT YOU HAVE FOR ME
BUT WHO YOU ARE
YOU ARE THE SONG THAT I SING
YOU ARE THE REASON I SING
MELODY IN MY HEART
YOU ARE THE SONG THAT I SING
I WILL PRAISE YOU LORD

LINK: https://fb.watch/hOCoHjyvzY/

WHAT WILL I GIVE TO YOU, MY PRAISE

WHAT WILL I GIVE TO YOU
MY PRAISE
WHAT WILL I GIVE TO YOU
MY PRAISE
I DON'T HAVE MONEY
MY PRAISE
WHAT WILL I GIVE TO YOU
MY PRAISE

LINK: https://youtu.be/ZAjhMlnXN1c

YOU ARE GREAT, YES YOU ARE

YOU ARE GREAT YES YOU ARE HOLY ONE
WALKED UPON THE SEA RISE THE DEAD
YOU REIGN IN MAJESTY MIGHTY GOD
EVERYTHING WRITTEN ABOUT YOU IS GREAT
YOU ARE GREAT YOU ARE GREAT 4X
EVERYTHING WRITTEN ABOUT YOU IS GREAT

LINK: https://youtu.be/q2KiwKlG85s

HAIL MY JESUS, POWERFUL WARRIOR

HAIL MY JESUS
POWERFUL POWER WARROIR
HAIL MY JESUS
POWERFUL POWER WARROIR

LINK: https://youtu.be/xh3yQKrjBls

AFRICAN: PRAISE AND WORSHIP – SET 36

WORSHIP-:

WHO IS LIKE UNTO THEE OH LORD

PRAISE-:

1. I WILL PRAISE THE LORD IN THE SANCTURAY
2. MASTER OF UNIVERSE
3. JEHOVAH REIGNS
4. HE'S A MIGHTY GOD
5. COME LET'S PRAISE

WORSHIP & PRAISE LYRICS

WHO IS LIKE UNTO THEE OH LORD

WHO IS LIKE UNTO THEE OH LORD
WHO IS LIKE UNTO THEE OH LORD
AMONGS THE GODS WHO IS LIKE THEE
GLORIOUS IN HOLINESS
FEARFUL IN PRAISES, DOING WONDERS
HALLELUJAH

LINK: https://youtu.be/_ZSRQGMk6N0

I WILL PRAISE THE LORD IN THE SANCTURAY

I WILL PRAISE THE LORD IN THE SANCTURAY
I WILL PRAISE THE LORD IN THE SANCTURAY
YOU ARE WORTHY OF MY PRAISE, I WILL DANCE AND CELEBRATE
I WILL PRAISE THE LORD IN THE SANCTURAY
LET THE PEOPLE NOW REJOICE FOR LORD IS GOOD
I WILL PRAISE THE LORD IN THE SANCTURAY

LINK: https://youtu.be/dDl1hWPCbTE

MASTER OF THE UNIVERSE

YOU ARE THE MASTER, MASTER OF THE UNIVERSE
CONQUEROR AND KING, LORD, MASTER OF THE UNIVERSE
YOU ARE THE EMPEROR ALWAYS, YOU ARE THE HEIR
OVER PRINCIPALITIES, YOU ARE THE HEIR,
OVERPOWERS, YOU ARE THE HEIR, OVER RULERS,
YOU ARE THE MASTER
MASTER OF THE UNIVERSE

LINK: https://youtu.be/kJ48XEDMBoY

JEHOVAH REIGNS, JEHOVAH REIGNS

JEHOVAH REIGNS, JEHOVAH REIGNS
JEHOVAH REIGNS, JEHOVAH REIGNS
YOU ARE LIFTED UP ABOVE OTHER GOD
YOU ARE LIFTED UP ABOVE OTHER GOD
YOU ARE LIFTED UP ABOVE OTHER GOD
YOU ARE LIFTED UP ABOVE OTHER GOD

LINK: https://youtu.be/SK9Uh_EV-b0

HE'S A MIGHTY GOD

HE'S A MIGHTY GOD
HE'S A MIGHTY GOD
JESUS, IS A MIGHTY GOD
EVERY POWER BOW BEFORE HIM
HE'S A MIGHTY GOD

LINK: https://youtu.be/OIUH6Sd_yCo

COME LET'S PRAISE THE LORD

COME LET'S PRAISE THE LORD
HE IS JEHOVAH (TALK ABOUT HIS FAITHFULNESS)
HE IS EL- SHADAI (TELL THE WORLD OF HIS SALVATION)
SPREAD THE NEWS AROUND (TELL THE WORLD OF HIS PRAISE)
LET US PRAISE LORD (PRAISE THE LORD)
FOREVER AND EVER MY GOS HEIS THE SAME
HE'LL NEVER CHANGE
FROM ETERNITY, TO ETRNITY
HE'LL BE MY GOD OOH
PRAISE HIM
LINK: https://youtu.be/YEXJ9N-qHSM

AFRICAN: PRAISE AND WORSHIP – SET 37

WORSHIP-:

ALPHA AND OMEGA, WE WORSHIP YOUR NAME

PRAISE-:

1. COME LET'S PRAISE
2. HEY, HEY MY GOD IS GOOD OH
3. AT THE MENTION OF YOUR NAME
4. JEHOVAH, YOU THE MOST HIGH
5. HE'S A MIGHTY GOD

WORSHIP & PRAISE LYRICS

ALPHA AND OMEGA, WE WORSHIP YOUR NAME

YOU ARE THE GOD THAT OPENS EVERY DOOR
YOU ARE THE GOD THAT MAKES THE LAME TO WALK
YOU ARE THE GOD WHO MAKES THE BLIND EYES SEE
YOU ARE THE GOD THAT GIVES ME VICTORY x2
ALPHA AND OMEGA,
WE WORSHIP YOUR NAME x 7

LINK: https://youtu.be/MEsC9U5izLg

COME LET'S PRAISE THE LORD

COME LET'S PRAISE THE LORD
HE IS JEHOVAH (TALK ABOUT HIS FAITHFULNESS)
HE IS EL-SHADAI (TELL THE WORLD OF HIS SALVATION)
SPREAD THE NEWS AROUND (TELL THE WORLD OF HIS PRAISE)
LET US PRAISE LORD (PRAISE THE LORD)
FOREVER AND EVER MY GOS HEIS THE SAME
HE'LL NEVER CHANGE
FROM ETERNITY, TO ETRNITY
HE'LL BE MY GOD OOH
PRAISE HIM

LINK: https://youtu.be/YEXJ9N-qHSM

HEY, HEY, MY GOD IS GOOD OH

HEY, HEY, MY GOD IS GOOD OH
HEY, HEY, MY GOD IS GOOD OH
EVERYTHING IS DOUBLE, DOUBLE OOO
MY BLESSINGS ARE DOUBLE, DOUBLE

LINK: https://youtu.be/d4J1ueG98lw

AT THE MENTION OF YOUR NAME

AT THE MENTION OF YOUR NAME
EVERY KNEE MUST BOW
AT THE MENTION OF YOUR NAME
EVERY TONGUE CONFESS
THAT YOU ARE LORD
YOU ARE LORD, YOU ARE LORD OF LORDS
YOU ARE KING, YOU ARE KING OF KINGS
AT THE MENTION OF YOUR NAME, EVERY KNEE MUST BOW

LINK: https://youtu.be/SpIL4YBBHfY

JEHOVAH, YOU ARE THE MOST HIGH

JEHOVAH, YOU ARE THE MOST HIGH
JEHOVAH, YOU ARE THE MOST HIGH GOD
JEHOVAH, YOU ARE THE MOST HIGH
JEHOVAH, YOU ARE THE MOST HIGH GOD

LINK: https://youtu.be/QPNlsEy7n5M

HE'S A MIGHTY GOD

HE'S A MIGHTY GOD
HE'S A MIGHTY GOD
JESUS, IS A MIGHTY GOD
EVERY POWER BOW BEFORE HIM
HE'S A MIGHTY GOD

LINK: https://youtu.be/OIUH6Sd_yCo

AFRICAN: PRAISE AND WORSHIP – SET 38

WORSHIP-:

UNTO THE LORD BE THE GLORY GREAT THINGS HE HAS DONE

PRAISE-:

1. ALL THE GLORY MUST BE TO THE LORD IN THE HIGHEST HALLELUJAH
2. OH LORD, WE PRAISE YOU
3. WE LIFT YOUR NAME ON HIGH, ALL THE GLORY TO YOU
4. THERE IS SOMETHING THAT MAKE COME INTO YOUR PRESENCE
5. YOU ARE GREAT, YES YOU ARE

WORSHIP & PRAISE LYRICS

UNTO THE LORD BE THE GLORY GREAT

UNTO THE LORD BE THE GLORY
GREAT THINGS HE HAS DONE
UNTO THE LORD BE THE GLORY
GREAT THINGS HE HAS DONE
GREAT THINGS, HE HAS DONE
GREATER THINGS HE WILL DO
UNTO THE LORD BE THE GLORY
GREAT THINGS HE HAS DONE
LINK: https://youtube.com/shorts/mRRLg58QwQg?featur

ALL THE GLORY MUST BE TO THE LORD IN THE HIGHEST

ALL THE GLORY MUST BE TO THE LORD
IN THE HIGHEST, HALLELUJAH
ALL THE GLORY MUST BE TO THE LORD
IN THE HIGHEST, HALLELUJAH
EVERYBODY, SHOUT HALLELU, HALLELUJAH
HALLELUJAH, HALLELUJAH
HALLELUJAH, HALLELUJAH
LINK: https://youtu.be/drmL-zAfdtg

OH LORD, WE PRAISE YOU

OH LORD, WE PRAISE YOU
OH LORD, WE PRAISE YOU
WE EXALT YOUR NAME x2
OH LORD, WE YOUR'RE WONDERFUL GOD AMEN
OH LORD, WE YOUR'RE WONDERFUL GOD AMEN

LINK: https://youtu.be/MPSnWLd3yR4

WE LIFT YOUR NAME ON HIGH, ALL THE GLORY TO YOU

WE LIFT YOUR NAME ON HIGH
ALL THE GLORY TO YOU
WE LIFT YOUR NAME ON HIGH
ALL THE GLORY TO YOU
ALL THE GLORY TO YOU, ALL THE GLORY TO YOU x2

THERE IS SOMETHING THAT MAKES ME COME INTO YOUR PRESENCE

THERE IS SOMETHING THAT MAKES ME COME INTO YOUR PRESENCE - MY HELPER
THERE IS SOMETHING THAT MAKES ME COME INTO YOUR PRESENCE - MY HELPER
MY HELPER O MY HELPER (2X)
THERE IS SOMETHING THAT MAKES ME COME INTO YOUR PRESENCE - MY HELPER
LINK: https://youtu.be/mT6B6eoAIug

YOU ARE GREAT, YES YOU ARE

YOU ARE GREAT YES YOU ARE HOLY ONE
WALKED UPON THE SEA RISE THE DEAD
YOU REIGN IN MAJESTY MIGHTY GOD
EVERYTHING WRITTEN ABOUT YOU IS GREAT
YOU ARE GREAT YOU ARE GREAT 4X
EVERYTHING WRITTEN ABOUT YOU IS GREAT

LINK: https://youtu.be/q2KiwKlG85s

AFRICAN: PRAISE AND WORSHIP – SET 39

WORSHIP-:

WE BOW DOWN AND WORSHIP, YAHWEH

PRAISE-:

1. WE ARE SAYING THANK YOU JESUS THANK YOU
2. THANK YOU LORD ALL WE HAVE TO SAY IS THANK YOU
3. OH LORD, WE PRAISE YOU
4. AWESOME GOD MIGHTY GOD
5. SOME PEOPLE SAY YOU SO GOOD

WORSHIP & PRAISE LYRICS

WE BOW DOWN AND WORSHIP, YAHWEH

WE BOW DOWN AND WORSHIP, YAHWEH
YAHWEH, YAHWEH, YAHWEH
YAHWEH, YAHWEH, YAHWEH
WE BOW DOWN AND WORSHIP, YAHWEH
WE BOW DOWN AND WORSHIP, YAHWEH

LINK: https://youtu.be/q0A6nHOspkc

WE ARE SAYING THANK, JESUS THANK

WE ARE SAYING THANK
JESUS THANK YOU
JEHOVAH THAN YOU
EVERYBODY IS SAYING THANK YOU
JESUS THANK YOU
THANK YOU, LORD,

LINK: https://youtu.be/Oy1SMGMB7Rw

THANK YOU, LORD, ALL WE HAVE TO SAY

THANK YOU, LORD
THANK YOU, LORD
ALL WE HAVE TO SAY IS THANK YOU LORD
THANK YOU, LORD
THANK YOU, LORD
ALL WE HAVE TO SAY IS THANK YOU LORD

LINK: https://youtu.be/bJlogO_rmeo

OH LORD, WE PRAISE YOU

OH LORD, WE PRAISE YOU
OH LORD, WE PRAISE YOU
WE EXALT YOUR NAME x2
OH LORD, WE YOUR'RE WONDERFUL GOD AMEN
OH LORD, WE YOUR'RE WONDERFUL GOD AMEN

LINK: https://youtu.be/MPSnWLd3yR4

AWESOME GOD, MIGHTY GOD

AWESOME GOD, MIGHTY GOD
AWESOME GOD, MIGHTY GOD
WE GIVE YOU PRAISE, AWESOME GOD
WE GIVE YOU PRAISE, MIGHTY GOD
YOU ARE HIGHLY LIFTED UP, AWESOME GOD
YOU ARE HIGHLY LIFTED UP, MIGHTY GOD

LINK: https://youtu.be/V5dcczS2GsE

YOU ARE BIGGER THAN WHAT PEOPLE SAY

YOU ARE BIGGER THAN WHAT PEOPLE SAY
JEHOVAH YOU ARE BIGGER THAN WHAT PEOPLE SAY
YOU ARE BIGGER THAN WHAT PEOPLE SAY
JEHOVAH YOU ARE BIGGER THAN WHAT PEOPLE SAY
JEHOVAH, YOU ARE GOOD, YOU ARE KIND
YOU ARE BIGGER THAN WHAT PEOPLE SAY

LINK: https://youtu.be/is_9GAbT0lI

AFRICAN: PRAISE AND WORSHIP – SET 40

WORSHIP-:

THANKS, THANKS, WE GIVE YOU THANKS

PRAISE-:

1. HOSSANA, HOSSANA, HOSSANA IN THE HIGHEST
2. ALMIGHTY FATHER WE GIVE GLORY
3. GIVE HIM PRAISE, GIVE HIM PRAISE
4. WE LIFT YOUR NAME ON HIGH ALL THE GLORY TO YOU
5. ALL THE GLORY MUST BE TO THE LORD IN THE HIGHEST

WORSHIP & PRAISE LYRICS

THANKS, THANKS, WE GIVE YOU THANKS

THANKS, THANKS, WE GIVE YOU THANKS
FOR ALL YOU HAVE DONE
WE ARE SO BLESSDED
OUR SOUL IS AT REST
OH LORD, WE GIVE YOU THANKS

LINK: https://youtu.be/MF4xWiFO980

ALL THE GLORY MUST BE TO THE LORD IN THE HIGHEST

ALL THE GLORY MUST BE
TO THE LORD IN THE HIGHEST, HALLELUJAH x2
EVERYBODY SHOUT HALLELU
HALLELUJAH
HALLELUJAH, HALLELUJAH x2

LINK: https://youtu.be/drmL-zAfdtg

ALMIGHTY FATHER WE GIVE GLORY

ALMIGHTY FATHER WE GIVE GLORY
MY GOD, YOU ARE GOOD
ALMIGHTY FATHER WE GIVE GLORY
MY GOD, YOU ARE GOOD
MY GOD, YOU ARE GOOD
MY GOD, YOU ARE GOOD

GIVE HIM PRAISE, GIVE HIM PRAISE

GIVE HIM PRAIS, GIVE HIM PRAISE
GIVE HIM PRAISE, GIVE HIM PRAISE
WE ARE HERE TO GIVE
ALL THE PRAISE TO THE LORD

WE LIFT YOUR NAME HIGHER

WE LIFT YOUR NAME HIGHER
WE LIFT YOUR NAME HIGHER
WE LIFT YOUR NAME HIGHER
JESUS, WE LIFT YOUR NAME HIGHER
WE LIFT YOUR NAME HIGHER

LINK: https://youtu.be/c5gOT8HzqnI

JEHOVAH, YOU ARE THE MOST HIGH

JEHOVAH, YOU ARE THE MOST HIGH
JEHOVAH, YOU ARE THE MOST HIGH GOD
JEHOVAH, YOU ARE THE MOST HIGH
JEHOVAH, YOU ARE THE MOST HIGH GOD

LINK: https://youtu.be/QPNIsEy7n5M

PART C

MIXED – CONTEMPORARY/AFRICAN: PRAISE AND WORSHIP – SET 1

WORSHIP-:

THAT IS WHY YOU ARE CALLED JEHOVAH

PRAISE-:

1. MASTER OF THE UNIVERSE
2. YOU ARE MY STRENGTH
3. I KNOW YOU RESCUED MY SOUL
4. IF YOU CALL TO HIM
5. HALLE, HALLE, HALLELUYAH, GLORY, GLORY, WE PRAISE YOUR NAME

WORSHIP & PRAISE LYRICS

THAT IS WHY YOU ARE CALLED JEHOVAH

THAT IS WHY YOU ARE CALLED JEHOVAH
THAT IS WHY YOU ARE CALLED JEHOVAH
WHAT YOU SAY YOU WILL DO
THAT IS WHAT YOU WILL DO
THAT IS WHY YOU ARE CALLED JEHOVAH

LINK: https://youtu.be/NH10ojwkWtk

MASTER OF THE UNIVERSE

YOU ARE THE MASTER, MASTER OF THE UNIVERSE
CONQUEROR AND KING, LORD, MASTER OF THE UNIVERSE
YOU ARE THE EMPEROR ALWAYS, YOU ARE THE HEIR
OVER PRINCIPALITIES, YOU ARE THE HEIR,
OVERPOWERS, YOU ARE THE HEIR, OVER RULERS, YOU ARE THE MASTER
MASTER OF THE UNIVERSE

LINK: https://youtu.be/kJ48XEDMBoY

YOU ARE MY STRENGTH

YOU ARE MY STRENGTH, STRENGTH LIKE NO OTHER
STRENGTH LIKE NO OTHER, REACHES TO ME
YOU ARE MY HOPE, HOPE LIKE NO OTHER
HOPE LIKE NO OTHER, REACHES TO ME
IN THE FULLNESS OF YOUR GRACE, IN THE POWER OF YOUR NAME
YOU LIFT ME UP, YOU LIFT ME UP (LET'S SING)

LINK: https://youtu.be/LA4eKhj-2ic

I KNOW YOU RESCUED MY SOUL

I KNOW HE RESCUED MY SOUL; HIS BLOOD HAS COVERED MY SIN
I BELIEVE, I BELIEVE, MY SHAME, HE'S TAKEN AWAY
MY PAIN IS HEALED IN HIS NAME, I BELIEVE, I BELIEVE, I'LL RAISE A BANNER 'CAUSE MY LORD HAS CONQUERED THE GRAVE
MY REDEEMER LIVES (4X)

LINK: https://youtu.be/3gIYEDzSyok

IF YOU CALL TO HIM

IF WE CALL TO HIM, HE WILL ANSWER US
IF WE RUN TO HIM, HE WILL RUN TO US
IF WE LIFT OUR HANDS, HE WILL LIFT US UP
COME NOW PRAISE HIS NAME, ALL YOU SAINTS OF GOD.
OH SING FOR JOY TO GOD OUR STRENGTH (2X)

LINK: https://youtu.be/Dd6QpIoIXFc

HALLE, HALLE HALLUYAH

HALLE, HALLE, HALLUYAH,
GLORY, GLORY, WE PRAISE YOUR NAME
YOU ARE THE KING OF KINGS AND THE LORD OF LORD, WE PRAISE YOUR NAME

LINK: https://youtu.be/2NszJzqbNlE

MIXED – CONTEMPORARY/AFRICAN: PRAISE AND WORSHIP – SET 2

WORSHIP-:

WE BOW DOWN AND WORSHIP, YAHWEH

PRAISE-:

1. EVERY PRAISE TO OUR GOD
2. YOU ARE GOOD AND YOUR MERCY IS FOREVER, HALLELUJAH
3. JEHOVAH, YOU ARE THE MOST HIGH
4. YOU'VE BEEN FAITHFUL LORD FROM THE AGES PAST
5. I SEARCHED ALL OVER

WORSHIP & PRAISE LYRICS

WE BOW DOWN AND WORSHIP, YAHWEH

WE BOW DOWN AND WORSHIP, YAHWEH
YAHWEH, YAHWEH, YAHWEH
YAHWEH, YAHWEH, YAHWEH
WE BOW DOWN AND WORSHIP, YAHWEH
WE BOW DOWN AND WORSHIP, YAHWEH

LINK: https://youtu.be/q0A6nHOspkc

EVERY PRAISE TO OUR GOD

EVERY PRAISE IS TO OUR GOD
EVERY WORD OF WORSHIP, WITH ONE ACCORD
EVERY PRAISE, EVERY PRAISE
IS TO OUR GOD
SING HALLELUJAH TO OUR GOD
GLORY HALLELUJAH IS DUE OUR GOD
EVERY PRAISE, EVERY PRAISE, IS TO OUR GOD

LINK: https://youtu.be/X48B8AbkmbA

YOU ARE GOOD AND YOUR MERCY IS FOREVER

YOU ARE GOOD AND YOUR MERCY IS FOREVER, HALLELUJAH!
YOU ARE GOOD AND YOUR MERCY IS FOREVER, HALLELUJAH!

LINK: : https://youtu.be/Wyo3kqNgcYQ

JEHOVAH, YOU ARE THE MOST HIGH

JEHOVAH, YOU ARE THE MOST HIGH
JEHOVAH, YOU ARE THE MOST HIGH GOD
JEHOVAH, YOU ARE THE MOST HIGH
JEHOVAH, YOU ARE THE MOST HIGH GOD

LINK: https://youtu.be/QPNIsEy7n5M

YOU'VE BEEN FAITHFUL LORD, FROM THE AGES PAST

YOU'VE BEEN FAITHFUL LORD, FROM THE AGES PAST
YOU ALONE ART WORTHY LORD
TO BE PRAISED AND ADORED
YOU'VE BEEN FAITHFUL LORD
THROUGH THE AGES PAST
THAT IS WHY YOUR NAME
IS FOREVER PRAISED.
LINK: https://youtu.be/uUicRWWcfig

I SEARCHED ALL OVER

SEARCHED ALL OVER, COULDN'T FIND NOBODY
I LOOKED HIGH AND LOW, STILL COULDN'T FIND NOBODY
NOBODY. GREATER, NOBODY GREATER
NOBODY GREATER THAN YOU
NOBODY GREATER, NOBODY GREATER JESUS
NOBODY GREATER THAN YOU
NOBODY GREATER, NOBODY GREATER NO
NOBODY GREATER THAN YOU
LINK: https://youtu.be/9QSbqSuwwx0

MIXED – CONTEMPORARY/AFRICAN: PRAISE AND WORSHIP – SET 3

WORSHIP-:

SAVOIUR, THE MAN YOU SAVED HAS COME TO HONOUR

PRAISE-:

1. PRAISE YE THE LORD OF MY SOUL
2. MY GOD WHO BEGAN IT HE WILL ACCOMPLISH IT
3. YOUR LOVE HAS TAKEN OVER ME
4. COME LET'S PRAISE THE LORD
5. THE LORD REIGNS

WORSHIP & PRAISE LYRICS

SAVOIUR, THE MAN YOU SAVED HAS COME TO HONOUR

SAVOIUR, THE MAN YOU SAVED HAS COME TO HONOUR
SAVOIUR, THE MAN YOU SAVED HAS COME TO WORSHIP
HELPER
HEALER
FATHER
LINK: https://youtu.be/TjDjPXBCzEY

MY GOD IS A GOOD GOD, YES HE IS

MY GOD IS A GOOD GOD, YES HE IS
HE LIFTS ME UP (HE LIFTS ME UP)
HE TURNS ME AROUND (HE TURNS ME AROUND)
HE SETS ME FEET, UPON THE SOLID ROCK
I FEEL LIKE DANCING, I FEEL LIKE CLAPPING

LINK: https://youtu.be/5RcwYmVRttA

PRAISE YE THE LORD OF MY SOUL

PRAISE YE THE LORD OF MY SOUL
THIS IS THE DAY HE HAS MADE
HALLELUJAH
HALLELUJAJ
PRAISE YE THE LORD

LINK: https://youtu.be/n5bCj5VetwI

YOUR LOVE HAS TAKEN OVER ME

YOUR LOVE HAS TAKEN OVER ME, FATHER I DEPEND ON YOU
I HAVE CONFIDENCE IN YOU, IN YOU OH LORD I PUT MY TRUST
YES YOU COVERED ME, UNDER THE CANOPY YES OH GIVE ME SECURITY
I AM THE RIGHTEOUSNESS OF GOD, OH YES YOU COVERED ME
UNDER THE CANOPY YES OH GIVE ME SECURITY, I AM THE RIGHTEOUSNESS OF GOD
LINK: https://youtu.be/_2xKfhSI_IQ

COME LET'S PRAISE THE LORD

COME LET'S PRAISE THE LORD
HE IS JEHOVAH (TALK ABOUT HIS FAITHFULNESS)
HE IS EL- SHADAI (TELL THE WORLD OF HIS SALVATION)
SPREAD THE NEWS AROUND (TELL THE WORLD OF HIS PRAISE)
LET US PRAISE LORD (PRAISE THE LORD)
FOREVER AND EVER MY GOS HEIS THE SAME
HE'LL NEVER CHANGE
FROM ETERNITY, TO ETRNITY
HE'LL BE MY GOD OOH
PRAISE HIM
LINK: https://youtu.be/YEXJ9N-qHSM

THE LORD REIGNS, LET THE EARTH REJOICE

THE LORD REIGNS., THE LORD REIGNS.
THE LORD REIGNS.MLET THE EARTH REJOICE.
LET THE EARTH REJOICE., LET THE EARTH REJOICE.
LET THE PEOPLE BE GLAD, THAT OUR GOD REIGNS

LINK: https://youtu.be/aAgVvh2WgMM

MIXED – CONTEMPORARY/AFRICAN: PRAISE AND WORSHIP – SET 4

WORSHIP-:

YOU DESERVE THE GLORY

PRAISE-:

1. THE LORD REIGNS, LET THE EARTH REJOICE
2. COME LET'S PRAISE THE LORD
3. JEHOVAH REIGNS
4. YOUR LOVE HAS TAKEN OVER ME
5. HAIL MY JESUS, POWERFUL WARRIOR

WORSHIP & PRAISE LYRICS

YOU DESERVE THE GLORY

YOU DESERVE THE GLORY AND THE HONOUR
LORD, WE LIFT OUR HANDS IN WORSHIP AS WE
LIFT YOUR HOLY NAME
FOR YOU ARE GREAT
YOU DO MIRACLES SO GREAT
THERE IS NO ONE ELSE LIKE YOU
THERE IS NO ONE ELSE LIKE YOU

LINK: https://youtu.be/LLseRHq-dA0

THE LORD REIGNS, LET THE EARTH REJOICE

THE LORD REIGNS., THE LORD REIGNS.
THE LORD REIGNS.MLET THE EARTH REJOICE.
LET THE EARTH REJOICE., LET THE EARTH REJOICE.
LET THE PEOPLE BE GLAD, THAT OUR GOD REIGNS

LINK: https://youtu.be/aAgVvh2WgMM

COME LET'S PRAISE THE LORD

COME LET'S PRAISE THE LORD
HE IS JEHOVAH (TALK ABOUT HIS FAITHFULNESS)
HE IS EL- SHADAI (TELL THE WORLD OF HIS SALVATION)
SPREAD THE NEWS AROUND (TELL THE WORLD OF HIS PRAISE)
LET US PRAISE LORD (PRAISE THE LORD)
FOREVER AND EVER MY GOS HEIS THE SAME
HE'LL NEVER CHANGE
FROM ETERNITY, TO ETRNITY
HE'LL BE MY GOD OOH
PRAISE HIM
LINK: https://youtu.be/YEXJ9N-qHSM

JEHOVAH REIGNS, JEHOVAH REIGNS

JEHOVAH REIGNS, JEHOVAH REIGNS
JEHOVAH REIGNS, JEHOVAH REIGNS
YOU ARE LIFTED UP ABOVE OTHER GOD
YOU ARE LIFTED UP ABOVE OTHER GOD
YOU ARE LIFTED UP ABOVE OTHER GOD
YOU ARE LIFTED UP ABOVE OTHER GOD

LINK: https://youtu.be/SK9Qh_EV-b0

YOUR LOVE HAS TAKEN OVER ME

YOUR LOVE HAS TAKEN OVER ME, FATHER I DEPEND ON YOU
I HAVE CONFIDENCE IN YOU, IN YOU OH LORD I PUT MY TRUST
YES YOU COVERED ME, UNDER THE CANOPY YES OH
GIVE ME SECURITY
I AM THE RIGHTEOUSNESS OF GOD, OH YES YOU
COVERED ME
UNDER THE CANOPY YES OH GIVE ME SECURITY, I AM
THE RIGHTEOUSNESS OF GOD
LINK: https://youtu.be/_2xKfhSI_IQ

HAIL MY JESUS, POWERFUL WARROIR

HAIL MY JESUS
POWERFUL POWER WARROIR
HAIL MY JESUS
POWERFUL POWER WARROIR

LINK: https://youtu.be/xh3yQKrjBls

MIXED – CONTEMPORARY/AFRICAN: PRAISE AND WORSHIP – SET 5

WORSHIP-:

NO OTHER NAME BUT THE NAME OF JESUS

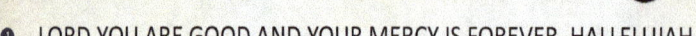

PRAISE-:

1. LORD YOU ARE GOOD AND YOUR MERCY IS FOREVER, HALLELUJAH
2. AWESOME GOD, MIGHTY GOD
3. EVERY PIRASE TO OUR GOD
4. WATER HE TURNED INTO WINE
5. ALL THE GLORY MUST BE TO THE LORD IN THE HIGHEST

WORSHIP & PRAISE LYRICS

NO OTHER NAME BUT THE NAME OF JESUS

WHEN ALL THE STORMS ARE RAGING
IN A WORLD WHERE PEACE CANNOT BE FOUND
AND TRUTH IS JUST SO HARD HERE
ABOVE THE DOUTHS, ABOVE THE FEARS
NO OTHER NAME BUT THE NAME OF JESUS
IS WORTHY OF GLORY
AND WORTHY OF HONOUR
AND WORTHY OF POWER
AND ALL PRAISE
LINK: https://youtu.be/QUgzowKz4Gw

LORD YOU ARE GOOD AND YOUR MERCY IS FOR FOREVER

LORD YOU ARE GOOD AND YOUR MERCY IS FOREVER HALLELUJAH,
LORD YOU ARE GOOD AND YOUR MERCY IS FOREVER HALLELUJAH,
HALLELUJAH, HALLELUJAH AMEN x3

LINK: https://youtu.be/Wyo3kqNgcYQ

AWESOME GOD, MIGHTY GOD

AWESOME GOD, MIGHTY GOD!
AWESOME GOD, MIGHTY GOD!
AWESOME GOD, MIGHTY GOD!
WE GIVE YOU PRAISE, AWESOME GOD!
WE GIVE YOU PRAISE, MIGHTY GOD!
YOU'RE HIGHLY LIFTED UP, AWESOME GOD!
YOU'RE HIGHLY LIFTED UP, MIGHTY GOD!

LINK: https://youtu.be/V5dcczS2GsE

EVERY PRAISE TO OUR GOD

EVERY PRAISE IS TO OUR GOD
EVERY WORD OF WORSHIP, WITH ONE ACCORD
EVERY PRAISE, EVERY PRAISE
IS TO OUR GOD
SING HALLELUJAH TO OUR GOD
GLORY HALLELUJAH IS DUE OUR GOD
EVERY PRAISE, EVERY PRAISE, IS TO OUR GOD

LINK: https://youtu.be/X48B8AbkmbA

WATER YOU TURN INTO WINE

WATER YOU TURNED INTO WINE, OPENED THE EYES OF THE BLIND
THERE'S NO ONE LIKE YOU, NONE LIKE YOU
INTO THE DARKNESS YOU SHINE, OUT OF THE ASHES
WE RISE, THERE'S NO ONE LIKE YOU, NONE LIKE YOU
OUR GOD IS GREATER, OUR GOD IS STRONGER
GOD YOU ARE HIGHER THAN ANY OTHER
OUR GOD IS HEALER, AWESOME IN POWER OUR GOD, OUR GOD
LINK: https://youtu.be/NJpt1hSYf2o

ALL THE GLORY MUST BE TO THE LORD IN THE HIGHEST

ONE THING WE ASK OF YOU, ONE THING THAT WE DESIRE
THAT AS WE WORSHIP YOU, LORD COME AND CHANGE OUR LIVES
SO, ARISE, ARISE, ARISE, ARISE, ARISE, TAKE YOUR PLACEBE ENTHRONED ON OUR PRAISE, ARISE
KING OF KINGS, HOLY GOD, AS WE SING ARISE
ARISE, ARISE, ARISE
LINK: https://youtu.be/RFoe8ZgNZEI

MIXED – CONTEMPORARY/AFRICAN: PRAISE AND WORSHIP – SET 6

WORSHIP-:

YOU'RE NOT A MAN OOH

PRAISE-:

1. WATER YOU TURNED INTO WINE
2. OPEN THE EYES OF MY HEART LORD
3. WE WILL HAIL YOUR NAME
4. JEHOVAH REIGNS
5. YOUR LOVE HAS TAKEN OVER ME

WORSHIP & PRAISE LYRICS

YOU'RE NOT A MAN OOH

YOU'RE NOT A MAN OOH
YOU'RE THE GOD WHO OPENS DOORS NO MAN CAN SHOT
YOU'RE NOT A MAN OOH x2
YOU'RE THE GOD OF EVERYTHING NO ONE LIKE YOU
NO ONE LIKE YOU JESUS
NO ONE LIKE YOU EZE, FATHER, MASTER
YOU'RE THE GOD OF EVERYTHING NO ONE LIKE YOU

LINK: https://youtu.be/1alCBQZqBiY

WATER YOU TURN INTO WINE

WATER YOU TURNED INTO WINE, OPENED THE EYES OF THE BLIND
THERE'S NO ONE LIKE YOU, NONE LIKE YOU
INTO THE DARKNESS YOU SHINE, OUT OF THE ASHES WE RISE, THERE'S NO ONE LIKE YOU, NONE LIKE YOU
OUR GOD IS GREATER, OUR GOD IS STRONGER
GOD YOU ARE HIGHER THAN ANY OTHER
OUR GOD IS HEALER, AWESOME IN POWER OUR GOD, OUR GOD

LINK: https://youtu.be/NJpt1hSYf2o

OPEN THE EYES OF MY HEART LORD

OPEN THE EYES OF MY HEART, LORD
OPEN THE EYES OF MY HEART, I WANT TO SEE YOU
TO SEE YOU HIGH AND LIFTED UP
SHININ' IN THE LIGHT OF YOUR GLORY
POUR OUT YOUR POWER AND LOVE
AS WE SING HOLY, HOLY, HOLY

LINK: https://youtu.be/fadU7b9aa78

WE WILL HAIL YOUR NAME

WE WILL HAIL,
HAIL YOUR NAME
DAY BY DAY
ALL THE WAY x2
WE WILL HAIL, HAIL, HAIL, HAIL
HAIL YOUR NAME, NAME, NAME
DAY BY DAY, DAY, DAY
ALL THE WAY, ALL WAY

LINK: https://youtu.be/1HgZNm1bjSI

JEHOVAH REIGNS, JEHOVAH REIGNS

JEHOVAH REIGNS, JEHOVAH REIGNS
JEHOVAH REIGNS, JEHOVAH REIGNS
YOU ARE LIFTED UP ABOVE OTHER GOD
YOU ARE LIFTED UP ABOVE OTHER GOD
YOU ARE LIFTED UP ABOVE OTHER GOD
YOU ARE LIFTED UP ABOVE OTHER GOD

LINK: https://youtu.be/SK9Qh_EV-b0

YOUR LOVE HAS TAKEN OVER ME

YOUR LOVE HAS TAKEN OVER ME, FATHER I DEPEND ON YOU
I HAVE CONFIDENCE IN YOU, IN YOU OH LORD I PUT MY TRUST
YES YOU COVERED ME, UNDER THE CANOPY YES OH
GIVE ME
SECURITY
I AM THE RIGHTEOUSNESS OF GOD, OH YES YOU COVERED ME
UNDER THE CANOPY YES OH GIVE ME SECURITY, I AM THE RIGHTEOUSNESS OF GOD

LINK: https://youtu.be/_2xKfhSI_IQ

MIXED – CONTEMPORARY/AFRICAN: PRAISE AND WORSHIP – SET 7

WORSHIP-:

YOU DESERVE THE GLORY AND THE HONOR

PRAISE-:

1. JEHOVAH REIGNS, HE REIGNS
2. JEHOVAH, YOU ARE THE MOST HIGH
3. YOU ARE GOD, YOU ARE NOT JUST BIG OH
4. I KNOW HE RESCUED MY SOUL
5. PRAISE YE THE LORD OH MY SOUL

WORSHIP & PRAISE LYRICS

YOU DESERVE THE GLORY AND THE HONOR

YOU DESERVE THE GLORY AND THE HONOR
LORD, WE LIFT OUR HANDS IN WORSHIP
AS WE LIFT YOUR HOLY NAME
FOR YOU ARE GREAT
YOU DO MIRACLE SO GREAT
THERE IS NO ONE LIKE YOU
THERE IS NO ONE ELSE LIKE YOU

LINK: https://youtu.be/LLseRHq-dA0

JEHOVAH REIGNS, JEHOVAH REIGNS

JEHOVAH REIGNS, JEHOVAH REIGNS
JEHOVAH REIGNS, JEHOVAH REIGNS
YOU ARE LIFTED UP ABOVE OTHER GOD
YOU ARE LIFTED UP ABOVE OTHER GOD
YOU ARE LIFTED UP ABOVE OTHER GOD
YOU ARE LIFTED UP ABOVE OTHER GOD

LINK: https://youtu.be/SK9Qh_EV-b0

JEHOVAH YOU ARE THE MOST HIGH

JEHOVAH YOU ARE THE MOST HIGH!
YOU ARE THE MOST HIGH GOD
JEHOVAH, YOU ARE THE MOST HIGH!
YOU ARE THE MOST HIGH GOD

LINK: https://youtu.be/QPNlsEy7n5M

YOU ARE GOD

YOU ARE GOD, YOU ARE NOT JUST BIG OH
YOU ARE NOT JUST LARGE OH
YOU ARE A GREAT GOD
YOU ARE BIG, BIG, BIG, BIG, BIG, BIG
LARGE, LARGE, LARGE, LARGE, LARGE
GREAT, GREAT, GREAT, GREAT, GREAT
YOU ARE A GREAT GOD

LINK: https://youtu.be/VZd2fQS8yLI

I KNOW YOU RESCUED MY SOUL

I KNOW HE RESCUED MY SOUL; HIS BLOOD HAS COVERED MY SIN
I BELIEVE, I BELIEVE, MY SHAME, HE'S TAKEN AWAY
MY PAIN IS HEALED IN HIS NAME, I BELIEVE, I BELIEVE,
I'LL RAISE A BANNER 'CAUSE MY LORD HAS CONQUERED THE GRAVE
MY REDEEMER LIVES (4X)

LINK: https://youtu.be/3glYEDzSyok

PRAISE YE THE LORD OF MY SOUL

THIS IS THE DAY HE HAS MADE
HALLELUJAH
HALLELUJAJ
PRAISE YE THE LORD

LINK: https://youtu.be/n5bCj5VetwI

MIXED – CONTEMPORARY/AFRICAN: PRAISE AND WORSHIP – SET 8

WORSHIP-:

HOSANNA IN THE HIGHEST, LET OUR KING BE LIFTED HIGH

PRAISE-:

1. I WILL BLESS THE LORD, OH MY SOUL
2. THE LORD REIGNS, THE LORD REIGNS LET THE EARTH REJOICE
3. JOY OVERFLOWS IN MY HEART SING A NEW SONG TO THE LORD
4. I'LL PRAISE YOU FOR THE REST OF THE DAYS, I WILL PRAISE YOU
5. JEHOVAH REIGNS

WORSHIP & PRAISE LYRICS

HOSANNA IN THE HIGHEST

HOSANNA
IN THE HIGHEST
LET OUR KING BE LIFTED HIGH, HOSANNA x 2
JESUS, YOU BE LIFTED HIGHER, HIGHER, HIGHER
LET OUR KING BE LIFTED HIGH
HOSANNA

LINK: https://youtu.be/sZ6utGRrsX4

I WILL BLESS THE LORD, OH MY SOUL

I WILL BLESS THE LORD, OH MY SOUL
AND ALL THT IS WITHIN ME, BLESS HIS HOLY NAME
I WILL BLESS THE LORD, OH MY SOUL
AND ALL THT IS WITHIN ME, BLESS HIS HOLY NAME
HE HAS DONE GREAT THINGS x3
BLESS HIS HOLY NAME

LINK: https://youtu.be/IYuibQ_tgDk

THE LORD REIGNS, LET THE EARTH REJOICE

THE LORD REIGNS., THE LORD REIGNS.
THE LORD REIGNS.MLET THE EARTH REJOICE.
LET THE EARTH REJOICE., LET THE EARTH REJOICE.
LET THE PEOPLE BE GLAD, THAT OUR GOD REIGNS

LINK: https://youtu.be/aAgVvh2WgMM

JOY OVERFLOW IN MY HEART

JOY OVERFLOWS IN MY HEART
SING A NEW SONG TO THE LORD
I WILL PRAISE YOUR NAME
I WILL WORSHIP YOU
GLORY HALLELUYAH SING A NEW SONG TO THE LORD (2X)

LINK: https://youtu.be/Aq4UDCRRdJc

I'LL PRAISE YOU FOR THE REST OF THE DAYS

I'LL PRAISE YOU FOR THE REST OF THE DAYS
I WILL PRAISE YOU

I'LL PRAISE YOU FOR THE REST OF THE DAYS
I WILL PRAISE YOU

I WILL PRAISE YOU; I WILL PRAISE YOU x3

JEHOVAH REIGNS, JEHOVAH REIGNS

JEHOVAH REIGNS, JEHOVAH REIGNS
JEHOVAH REIGNS, JEHOVAH REIGNS
YOU ARE LIFTED UP ABOVE OTHER GOD
YOU ARE LIFTED UP ABOVE OTHER GOD
YOU ARE LIFTED UP ABOVE OTHER GOD
YOU ARE LIFTED UP ABOVE OTHER GOD

LINK: https://youtu.be/SK9Qh_EV-b0

MIXED - CONTEMPORARY/AFRICAN: PRAISE AND WORSHIP - SET 9

WORSHIP -:

THANKS, THANKS, WE GIVE YOU THANKS FOR ALL YOU HAVE DONE

PRAISE -:

1. YOUR LOVE HAVE TAKEN OVER ME
2. CREATOR OF THE UNIVERSE
3. WATER HE TURNED INTO WINE
4. MY GOD IS A GOOD GOD
5. YOU ARE GOD, YOU ARE NOT JUST BIG

WORSHIP & PRAISE LYRICS

THANKS, THANKS, WE GIVE YOU THANKS

THANKS, THANKS, WE GIVE YOU THANKS
FOR ALL YOU HAVE DONE
WE ARE SO BLESSDED
OUR SOUL IS AT REST
OH LORD, WE GIVE YOU THANKS

LINK: https://youtu.be/MF4xWiFO980

YOUR LOVE HAS TAKEN OVER ME

YOUR LOVE HAS TAKEN OVER ME, FATHER I DEPEND ON YOU
I HAVE CONFIDENCE IN YOU, IN YOU OH LORD I PUT MY TRUST
YES YOU COVERED ME, UNDER THE CANOPY YES OH GIVE ME
SECURITY
I AM THE RIGHTEOUSNESS OF GOD, OH YES YOU COVERED ME
UNDER THE CANOPY YES OH GIVE ME SECURITY, I AM
THE RIGHTEOUSNESS OF GOD

LINK: https://youtu.be/_2xKfhSI_IQ

CREATOR OF THE UNIVERSE

CREATOR OF THE UNIVERSE WHAT CANT YOU DO
WHAT CAN'T YOU DO WHAT CAN'T YOU DO
WHAT CAN'T YOU DO JESUS, NAME ABOVE EVERY
NAME ABOVE EVERY OTHER NAME EVERY OTHER NAME
WHAT CAN'T YOU CHANGE, WHAT CAN'T YOU
CHANGE JESUS
LIFT YOUR HANDS AND SAY YOU'RE ABLE
YOU ARE ABLE GREAT AND MIGHTY GREAT AND
MIGHTY GOD
YOU'RE ABLE JESUS

LINK: https://youtu.be/HPqDaKajSnQ

WATER YOU TURN INTO WINE

WATER YOU TURNED INTO WINE, OPENED THE EYES
OF THE BLIND
THERE'S NO ONE LIKE YOU, NONE LIKE YOU
INTO THE DARKNESS YOU SHINE, OUT OF THE ASHES
WE RISE, THERE'S NO ONE LIKE YOU, NONE LIKE YOU
OUR GOD IS GREATER, OUR GOD IS STRONGER
GOD YOU ARE HIGHER THAN ANY OTHER
OUR GOD IS HEALER, AWESOME IN POWER OUR GOD, OUR GOD

LINK: https://youtu.be/NJpt1hSYf2o

MY GOD IS A GOOD GOD, YES HE IS

MY GOD IS A GOOD GOD, YES HE IS
HE LIFTS ME UP (HE LIFTS ME UP)
HE TURNS ME AROUND (HE TURNS ME AROUND)
HE SETS ME FEET, UPON THE SOLID ROCK
I FEEL LIKE DANCING, I FEEL LIKE CLAPPING

LINK: https://youtu.be/5RcwYmVRttA

YOU ARE GOD

YOU ARE GOD, YOU ARE NOT JUST BIG OH
YOU ARE NOT JUST LARGE OH
YOU ARE A GREAT GOD
YOU ARE BIG, BIG, BIG, BIG, BIG, BIG, BIG
LARGE, LARGE, LARGE, LARGE, LARGE, LARGE
GREAT, GREAT, GREAT, GREAT, GREAT
YOU ARE A GREAT GOD

LINK: https://youtu.be/VZd2fQS8yLI

MIXED – CONTEMPORARY/AFRICAN: PRAISE AND WORSHIP – SET 10

WORSHIP-:

YOU ARE GOD FROM BEGINNING

PRAISE-:

1. MASTER OF THE UNIVERSE
2. COME LET'S PRAISE THE LORD
3. HOLY ARE YOU LORD
4. CREATOR OF THE UNIVERSE
5. HAIL MY JESUS, POWERFUL WARROIR

WORSHIP & PRAISE LYRICS

YOU ARE GOD FROM BEGINNING

YOU ARE GOD FROM BEGINNING TO THE END
THERE'S NO PLACE FOR ARGUMENT, YOU ARE
GOD ALL BY YOURSELF
YOU'VE GOT TIMES AND SEASONS IN YOUR HANDS
YOU CALLED FOR LIGHT OUT OF DARKNESS
YOU DON'T NEED A MAN TO BE THE GOD YOU ARE
BUT YOU HAVE CHOSEN TO CALL ME YOUR OWN

LINK: https://youtu.be/pJMNagqzDVM

MASTER OF THE UNIVERSE

YOU ARE THE MASTER, MASTER OF THE UNIVERSE
CONQUEROR AND KING, LORD! MASTER OF THE UNIVERSE
YOU ARE THE EMPEROR ALWAYS, YOU ARE THE HEIR
OVER PRINCIPALITIES, YOU ARE THE HEIR, OVER
POWERS, YOU ARE THE HEIR, OVER RULERS, YOU ARE
THE MASTER
MASTER OF THE UNIVERSE

LINK: https://youtu.be/kJ48XEDMBoY

COME LET'S PRAISE THE LORD

COME LET'S PRAISE THE LORD
HE IS JEHOVAH (TALK ABOUT HIS FAITHFULNESS)
HE IS EL- SHADAI (TELL THE WORLD OF HIS SALVATION)
SPREAD THE NEWS AROUND (TELL THE WORLD OF HIS PRAISE)
LET US PRAISE LORD (PRAISE THE LORD)
FOREVER AND EVER MY GOS HEIS THE SAME
HE'LL NEVER CHANGE
FROM ETERNITY, TO ETRNITY
HE'LL BE MY GOD OOH
PRAISE HIM
LINK: https://youtu.be/YEXJ9N-qHSM

HOLY ARE YOU LORD

HOLY ARE YOU LORD, ALL CREATION CALL YOU
GODWORTHY IS YOUR NAME, WE WORSHIP YOUR MAJESTY
AWESOME GOD, HOW GREAT THOU ART
YOU ARE GOD, MIGHTY ARE YOUR MIRACLES
WE STAND IN AWE OF YOUR HOLY NAME
LORD WE BOW AND WORSHIP YOU

LINK: https://youtu.be/qnLvi392hhE

CREATOR OF THE UNIVERSE

CREATOR OF THE UNIVERSE WHAT CANT YOU DO
WHAT CAN'T YOU DO WHAT CAN'T YOU DO
WHAT CAN'T YOU DO JESUS, NAME ABOVE EVERY
NAME ABOVE EVERY OTHER NAME EVERY OTHER NAME
WHAT CAN'T YOU CHANGE, WHAT CAN'T YOU CHANGE JESUS
LIFT YOUR HANDS AND SAY YOU'RE ABLE
YOU ARE ABLE GREAT AND MIGHTY GREAT AND
MIGHTY GOD
YOU'RE ABLE JESUS
LINK: https://youtu.be/HPqDaKajSnQ

HAIL MY JESUS, POWERFUL, POWERFUL

HAIL MY JESUS
POWERFUL POWER WARRIOR
HAIL MY JESUS
POWERFUL POWER WARRIOR

LINK: https://youtu.be/xh3yQKrjBls

MIXED – CONTEMPORARY/AFRICAN: PRAISE AND WORSHIP – SET 11

WORSHIP-:

JEHOVAH IS YOUR NAME

PRAISE-:

1. BLESSED JESUS WE'VE COME TO GIVE YOU PRAISE
2. HOSSANA, HOSSANA, IN THE HIGHEST
3. JOY OVERFLOWS IN MY HEART SING A NEW SONG TO THE LORD
4. I'LL PRAISE YOU FOR THE REST OF THE DAYS, I WILL PRAISE YOU
5. AWESOME GOD, MIGHTY GOD

WORSHIP & PRAISE LYRICS

JEHOVAH IS YOUR NAME

JEHOVAH IS YOUR NAME
JEHOVAH IS YOUR NAME
MIGHTY WARRIOR, GREAT IN BATTLE
JEHOVAH IS YOUR NAME

LINK: https://youtu.be/Ro9KtH6cSVU

BLESSED JESUS WE'VE COME TO GIVE PRAISE

BLESSED JESUS
WE'VE COME TO GIVE PRAISE
YOU SRE WORTHY
AND BLESSED BE YOUR NAME
WE LOVE YOU LORD
WE LOVE YOU LORD

LINK: https://youtu.be/tHQxyREYj-c

HOSSANA, HOSSANA, HOSSANA IN THE HIGHEST

HOSSANA, HOSSANA, HOSSAN IN THE HIGHEST
HOSSANA, HOSSANA, HOSSAN IN THE HIGHEST
LORD WE LIGT UP YOUR NAME
WITH THE HEAT FULL OF PRAISE
BE EXALTED OH LORD MY GOD
HOSSANA IN THE HIGHEST

LINK: https://youtu.be/E1X-VDCMyAc

JOY OVERFLOW IN MY HEART

JOY OVERFLOWS IN MY HEART
SING A NEW SONG TO THE LORD
I WILL PRAISE YOUR NAME
I WILL WORSHIP YOU
GLORY HALLELUYAH SING A NEW SONG TO THE LORD (2X)

LINK: https://youtu.be/Aq4UDCRRdJc

I'LL PRAISE YOU FOR THE REST OF THE DAYS

I'LL PRAISE YOU FOR THE REST OF THE DAYS
I WILL PRAISE YOU

I'LL PRAISE YOU FOR THE REST OF THE DAYS
I WILL PRAISE YOU

I WILL PRAISE YOU; I WILL PRAISE YOU x3

AWESOME GOD, MIGHTY GOD

AWESOME GOD, MIGHTY GOD!
AWESOME GOD, MIGHTY GOD!
AWESOME GOD, MIGHTY GOD!
WE GIVE YOU PRAISE, AWESOME GOD!
WE GIVE YOU PRAISE, MIGHTY GOD!
YOU'RE HIGHLY LIFTED UP, AWESOME GOD!
YOU'RE HIGHLY LIFTED UP, MIGHTY GOD!

LINK: https://youtu.be/V5dcczS2GsE

MIXED - CONTEMPORARY/AFRICAN: PRAISE AND WORSHIP - SET 12

WORSHIP-:

AT THE CENTRE OF IT ALL, ITS YOU THAT I SEE

PRAISE-:

1. HALLELUJAH TO THE LORD GOD ALMIGHTY REIGN
2. WE GIVE YOU ALL THE PRAISE; YOU ARE LORD THERE IS NO OTHER
3. WATER YOU TURNED IN THE WINE
4. OH LORD, WE PRAISE YOU
5. THERE IS SOMETHING THAT MAKES ME COME INTO YOUR PRESENCE

WORSHIP & PRAISE LYRICS

AT THE CENTRE OF IT ALL, ITS YOU THAT I SEE

AT THE CENTRE OF IT ALL
ITS YOU THAT I SEE
ITS YOU THAT I SEE
THERE ISPOWER IN YOUR NAME
MIRACLES HAPPEN IN YOUR NAME
AS WE LIFT OUR VOICE IN PRAISE
ITS YOU THAT I SEE
ITS YOU THAT I SEE
LINK: https://youtu.be/_GzvFn-oyII

HALLELUJAH TO THE LORD GOD ALMIGHTY REIGN

HALLELUJAH TO THE LORD GOD ALMIGHTY REIGN
HALLELUJAH TO THE LORD GOD ALMIGHTY REIGN
HALLELUJAH, HOSSANA
HALLELUJAH, HOSSANA
HALLELUJAH TO THE LORD GOD ALMIGHTY REIGN

LINK: https://youtu.be/HRPtXuFpV9U

WE GIVE YOU ALL THE PRAISE

WE GIVE YOU ALL THE PRAISE
WE GIVE YOU ALL THE PRAISE

YOU ARE LORD THERE IS NO OTHER
WE GIVE YOU ALL THE PRAISE

WATER YOU TURN INTO WINE

WATER YOU TURNED INTO WINE, OPENED THE EYES
OF THE BLIND
THERE'S NO ONE LIKE YOU, NONE LIKE YOU
INTO THE DARKNESS YOU SHINE, OUT OF THE ASHES
WE RISE, THERE'S NO ONE LIKE YOU, NONE LIKE YOU
OUR GOD IS GREATER, OUR GOD IS STRONGER
GOD YOU ARE HIGHER THAN ANY OTHER
OUR GOD IS HEALER, AWESOME IN POWER OUR GOD, OUR GOD
LINK: https://youtu.be/NJpt1hSYf2o

OH LORD, WE PRAISE YOU

OH LORD, WE PRAISE YOU
OH LORD, WE PRAISE YOU
WE EXALT YOUR NAME x2
OH LORD, WE YOUR'RE WONDERFUL GOD AMEN
OH LORD, WE YOUR'RE WONDERFUL GOD AMEN

LINK: https://youtu.be/MPSnWLd3yR4

THERE IS SOMETHING THAT MAKES ME COME INTO

THERE IS SOMETHING THAT MAKES ME COME INTO
YOUR PRESENCE - MY HELPER
THERE IS SOMETHING THAT MAKES ME COME INTO
YOUR PRESENCE - MY HELPER
MY HELPER O MY HELPER (2X)
THERE IS SOMETHING THAT MAKES ME COME INTO
YOUR PRESENCE - MY HELPER
LINK: https://youtu.be/mT6B6eoAIug

MIXED – CONTEMPORARY/AFRICAN: PRAISE AND WORSHIP – SET 13

WORSHIP-:

CASTING CROWNS

PRAISE-:

1. AT THE MENTION OF YOUR NAME
2. WHAT WILL I GIVE TO YOU, MY PRAISE
3. ARISE, ARISE, ARISE
4. WHO HAS THE FINAL SAY, JEHOHAH, WE LIFT YOU UP
5. HOLY ARE YOU LORD, ALL CREATION CALL YOU LORD

WORSHIP & PRAISE LYRICS

CASTING CROWNS

CASTING CROWNS, LIFTING HANDS
BOWING HEARTS, IS ALL WE'VE COME TO DO
ADONAI, ADONAI, ADONAI, YOU REIGN ON HIGH
WE WILL RISE, IN YOUR NAME, ADONAI, YOU REIGN ON HIGH

LINK: https://youtu.be/2P-FIceZIDo

AT THE MENTION OF YOUR NAME

AT THE MENTION OF YOUR NAME
EVERY KNEE MUST BOW
AT THE MENTION OF YOUR NAME
EVERY TONGUE CONFESS
THAT YOU ARE LORD
YOU ARE LORD, YOU ARE LORD of LORDS
YOU ARE KING, YOU ARE KING OF KINGS

LINK: https://youtu.be/SplL4YBBHfY

WHAT WILL I GIVE TO YOU, MY PRAISE

WHAT WILL I GIVE TO YOU, MY PRAISE
WHAT WILL I GIVE TO YOU, MY PRAISE
I DON'T HAVE MONEY, MY PRAISE
WHAT WILL I GIVE TO YOU, MY PRAISE
WHAT WILL I GIVE TO YOU, MY PRAISE

LINK: https://youtu.be/ZAjhMlnXN1c

ARISE, ARISE, ARISE

ONE THING WE ASK OF YOU, ONE THING THAT WE DESIRE
THAT AS WE WORSHIP YOU, LORD COME AND CHANGE OUR LIVES
SO, ARISE, ARISE, ARISE, ARISE, ARISE, TAKE YOUR PLACEBE ENTHRONED ON OUR PRAISE, ARISE
KING OF KINGS, HOLY GOD, AS WE SING ARISE
ARISE, ARISE, ARISE

LINK: https://youtu.be/RFoe8ZgNZEI

WHO HAS THE FINAL SAY, JEHOHAH, WE LIFT YOU UP

WHO HAS THE FINAL SAY
JEHOVAH, HAS THE FINAL SAY
WHO HAS THE FINAL SAY
JEHOVAH, HAS THE FINAL SAY
JEHOVAH, TURNED MY LIFE AROUND x2
HE MAKES A WAY, WHERE THERE IS NO WAY
JEHOVAH, HAS THE FINAL SAY
WE LIFT YOU UP
LINK: https://youtu.be/Bx2T8aunyvs

HOLY ARE YOU LORD (AWESOME GOD)

HOLY ARE YOU LORD
ALL CREATION CALL YOU GOD
WORTHY IS YOUR NAME, WE WORSHIP YOUR MAJESTY
AWESOME GOD, HOW GREAT THOU ART
YOU ARE GOD, MIGHTY ARE YOUR MIRACLES
WE STAND IN AWE OF YOUR HOLY NAME
LORD, WE BOW DOWN AND WORSHIP YOU

LINK: https://youtu.be/qnLvi392hhE

MIXED – CONTEMPORARY/AFRICAN: PRAISE AND WORSHIP – SET 14

WORSHIP-:

AT THE CENTER OF IT ALL

PRAISE-:

1. LORD YOU ARE SO GOOD, BLESSDED BE YOUR NEME, IN HEAVEN YOU'RE THE LORD
2. BLESSED BE THE NAME OF THE LORD, THE NAME OF THE LORD IS
3. SOME PEOPLE SAY YOU ARE GOOD, YOUR KIND
4. HIAL MY JESUS, POWERFUL, POWERFUL
5. GIVE HIM PRAISE, GIVE HIM PRAISE

WORSHIP & PRAISE LYRICS

AT THE CENTER OF IT ALL

AT THE CENTER OF IT ALL
IT'S YOU THAT I SEE x2
THERE IS POWER IN YOUR NAME
MIRACLE HAPPEN IN YOUR NAME
AS WE LIFT OUR VOICE IN PRASE
IT'S YOU THAT I SEE x2
YOUR BIGGER, STRONGER, HIGHER, GREATER

LINK: https://youtu.be/_GzvFn-oyII

LORD YOU ARE SO GOOD, BLESSDED BE YOUR NAME

LORD YOU ARE SO GOOD, BLESSDED BE YOUR NAME
IN HEAVEN YOU'RE THE LORD
ON EARTH YOU REIGN FOREVER
OH LORD, HOW GREAT THOU ART
BLESSED BY YOUR NAME

LINK: https://youtu.be/QhxObPYSWS8

BLESSED BE THE NAME OF THE LORD

BLESSED BE THE NAME OF THE LORD
BLESSED BE THE NAME OF THE LORD
BLESSED BE THE NAME OF THE LORD
THE NAME OF THE LORD IS A STRONG TOWER
THE RIGHTEOUS RUN INTO IT THEY ARE SAVED

LINK: https://youtu.be/bYrcrP1ysjw

SOME PEOPLE SAY YOU ARE GOOD, YOUR KIND OO

SOME PEOPLE SAY YOU ARE GOOD,
SOME PEAOPLE SAY YOU ARE KIND,
YOU ARE BIGGER THAN WHAT PEOPLE SAY
JEHOHAH, YOU THE MOST - HIGH GOD
YOU ARE BIGGER THAN WHAT PEOPLE SAY
JEHOHAH, YOU THE MOST - HIGH GOD

LINK: https://youtu.be/is_9GAbT0II

HAIL MY JESUS, POWERFUL, POWERFUL

HAIL MY JESUS
POWERFUL POWER WARROIR
HAIL MY JESUS
POWERFUL POWER WARROIR

LINK: https://youtu.be/xh3yQKrjBls

GIVE HIM PRAISE, GIVE HIM PRAISE

GIVE HIM PRAISE, GIVE HIM PRAISE
WE ARE HERE TO GIVE
ALL THE PRAISE TO THE LORD
GIVE HIM PRAISE, GIVE HIM PRAISE
WE ARE HERE TO GIVE
ALL THE PRAISE TO THE LORD

MIXED – CONTEMPORARY/AFRICAN: PRAISE AND WORSHIP – SET 15

WORSHIP-:

OH, BE LIFTED, ABOVE ALL OTHER GOD'S

PRAISE-:

1. EVERY PRAISE IS TO OUR GOD
2. WATER YOU TURN INTO WINE
3. BLESSED BE THE NAME OF THE LORD, MOST HIGH
4. THEY CALL YOU MIGHTY WARRIOR JEHOVAH JIREH, MIGHTY WARRIOR
5. ALL THE GLORY BE TO THE LORD IN THE HIGHEST, HALLELUJAH

WORSHIP & PRAISE LYRICS

OH, BE LIFTED, ABOVE ALL OTHER GOD'S

OH, BE LIFTED, ABOVE ALL OTHER GOD'S
WE LAY OUR CROWNS, AND WORSHIP YOU
OH, BE LIFTED, ABOVE ALL OTHER GOD'S
WE LAY OUR CROWNS, AND WORSHIP YOU
OH, GLORIOUS GOD, WE PRAISE YOUR NAME
WE LAY OUR CROWNS, AND WORSHIP YOU
OH, GLORIOUS GOD, WE PRAISE YOUR NAME
WE LAY OUR CROWNS, AND WORSHIP YOU

LINK: https://youtu.be/yH1FJEQBzss

EVERY PRAISE TO OUR GOD

EVERY PRAISE IS TO OUR GOD
EVERY WORD OF WORSHIP, WITH ONE ACCORD
EVERY PRAISE, EVERY PRAISE
IS TO OUR GOD
SING HALLELUJAH TO OUR GOD
GLORY HALLELUJAH IS DUE OUR GOD
EVERY PRAISE, EVERY PRAISE, IS TO OUR GOD

LINK: https://youtu.be/X48B8AbkmbA

WATER YOU TURN INTO WINE

WATER YOU TURNED INTO WINE, OPENED THE
EYES OF THE BLIND
THERE'S NO ONE LIKE YOU, NONE LIKE YOU
INTO THE DARKNESS YOU SHINE, OUT OF THE
ASHES WE RISE, THERE'S NO ONE LIKE YOU, NONE LIKE YOU
OUR GOD IS GREATER, OUR GOD IS STRONGER
GOD YOU ARE HIGHER THAN ANY OTHER
OUR GOD IS HEALER, AWESOME IN POWER OUR GOD, OUR GOD

LINK: https://youtu.be/NJpt1hSYf2o

BLESSED BE THE NAME OF THE LORD

BLESSED BE THE NAME OF THE LORD x2
BLESSED BE THE NAME OF THE LORD, MOST HIGH
THE NAME OF THE LORD IS, A STRONG TOWER
THE RIGHTEOUS RUN INTO IT AND THEY ARE SAVED
THE NAME OF THE LORD IS, A STRONG TOWER
THE RIGHTEOUS RUN INTO IT AND THEY ARE SAVED

LINK: https://youtu.be/bYrcrP1ysjw

THEY CALL YOU MIGHTY WARRIOR JEHOVAH JIREH

THEY CALL YOU MIGHTY WARRIOR JEHOVAH JIREH,
MIGHTY WARRIOR
AHE HEE, JEHOVA, MIGHTY WARRIOR
THEY CALL YOU MIGHTY WARRIOR JEHOVAH JIREH,
MIGHTY WARRIOR
AHE HEE, JEHOVA, MIGHTY WARRIOR

SOMEBODY, CALL HIM MIGHTY WARRIOR x 3

ALL THE GLORY BE TO THE LORD IN THE HIGHEST

ALL THE GLORY BE TO THE LORD IN THE HIGHEST,
HALLELUJAH
ALL THE GLORY BE TO THE LORD IN THE HIGHEST,
HALLELUJAH
EVERYBODY, SHOUT, HALLELU, HALLELUJAH
SHOUT, HALLELU, HALLELUJAH
EVERYBODY, SHOUT, HALLELU, HALLELUJAH

LINK: https://youtu.be/drmL-zAfdtg

MIXED - CONTEMPORARY/AFRICAN: PRAISE AND WORSHIP - SET 16

WORSHIP-:

HOLY ARE YOU LORD, ALL CREATION CALL YOU LORD

PRAISE-:

1. BLESSED BE THE NAME OF THE LORD, MOST HIGH
2. EVERY PRAISE IS TO OUR GOD
3. HEY, HEY, MY GOD IS GOOD OH
4. WE ARE SAYING THANK, JESUS THANK YOU, JEHOVAH THAN YOU
5. WE GIVE YOU ALL THE PRAISE, YOU ARE LORD THERE IS NO OTHER

WORSHIP & PRAISE LYRICS

HOLY ARE YOU LORD (AWESOME GOD)

HOLY ARE YOU LORD
ALL CREATION CALL YOU GOD
WORTHY IS YOUR NAME, WE WORSHIP YOUR MAJESTY
AWESOME GOD, HOW GREAT THOU ART
YOU ARE GOD, MIGHTY ARE YOUR MIRACLES
WE STAND IN AWE OF YOUR HOLY NAME
LORD, WE BOW DOWN AND WORSHIP YOU

LINK: https://youtu.be/qnLvi392hhE

BLESSED BE THE NAME OF THE LORD

BLESSED BE THE NAME OF THE LORD x2
BLESSED BE THE NAME OF THE LORD, MOST HIGH
THE NAME OF THE LORD IS, A STRONG TOWER
THE RIGHTEOUS RUN INTO IT AND THEY ARE SAVED
THE NAME OF THE LORD IS, A STRONG TOWER
THE RIGHTEOUS RUN INTO IT AND THEY ARE SAVED

LINK: https://youtu.be/bYrcrP1ysjw

EVERY PRAISE TO OUR GOD

EVERY PRAISE IS TO OUR GOD
EVERY WORD OF WORSHIP, WITH ONE ACCORD
EVERY PRAISE, EVERY PRAISE
IS TO OUR GOD
SING HALLELUJAH TO OUR GOD
GLORY HALLELUJAH IS DUE OUR GOD
EVERY PRAISE, EVERY PRAISE, IS TO OUR GOD

LINK: https://youtu.be/X48B8AbkmbA

HEY, HEY, MY GOD IS GOOD OH

HEY, HEY, MY GOD IS GOOD OH
HEY, HEY, MY GOD IS GOOD OH
EVERYTHING IS DOUBLE, DOUBLE OOO
MY BLESSINGS ARE DOUBLE, DOUBLE

LINK: https://youtu.be/d4J1ueG98lw

WE ARE SAYING THANK, JESUS THANK

WE ARE SAYING THANK
JESUS THANK YOU
JEHOVAH THAN YOU
EVERYBODY IS SAYING THANK YOU
JESUS THANK YOU
THANK YOU, LORD,

LINK: https://youtu.be/Oy1SMGMB7Rw

WE GIVE YOU ALL THE PRAISE

WE GIVE YOU ALL THE PRAISE
WE GIVE YOU ALL THE PRAISE
YOU ARE LORD THEREIS NO OTHER YOU ARE LORD
LORD, WE GIVE YOU ALL THE PRAISE
WE GIVE YOU ALL THE PRAISE

YOU ARE LORD THEREIS NO OTHER YOU ARE LORD
LORD, WE GIVE YOU ALL THE PRAISE
WE GIVE YOU ALL THE PRAISE

MIXED - CONTEMPORARY/AFRICAN: PRAISE AND WORSHIP - SET 17

WORSHIP-:

YOU DESERVE THE GLORY AND THE HONOUR

PRAISE-:

1. HOSSANA, HOSSANA, HOSSANA IN THE HIGHEST
2. WE GIVE YOU ALL THE PRAISE, YOU ARE THE LORD THERE IS NO OTHER
3. YOU ARE GOOD AND YOUR MERCIES ARE FOREVER, HALLELUJAH
4. YOU ARE GOD, YOU ARE NOT JUST BIG
5. JEHOVAH, YOU ARE THE MOST HIGH

WORSHIP & PRAISE LYRICS

YOU DESERVE THE GLORY AND THE HONOR

YOU DESERVE THE GLORY AND THE HONOR
LORD, WE LIFT OUR HANDS IN WORSHIP
AS WE LIFT YOUR HOLY NAME
FOR YOU ARE GREAT
YOU DO MIRACLE SO GREAT
THERE IS NO ONE LIKE YOU
THERE IS NO ONE ELSE LIKE YOU

LINK: https://youtu.be/LLseRHq-dA0

HOSSANA, HOSSANA, HOSSANA IN THE HIGHEST

HOSSANA, HOSSANA, HOSSAN IN THE HIGHEST
HOSSANA, HOSSANA, HOSSAN IN THE HIGHEST
LORD WE LIGT UP YOUR NAME
WITH THE HEAT FULL OF PRAISE
BE EXALTED OH LORD MY GOD
HOSSANA IN THE HIGHEST

LINK: https://youtu.be/E1X-VDCMyAc

EVERY PRAISE TO OUR GOD

EVERY PRAISE IS TO OUR GOD
EVERY WORD OF WORSHIP, WITH ONE ACCORD
EVERY PRAISE, EVERY PRAISE
IS TO OUR GOD
SING HALLELUJAH TO OUR GOD
GLORY HALLELUJAH IS DUE OUR GOD
EVERY PRAISE, EVERY PRAISE, IS TO OUR GOD

LINK: https://youtu.be/X48B8AbkmbA

YOU ARE GOOD AND YOUR MERCY IS FOREVER

YOU ARE GOOD AND YOUR MERCY IS FOREVER, HALLELUJAH!
YOU ARE GOOD AND YOUR MERCY IS FOREVER, HALLELUJAH!
YOU ARE GOOD AND YOUR MERCY IS FOREVER, HALLELUJAH!

LINK: : https://youtu.be/Wyo3kqNgcYQ

YOU ARE GOD

YOU ARE GOD, YOU ARE NOT JUST BIG OH
YOU ARE NOT JUST LARGE OH
YOU ARE A GREAT GOD
YOU ARE BIG, BIG, BIG, BIG, BIG, BIG
LARGE, LARGE, LARGE, LARGE, LARGE
GREAT, GREAT, GREAT, GREAT, GREAT
YOU ARE A GREAT GOD

LINK: https://youtu.be/VZd2fQS8yLI

JEHOVAH YOU ARE THE MOST HIGH

JEHOVAH YOU ARE THE MOST HIGH!
YOU ARE THE MOST HIGH GOD
JEHOVAH, YOU ARE THE MOST HIGH!
YOU ARE THE MOST HIGH GOD

LINK: https://youtu.be/QPNIsEy7n5M

MIXED – CONTEMPORARY/AFRICAN: PRAISE AND WORSHIP – SET 18

WORSHIP-:

WE GIVE YOU GLORY LORD, AS WE HONOUR YOU, YOU ARE WONDERFUL

PRAISE-:

1. BLESSED JESUS, WE HAVE COME TO GIVE YOU PRAISE
2. BLESSED BE THE NAME OF THE LORD
3. HOSANNA, HOSANNA, HOSANNA IN THE HIGHEST
4. YOU'VE BEEN FAITHFUL LORD FROM THE AGES PAST
5. WE GIVE YOU ALL THE PRAISE, YOU ARE LORD THERE IS NO OTHER

WORSHIP & PRAISE LYRICS

WE GIVE YOU GLORY LORD, AS WE HONOUR YOU

WE GIVE YOU GLORY LORD, AS WE HONOUR YOU
WE GIVE YOU GLORY LORD, AS WE HONOUR YOU
YOU ARE WONDERFUL, YOU ARE WORTHY OH LORD
YOU ARE WONDERFUL, YOU ARE WORTHY OH LORD
YOU ARE WONDERFUL, YOU ARE WORTHY OH LORD

LINK: https://youtu.be/vHxBleOPX_M

BLESSED JESUS WE'VE COME TO GIVE PRAISE

BLESSED JESUS
WE'VE COME TO GIVE PRAISE
YOU SRE WORTHY
AND BLESSED BE YOUR NAME
WE LOVE YOU LORD
WE LOVE YOU LORD

LINK: https://youtu.be/tHQxyREYj-c

BLESSED BE THE NAME OF THE LORD

BLESSED BE THE NAME OF THE LORD x2
BLESSED BE THE NAME OF THE LORD, MOST HIGH
THE NAME OF THE LORD IS, A STRONG TOWER
THE RIGHTEOUS RUN INTO IT AND THEY ARE SAVED
THE NAME OF THE LORD IS, A STRONG TOWER
THE RIGHTEOUS RUN INTO IT AND THEY ARE SAVED

LINK: https://youtu.be/bYrcrP1ysjw

HOSSANA, HOSSANA, HOSSANA IN THE HIGHEST

HOSSANA, HOSSANA, HOSSAN IN THE HIGHEST
HOSSANA, HOSSANA, HOSSAN IN THE HIGHEST
LORD WE LIGT UP YOUR NAME
WITH THE HEAT FULL OF PRAISE
BE EXALTED OH LORD MY GOD
HOSSANA IN THE HIGHEST

LINK: https://youtu.be/E1X-VDCMyAc

YOU'VE BEEN FAITHFUL LORD FROM THE AGES PAST

YOU'VE BEEN FAITHFUL LORD
FROM THE AGES PAST
THAT IS WHY YOUR NAME IS FOREVERMORE
YOU ALONE ARE WORTHY LORD
TO BE PRAISED AND ADORE
YOU ALONE ARE WORTHY LORD
TO BE PRAISED AND ADORE
LINK: https://youtu.be/uUicRWWcfig

WE GIVE YOU ALL THE PRAISE

WE GIVE YOU ALL THE PRAISE
WE GIVE YOU ALL THE PRAISE
YOU ARE LORD THEREIS NO OTHER YOU ARE LORD
LORD, WE GIVE YOU ALL THE PRAISE
WE GIVE YOU ALL THE PRAISE

YOU ARE LORD THEREIS NO OTHER YOU ARE LORD
LORD, WE GIVE YOU ALL THE PRAISE
WE GIVE YOU ALL THE PRAISE

MIXED – CONTEMPORARY/AFRICAN: PRAISE AND WORSHIP – SET 19

WORSHIP-:

YOU ARE GOD FROM BEGINNING TO THE END

PRAISE-:

1. HOSANNA, HOSANNA, HOSANNA IN THE HIGHEST
2. JESUS YOU ARE MY FIRM FOUNDATION
3. PRAISE YE THE LORD, OH MY SOUL
4. JEHOVAH, YOU TURN MY LIFE AROUND
5. COME LET'S PRAISE THE LORD

WORSHIP & PRAISE LYRICS

YOU ARE GOD FROM BEGINNING TO THE END

YOU'VE GOT TIMES AND SEASONS IN YOUR HANDS
YOU CALLED FOR LIGT OUT OF DARKNESS
YOU DON'T NEED A MAN TO BE THE GOD YOU ARE
BUT YOU HAVE CHOOSEN TO CALL ME YOUR OWN
YOU ARE GOD FROM BEGINNING TO THE END
THERE'S NO PLACE FOR ARGUMENT
YOU ARE GOD ALL BY YOUSELF x 2

LINK: https://youtu.be/pJMNagqzDVM

HOSSANA, HOSSANA< HOSSANA IN THE HIGHEST

HOSSANA, HOSSANA, HOSSAN IN THE HIGHEST
HOSSANA, HOSSANA, HOSSAN IN THE HIGHEST
LORD WE LIGT UP YOUR NAME
WITH THE HEAT FULL OF PRAISE
BE EXALTED OH LORD MY GOD
HOSSANA IN THE HIGHEST

LINK: https://youtu.be/E1X-VDCMyAc

JESUS YOU ARE MY FIRM FOUNDATION

JESUS, YOU'RE MY FIRM FOUNDATION, I KNOW I CAN STAND SECURE;
JESUS, YOU'RE MY FIRM FOUNDATION, I PUT MY HOPE IN YOUR HOLY WORD,
I PUT MY HOPE IN YOUR HOLY WORD.
I HAVE A LIVING HOPE, I HAVE A FUTURE;
GOD HAS A PLAN FOR ME, OF THIS I'M SURE(2X)

LINK: https://youtu.be/KVPsW4csPs0

PRAISE YE THE LORD OF MY SOUL

THIS IS THE DAY HE HAS MADE
HALLELUJAH
HALLELUJAJ
PRAISE YE THE LORD

LINK: https://youtu.be/n5bCj5VetwI

JEHOVAH, HE TURNED MY LIFE AROUND

JEHOVAH TURNED MY LIFE AROUND (2X)
HE MAKES A WAY WHERE THERE SEEMS NO WAY, JEHOVAH
JEHOVAH, TURNED MY LIFE AROUND
JEHOVAH TURNED MY LIFE AROUND OOOHH.
HE MAKES A WAY WHERE THERE SEEMS NO WAY

LINK: https://youtu.be/PYnt_KhKodA

COME LET'S PRAISE THE LORD

COME LET'S PRAISE THE LORD
HE IS JEHOVAH (TALK ABOUT HIS FAITHFULNESS)
HE IS EL- SHADAI (TELL THE WORLD OF HIS SALVATION)
SPREAD THE NEWS AROUND (TELL THE WORLD OF HIS PRAISE)
LET US PRAISE LORD (PRAISE THE LORD)
FOREVER AND EVER MY GOS HEIS THE SAME
HE'LL NEVER CHANGE
FROM ETERNITY, TO ETRNITY
HE'LL BE MY GOD OOH
PRAISE HIM
LINK: https://youtu.be/YEXJ9N-qHSM

MIXED – CONTEMPORARY/AFRICAN: PRAISE AND WORSHIP – SET 20

WORSHIP-:

AMAZING GOD, YOU DO MIND BLOWING THINGS

PRAISE-:

1. HALLE, HALLE, HALLELUJAH, GLORY, GLORY, WE PRAISE YOUR NAME
2. YOU ARE GREAT, YES YOU ARE
3. HOLY ARE YOU LORD, ALL CREATION
4. YOU ARE GOD, YOU ARE NOT JUST BIG
5. EVERY PRAISE TO OUR GOD

WORSHIP & PRAISE LYRICS

AMAZING GOD, YOU DO MIND BLOWING THINGS

AMAZING GOD
AMAZING GOD
YOU DO MIND BLOWING THINGS
AMAZING GOD x3
YOU COME THROUGH FOR ME
YOU COME THROUGH FOR ME
YOU DO MIND BLOWING THINGS
AMAZING GOD
LINK: https://youtu.be/S1NrvLijq10

HALLE, HALLE, HALLELUJAH

HALLE, HALLE, HALLELUJAH, GLORY, GLORY
WE PRAISE YOUR NAME
YOU ARE THE KING OF KINGS
AND THE LORD OF LORDS
WE PRAISE YOUR NAME
LINK: https://youtu.be/2NszJzqbNlE

YOU ARE GREAT, YES YOU ARE

YOU ARE GREAT YES YOU ARE HOLY ONE
WALKED UPON THE SEA RISE THE DEAD
YOU REIGN IN MAJESTY MIGHTY GOD
EVERYTHING WRITTEN ABOUT YOU IS GREAT
YOU ARE GREAT YOU ARE GREAT 4X
EVERYTHING WRITTEN ABOUT YOU IS GREAT

LINK: https://youtu.be/q2KiwKlG85s

HOLY ARE YOU LORD (AWESOME GOD)

HOLY ARE YOU LORD
ALL CREATION CALL YOU GOD
WORTHY IS YOUR NAME, WE WORSHIP YOUR MAJESTY
AWESOME GOD, HOW GREAT THOU ART
YOU ARE GOD, MIGHTY ARE YOUR MIRACLES
WE STAND IN AWE OF YOUR HOLY NAME
LORD, WE BOW DOWN AND WORSHIP YOU

LINK: https://youtu.be/qnLvi392hhE

YOU ARE GOD

YOU ARE GOD, YOU ARE NOT JUST BIG OH
YOU ARE NOT JUST LARGE OH
YOU ARE A GREAT GOD
YOU ARE BIG, BIG, BIG, BIG, BIG, BIG
LARGE, LARGE, LARGE, LARGE, LARGE, LARGE
GREAT, GREAT, GREAT, GREAT, GREAT
YOU ARE A GREAT GOD

LINK: https://youtu.be/VZd2fQS8yLI

EVERY PRAISE TO OUR GOD

EVERY PRAISE IS TO OUR GOD
EVERY WORD OF WORSHIP, WITH ONE ACCORD
EVERY PRAISE, EVERY PRAISE
IS TO OUR GOD
SING HALLELUJAH TO OUR GOD
GLORY HALLELUJAH IS DUE OUR GOD
EVERY PRAISE, EVERY PRAISE, IS TO OUR GOD

LINK: https://youtu.be/X48B8AbkmbA

MIXED – CONTEMPORARY/AFRICAN: PRAISE AND WORSHIP – SET 21

WORSHIP-:

YOU ARE AWESOME IN THIS PLACE MIGHTY GOD

PRAISE-:

1. LORD YOU ARE SO GOOD, BLESSDED BE YOUR NAME
2. ARISE, ARISE, ARISE
3. WATER HE TURNED INTO WINE
4. YOU ARE GOD, YOU ARE NOT JUST BIG
5. YOU ARE GREAT, YES YOU ARE, HOLY ONE

WORSHIP & PRAISE LYRICS

YOU ARE AWESOME IN THIS PLACE MIGHTY GOD

YOU ARE AWESOME IN THIS PLACE MIGHTY GOD
YOU ARE AWESOME IN THIS PLACE MIGHTY GOD
ABBA FATHER, YOU ARE WORTHY OF OUR PRAISE
TO YOU OUR LIFE WE RAISE
YOU ARE AWESOME IN THIS MIGHTY GOD

LINK: https://youtu.be/faiLQCuoskM

LORD YOU ARE SO GOOD, BLESSDED BE YOUR NAME

LORD YOU ARE SO GOOD, BLESSDED BE YOUR NAME
IN HEAVEN YOU'RE THE LORD
ON EARTH YOU REIGN FOREVER
OH LORD, HOW GREAT THOU ART
BLESSED BY YOUR NAME

LINK: https://youtu.be/QhxObPYSWS8

ARISE, ARISE, ARISE

ONE THING WE ASK OF YOU, ONE THING THAT WE DESIRE
THAT AS WE WORSHIP YOU, LORD COME AND CHANGE OUR LIVES
SO, ARISE, ARISE, ARISE, ARISE, ARISE, TAKE YOUR PLACEBE ENTHRONED ON OUR PRAISE, ARISE
KING OF KINGS, HOLY GOD, AS WE SING ARISE
ARISE, ARISE, ARISE

LINK: https://youtu.be/RFoe8ZgNZEI

WATER HE TURNED INTO WINE

WATER YOU TURNED INTO WINE, OPENED THE EYES OF THE BLIND
THERE'S NO ONE LIKE YOU, NONE LIKE YOU
INTO THE DARKNESS YOU SHINE, OUT OF THE ASHES WE RISE, THERE'S NO ONE LIKE YOU, NONE LIKE YOU
OUR GOD IS GREATER, OUR GOD IS STRONGER
GOD YOU ARE HIGHER THAN ANY OTHER
OUR GOD IS HEALER, AWESOME IN POWER OUR GOD, OUR GOD
LINK: https://youtu.be/NJpt1hSYf2o

YOU ARE GOD

YOU ARE GOD, YOU ARE NOT JUST BIG OH
YOU ARE NOT JUST LARGE OH
YOU ARE A GREAT GOD
YOU ARE BIG, BIG, BIG, BIG, BIG, BIG
LARGE, LARGE, LARGE, LARGE, LARGE
GREAT, GREAT, GREAT, GREAT, GREAT
YOU ARE A GREAT GOD

LINK: https://youtu.be/VZd2fQS8yLI

YOU ARE GREAT, YES YOU ARE

YOU ARE GREAT YES YOU ARE HOLY ONE
WALKED UPON THE SEA RISE THE DEAD
YOU REIGN IN MAJESTY MIGHTY GOD
EVERYTHING WRITTEN ABOUT YOU IS GREAT
YOU ARE GREAT YOU ARE GREAT 4X
EVERYTHING WRITTEN ABOUT YOU IS GREAT

LINK: https://youtu.be/q2KiwKlG85s

MIXED – CONTEMPORARY/AFRICAN: PRAISE AND WORSHIP – SET 22

WORSHIP-:

BLESS THE LORD OH MY SOUL, WORSHIP HIS HOLY NAME

PRAISE-:

1. I HAVE COME TO GIVE BACK TO YOU
2. BLESSED JESUS, WE'VE COME TO GIVE PRAISE
3. LORD YOU ARE GOOD AND MERCY IF FOREVER, HALLELUJAH
4. JEHOVAH, YOU ARE THE MOST HIGH
5. JEHOVAH EEH JEHOVAH AAH

WORSHIP & PRAISE LYRICS

BLESS THE LORD OH MY SOUL, OH MY SOUL

BLESS THE LORD OH MY SOUL, OH MY SOUL
WORSHIP HIS HOLY NAME
SING LIKE NEVER BEFORE
OH, MY SOUL, WORSHIP HIS HOLY NAME
SING LIKE NEVER BEFORE
OH, MY SOUL, WORSHIP HIS HOLY NAME

LINK: https://youtu.be/7utzmfkQmJA

I HAVE COME TO GIVE BACK TO YOU

I HAVE COME TO GIVE BACK TO YOU
I HAVE COME TO SAY THANK YOU LORD x2
TAKE ALL THE PRAISE x 3
TAKE ALL THE PRAISE, YOU DESERVE
TAKE ALL THE PRAISE
TAKE ALL THE PRAISE
I HAVE COME TO SAY THANK YOU LORD

LINK: https://youtu.be/07dgTV33pTA

BLESSED JESUS WE'VE COME TO GIVE PRAISE

BLESSED JESUS
WE'VE COME TO GIVE PRAISE
YOU SRE WORTHY
AND BLESSED BE YOUR NAME
WE LOVE YOU LORD
WE LOVE YOU LORD

LINK: https://youtu.be/tHQxyREYj-c

YOU ARE GOOD AND YOUR MERCY IS FOREVER

YOU ARE GOOD AND YOUR MERCY IS FOREVER, HALLELUJAH!
YOU ARE GOOD AND YOUR MERCY IS FOREVER, HALLELUJAH!
YOU ARE GOOD AND YOUR MERCY IS FOREVER, HALLELUJAH!

LINK: : https://youtu.be/Wyo3kqNgcYQ

JEHOVAH YOU ARE THE MOST HIGH

JEHOVAH YOU ARE THE MOST HIGH!
YOU ARE THE MOST HIGH GOD
JEHOVAH, YOU ARE THE MOST HIGH!
YOU ARE THE MOST HIGH GOD

LINK: https://youtu.be/QPNIsEy7n5M

JEHOVAH EEH JEHOVAH AAH (LORD, SAVOIUR)

JEHOVAH LORD, JEHOVAH AA
JEHOVAH EEH JEHOVAH AAH
JEHOVAH LORD, JEHOVAH AA
JEHOVAH EEH JEHOVAH AAH

LINK: https://youtu.be/o8pGlMRqKMM

MIXED – CONTEMPORARY/AFRICAN: PRAISE AND WORSHIP – SET 23

WORSHIP-:

THAT IS WHY YOU ARE CALLED JEHOVAH

PRAISE-:

1. OPEN THE EYES OF MY HEART
2. YOU ARE GOOD AND YOUR MERCY IS FOREVER, HALLELUJAH
3. HALLE, HALLE, HALLELUJAH, GLORY, GLORY WE PRAISE YOUR NAME
4. JEHOVAH, YOU ARE THE MOST HIGH
5. HALLELUJAH EH

WORSHIP & PRAISE LYRICS

THAT IS WHY YOU ARE CALLED JEHOVAH

THAT IS WHY YOU ARE CALLED JEHOVAH
THAT IS WHY YOU ARE CALLED JEHOVAH
WHAT YOU SAY YOU WILL DO
THAT IS WHAT YOU WILL DO
THAT IS WHY YOU ARE CALLED JEHOVAH

LINK: https://youtu.be/NH1OojwkWtk

OPEN THE EYES OF MY HEART LORD

OPEN THE EYES OF MY HEART, LORD
OPEN THE EYES OF MY HEART, I WANT TO SEE YOU
TO SEE YOU HIGH AND LIFTED UP
SHININ' IN THE LIGHT OF YOUR GLORY
POUR OUT YOUR POWER AND LOVE
AS WE SING HOLY, HOLY, HOLY

LINK: https://youtu.be/fadU7b9aa78

YOU ARE GOOD AND YOUR MERCY IS FOREVER

YOU ARE GOOD AND YOUR MERCY IS FOREVER
HALLELUJAH
YOU ARE GOOD AND YOUR MERCY IS FOREVER
HALLELUJAH
HALLELUJAH, HALLELUJAH AMEN x3

LINK: https://youtu.be/Wyo3kqNgcYQ

HALLE, HALLE, HALLELUJAH, GLORY

HALLE, HALLE, HALLELUJAH,
GLORY, GLORY WE PRAISE YOUR NAME
YOU ARE THE KING OF KINGS
AND THE LORD OF LORDS
WE PRAISE YOUR NAME

LINK: https://youtu.be/2NsZJzybNlE

JEHOVAH YOU ARE THE MOST HIGH

JEHOVAH YOU ARE THE MOST HIGH!
YOU ARE THE MOST HIGH GOD
JEHOVAH, YOU ARE THE MOST HIGH!
YOU ARE THE MOST HIGH GOD

LINK: https://youtu.be/QPNlsEy7n5M

HALLELUJAH EH

HALLELUJAH EH! HALLELUJAH O OH!
HALLELUJAH EH! IT'S THE SOUND OF VICTORY
HALLELUJAH EH! HALLELUJAH O OH!
LET THE SOUND OF REJOICING FILL THIS HOUSE

LINK: https://youtu.be/BgGkIjd7qe4

MIXED – CONTEMPORARY/AFRICAN: PRAISE AND WORSHIP – SET 24

WORSHIP-:

JEHOVA IS YOUR NAME (MIGHTY WARRIOR)

PRAISE-:

1. JEHOVAH JIREH, JEHOVAH NISSI, YOU ARE MY EBENEZER
2. HALLELUJAH EE
3. I KNOW HE RESCUED MY SOUL
4. CASTING CROWN
5. HALLELUJAH THAT'S WHAT OUR SONG WILL BE

WORSHIP & PRAISE LYRICS

JEHOVA IS YOUR NAME (MIGHTY WARRIOR)

JEHOVA IS YOUR NAME
JEHOVA IS YOUR NAME
MIGHTY WARRIOR, GREAT IN BATTLE
JEHOVA IS YOUR NAME
MIGHTY WARRIOR, GREAT IN BATTLE
JEHOVA IS YOUR NAME

LINK: https://youtu.be/Ro9KtH6cSVU

JEHOVAH SHAMMAH, JEHOVAH NISSI, YOU ARE MY EBENEZER

JEHOVAH JIREH
JEHOVAH NISSI
YOU ARE MY EBENEZAR
YOU ARE MY ADONAI
I GIVE YOU GLORY HONOUR POWER MAJESTY
YOU ARE MY LORD, FOREVER

LINK: https://youtu.be/jul4xzRwMmw

HALLELUJAH EH

HALLELUJAH EH! HALLELUJAH O OH!
HALLELUJAH EH! IT'S THE SOUND OF VICTORY
HALLELUJAH EH! HALLELUJAH O OH!
LET THE SOUND OF REJOICING FILL THIS HOUSE

LINK: https://youtu.be/BgGkIjd7qe4

I KNOW YOU RESCUED MY SOUL

I KNOW HE RESCUED MY SOUL; HIS BLOOD HAS COVERED MY SIN
I BELIEVE, I BELIEVE, MY SHAME, HE'S TAKEN AWAY
MY PAIN IS HEALED IN HIS NAME, I BELIEVE, I BELIEVE, I'LL RAISE A BANNER 'CAUSE MY LORD HAS CONQUERED THE GRAVE
MY REDEEMER LIVES (4X)

LINK: https://youtu.be/3glYEDzSyok

CASTING CROWNS

CASTING CROWNS, LIFTING HANDS
BOWING HEARTS, IS ALL WE'VE COME TO DO
ADONAI, ADONAI, ADONAI, YOU REIGN ON HIGH
WE WILL RISE, IN YOUR NAME, ADONAI, YOU REIGN ON HIGH

LINK: https://youtu.be/2P-FIceZIDo

HALLELUJAH THAT'S WHAT OUR SONG WILL BE

HALLELUJAH,
THAT'S WHAT OUR SONG WILL BE
THAT'S WHAT OUR SONG WILL BE
THAT'S WHAT OUR SONG WILL BE

LINK: https://youtu.be/eYJpUgTXOUk

MIXED – CONTEMPORARY/AFRICAN: PRAISE AND WORSHIP- SET 25

WORSHIP-:

YOU ARE GOD ALL BY YOURSELF

PRAISE-:

1. JESUS, YOU ARE MY FIRM FOUNDATION
2. MASTER OF THE UNIVERSE
3. YOU ARE GOOD, AND YOUR MERCY IS FORVER, HALLELUJAH
4. HALLELUJAH THAT'S WHAT OUR SONG WILL BE
5. HALLELUJAH, FOR THE LORD OUR GOD THE ALMIGHTY REIGNS

WORSHIP & PRAISE LYRICS

YOU ARE GOD ALL BY YOURSELF

YOU'VE GOT TIMES AND SEASONS IN YOUR HANDS
YOU CALLED FOR LIGHT OUT OF DARKNESS
YOU DON'T NEED A MAN TOBE THE GOD YOU ARE
BUT YOU HAVE CHOOSEN TO CALL ME YOUR OWN
YOU ARE GOD FROM BEGINNING TO THE END
THERE'S NO PLACE FOR ARGUMENT
YOU ARE GOD ALL BY YOURSELF x2

LINK: https://youtu.be/pJMNagqzDVM

JESUS YOU ARE MY FIRM FOUNDATION

JESUS, YOU'RE MY FIRM FOUNDATION, I KNOW I
CAN STAND SECURE;
JESUS, YOU'RE MY FIRM FOUNDATION, I PUT MY
HOPE IN YOUR HOLY WORD,
I PUT MY HOPE IN YOUR HOLY WORD.
I HAVE A LIVING HOPE, I HAVE A FUTURE;
GOD HAS A PLAN FOR ME, OF THIS I'M SURE(2X)

LINK: https://youtu.be/KVPsW4csPs0

MASTER OF THE UNIVERSE

YOU ARE THE MASTER, MASTER OF THE UNIVERSE
CONQUEROR AND KING, LORD! MASTER OF THE UNIVERSE
YOU ARE THE EMPEROR ALWAYS, YOU ARE THE HEIR
OVER PRINCIPALITIES, YOU ARE THE HEIR, OVER
POWERS, YOU ARE THE HEIR, OVER RULERS, YOU
ARE THE MASTER
MASTER OF THE UNIVERSE

LINK: https://youtu.be/kJ48XEDMBoY

YOU ARE GOOD AND YOUR MERCY IS FOREVER

YOU ARE GOOD AND YOUR MERCY IS FOREVER
HALLELUJAH
YOU ARE GOOD AND YOUR MERCY IS FOREVER
HALLELUJAH
HALLELUJAH, HALLELUJAH AMEN x3

LINK: https://youtu.be/Wyo3kqNgcYQ

HALLELUJAH THAT'S WHAT OUR SONG WILL BE

HALLELUJAH,
THAT'S WHAT OUR SONG WILL BE
THAT'S WHAT OUR SONG WILL BE
THAT'S WHAT OUR SONG WILL BE

LINK: https://youtu.be/eYJpUgTXOUk

HALLELUJAH, FOR THE LORD OUR GOD

HALLELUJAH, FOR THE LORD OUR GOD THE
ALMIGHTY REIGNS
HALLELUJAH, FOR THE LORD OUR GOD THE
ALMIGHTY REIGNS
HOSSANA, HALLELUJAH
HOSSANA, HALLELUJAH

LINK: https://youtu.be/HRPtXuFpV9U

MIXED – CONTEMPORARY/AFRICAN: PRAISE AND WORSHIP - SET 26

WORSHIP-:

OPEN THE FLOODGATES, IN ABUNDANCE

PRAISE-:

1. HOSSANA, HOSSANA, HOSSANA IN THE HIGHEST
2. WATER HE TUNRNED INTO WINE
3. THE LORD REIGNS, LET THE EARTH REJOICE
4. JEHOVAH YOU ARE THY MOST HIGH
5. I SEARCHED ALL OVER

WORSHIP & PRAISE LYRICS

OPEN THE FLOODGATES, IN ABUNDANCE

FATHER, WE ARE IN YOUR PRESENCE
LET IT RAIN, CAUSE YOUR RAIN, CAUSE YOUR RAIN
LET IT FALL ON ME
OPEN THE FLOOD GATES IN ABUNDANCE AND
CAUSE YOUR RAIN
OPEN THE FLOOD GATES IN ABUNDANCE AND
CAUSE YOUR RAIN
TO FALL ON ME (SAY BABA OH!)
FATHER OH... OH, OH OH OH OH
FATHER OH... OH OH OH OH
LINK: https://youtu.be/63nyGawcJbQ

HOSSANA, HOSSANA, HOSSANA IN THE HIGHEST

HOSSANA, HOSSANA, HOSSANA
IN THE HIGHEST
LORD, WE LIFT UP YOUR NAME
WITH THE HEART FULL OF PRAISE
BE EXALTED, OH LORD MY GOD
HOSSANA IN THE HIGHEST

LINK: https://youtu.be/E1X-VDCMyAc

WATER YOU TURNED INTO WINE

WATER YOU TURNED INTO WINE, OPENED THE
EYES OF THE BLIND
THERE'S NO ONE LIKE YOU, NONE LIKE YOU
INTO THE DARKNESS YOU SHINE, OUT OF THE
ASHES WE RISE, THERE'S NO ONE LIKE YOU, NONE LIKE YOU
OUR GOD IS GREATER, OUR GOD IS STRONGER
GOD YOU ARE HIGHER THAN ANY OTHER
OUR GOD IS HEALER, AWESOME IN POWER OUR GOD, OUR GOD
LINK: https://youtu.be/NJpt1hSYf2o

THE LORD REIGNS, LET THE EARTH REJOICE

THE LORD REIGNS., THE LORD REIGNS.
THE LORD REIGNS.MLET THE EARTH REJOICE.
LET THE EARTH REJOICE., LET THE EARTH REJOICE.
LET THE PEOPLE BE GLAD, THAT OUR GOD REIGNS

LINK: https://youtu.be/aAgVvh2WgMM

JEHOVAH YOU ARE THY MOST HIGH

JEHOVAH YOU ARE THY MOST HIGH
JEHOVAH YOU ARE THY MOST HIGH
JEHOVAH YOU ARE THY MOST HIGH
YOU ARE MOST HIGH
YOU MOST GOD
YOU THE MOST HIGH
YOU ARE THE MOST

LINK: https://youtu.be/QPNlsEy7n5M

I SEARCHED ALL OVER

SEARCHED ALL OVER, COULDN'T FIND NOBODY
I LOOKED HIGH AND LOW, STILL COULDN'T FIND NOBODY
NOBODY. GREATER, NOBODY GREATER
NOBODY GREATER THAN YOU
NOBODY GREATER, NOBODY GREATER JESUS
NOBODY GREATER THAN YOU
NOBODY GREATER, NOBODY GREATER NO
NOBODY GREATER THAN YOU
LINK: https://youtu.be/9QSbqSuwwx0

MIXED - CONTEMPORARY/AFRICAN: PRAISE AND WORSHIP - SET 27

WORSHIP-:

MY HALLELUJAH, BELONGS TO YOU (YOU DESERVE IT)

PRAISE-:

1. WHAT SHALL WE SAY UNTO THE LORD, (THANK YOU LORD)
2. WHO HAS THE FINAL SAY
3. GLORY, GLORY, HALLELUJAH, GLORY, GLORY
4. WHEN JESUS SAY YES, NOBODY CAN SAY NO
5. EVERY PRAISE TO OUR GOD

WORSHIP & PRAISE LYRICS

YOU DESERVE IT

MY HALLELUJAH BELONGS TO YOU
MY HALLELUJAH BELONGS TO YOU
MY HALLELUJAH BELONGS TO YOU
MY HALLELUJAH BELONGS TO YOU
YOU DESERVE IT x 6

LINK: https://youtu.be/zxL1m0uG8x4

WHAT SHALL WE SAY UNTO THE LORD

WHAT SHALL WE SAY UNTO THE LORD
ALL WE HAVE TO SAY IS THANK YOU LORD
WHAT SHALL WE SAY UNTO THE LORD
ALL WE HAVE TO SAY IS THANK YOU LORD
THANK YOU LORD x2
ALL WE HAVE TO SAY IS THANK YOU LORD
THANK YOU LORD x2
ALL WE HAVE TO SAY IS THANK YOU LORD

LINK: https://youtu.be/bJIogO_rmeo

WHO HAS THE FINAL SAY

WHO HAS THE FINAL SAY
JEHOAH HAS THE FINAL SAY
JEHOVAH, TURNED MY LIFE AROUND, HE TURNED MY LIFE AROUND
HE MAKES A WAY, WHERE THERE IS NO WAY
JEHOVAH, HAS THE FINAL SAY

LINK: https://youtu.be/Bx2T8aunyvs

I WILL PRAISE THE LORD IN THE SANCTURAY

I WILL PRAISE THE LORD IN THE SANCTURAY
I WILL PRAISE THE LORD IN THE SANCTURAY
YOU ARE WORTHY OF MY PRAISE, I WILL DANCE AND CELEBRATE
I WILL PRAISE THE LORD IN THE SANCTURAY
LET THE PEOPLE NOW REJOICE FOR LORD IS GOOD
I WILL PRAISE THE LORD IN THE SANCTURAY

LINK: https://youtu.be/dDI1hWPCbTE

WHEN JESUS SAY YES, NOBODY CAN SAY NO

WHEN JESUS SAY YES, NOBODY CAN SAY NO
WHEN JESUS SAY YES, NOBODY CAN SAY NO
WHEN JESUS SAY YES, NOBODY CAN SAY NO
THERE'S NO LIMIT TO WHAT YOU CAN DO
CAUSE IT ALL BELONGS TO YOU
YES, IT ALL BELONGS TO YOU
YOU'RE ALMIGHTY AND ALL POWERFUL
AND IT ALL BELONG TO YOU
YES, IT ALL BELONGS TO YOU

LINK: https://youtu.be/BK-tNGf0e20

EVERY PRAISE TO OUR GOD

EVERY PRAISE IS TO OUR GOD
EVERY WORD OF WORSHIP, WITH ONE ACCORD
EVERY PRAISE, EVERY PRAISE
IS TO OUR GOD
SING HALLELUJAH TO OUR GOD
GLORY HALLELUJAH IS DUE OUR GOD
EVERY PRAISE, EVERY PRAISE, IS TO OUR GOD

LINK: https://youtu.be/X48B8AbkmbA

MIXED – CONTEMPORARY/AFRICAN: PRAISE AND WORSHIP- SET 28

WORSHIP-:

YOU ARE WORTHY TO BE GLORIFIED, YOU ARE WORTHY JEHOVAH

PRAISE-:

1. JEHOVAH SHAMMAH, JEHOVAH NISSI
2. CASTING CROWNS
3. CREATOR OF THE UNIVERSE
4. ARISE, ARISE, ARISE
5. YES YOU ARE THE LORD

WORSHIP & PRAISE LYRICS

YOU ARE WORTHY TO BE GLORIFIED

YOU ARE WORTHY TO BE GLORIFIED
YOU ARE WORTHY JEHOVAH
YOU ARE WORTHY TO BE GLORIFIED
YOU ARE WORTHY LORD

LINK: https://youtu.be/nFpU1BlG-hA

CASTING CROWNS

CASTING CROWNS, LIFTING HANDS
BOWING HEARTS, IS ALL WE'VE COME TO DO
ADONAI, ADONAI, ADONAI, YOU REIGN ON HIGH
WE WILL RISE, IN YOUR NAME, ADONAI, YOU REIGN ON HIGH

LINK: https://youtu.be/2P-FlceZIDo

JEHOVAH SHAMMAH, JEHOVAH NISSI, YOU ARE MY EBENEZER

JEHOVAH SHAMAH
JEHOVAH NISSI
YOU ARE MY EBENEZAR
YOU ARE MY ADONAI
I GIVE YOU GLORY HONOUR POWER MAJESTY
YOU ARE MY LORD

LINK: https://youtu.be/jul4xzRwMmw

CREATOR OF THE UNIVERSE

YOU ARE WORTHY TO BE GLORIFIED
YOU ARE WORTHY JEHOVAH
YOU ARE WORTHY TO BE GLORIFIED
YOU ARE WORTHY LORD

LINK: https://youtu.be/nFpU1BlG-hA

ARISE, ARISE, ARISE

ONE THING WE ASK OF YOU, ONE THING THAT WE DESIRE
THAT AS WE WORSHIP YOU, LORD COME AND CHANGE OUR LIVES
SO, ARISE, ARISE, ARISE, ARISE, ARISE, TAKE YOUR PLACEBE ENTHRONED ON OUR PRAISE, ARISE
KING OF KINGS, HOLY GOD, AS WE SING ARISE
ARISE, ARISE, ARISE

LINK: https://youtu.be/RFoe8ZgNZEI

YES, YOU ARE THE LORD, MOST HIGH

YES, YOU ARE THE LORD, MOST HIGH
YES, YOU ARE THE LORD, MOST HIGH
YES, YOU ARE THE LORD
YES, YOU ARE THE LORD, MOST HIGH
YES, YOU ARE THE LORD, MOST HIGH

LINK: https://youtu.be/MpCKY9WfaA8

MIXED – CONTEMPORARY/AFRICAN: PRAISE AND WORSHIP – SET 29

WORSHIP-:

NO OTHER NAME BUT THE NAME OF JESUS

PRAISE-:

1. HIGHER, HIGHER, HIGHER (6X) LIFT JESUS HIGHER
2. YOU ARE GOD; YOU ARE NOT JUST BIG OO...
3. ARISE, ARISE, ARISE
4. AM TRADING MY SORROW (YES LORD)
5. AWESOME GOD, MIGHTY GOD

WORSHIP & PRAISE LYRICS

NO OTHER NAME BUT THE NAME OF JESUS

NO OTHER NAME BUT THE NAME OF JESUS
NO OTHER NAME BUT THE NAME OF LORD
NO OTHER NAME BUT THE NAME OF JESUS
HIS WORTHY OF GLORY
AND WORTHY OF HONOUR
AND WPRTHY OF PWERR
AND ALL PRAISE

LINK: https://youtu.be/QUgzowKz4Gw

HIGHER, HIGHER, HIGHER (6X) LIFT JESUS HIGHER

HIGHER, HIGHER
HIGHER, HIGHER, HIGHER, HIGHER, HIGHER, HIGHER,
HIGHER, HIGHER
HIGHER, HIGHER, HIGHER, HIGHER, HIGHER, HIGHER,
HIGHER, HIGHER
HIGHER, HIGHER, HIGHER, HIGHER, HIGHER,
LIFT JESUS HIGHER

LINK: https://youtu.be/Hq9Mq0WMuSc

YOU ARE GOD

YOU ARE GOD, YOU ARE NOT JUST BIG OH
YOU ARE NOT JUST LARGE OH
YOU ARE A GREAT GOD
YOU ARE BIG, BIG, BIG, BIG, BIG, BIG, BIG
LARGE, LARGE, LARGE, LARGE, LARGE, LARGE
GREAT, GREAT, GREAT, GREAT, GREAT
YOU ARE A GREAT GOD

LINK: https://youtu.be/VZd2fQS8yLI

ARISE, ARISE, ARISE

ONE THING WE ASK OF YOU, ONE THING THAT WEDESIRE
THAT AS WE WORSHIP YOU, LORD COME AND
CHANGE OUR LIVES
SO, ARISE, ARISE, ARISE, ARISE, ARISE, TAKE YOUR
PLACEBE ENTHRONED ON OUR PRAISE, ARISE
KING OF KINGS, HOLY GOD, AS WE SING ARISE
ARISE, ARISE, ARISE

LINK: https://youtu.be/RFoe8ZgNZEI

YES LORD, YES LORD (AM TRADING)

I'M TRADING MY SORROWS
I'M TRADING MY SHAME
I'M LAYING THEM DOWN
FOR THE JOY OF THE LORD
I'M TRADING MY SICKNESS
I'M TRADING MY PAIN
I'M LAYING THEM DOWN
FOR THE JOY OF THE LORD
YES LORD YES LORD
YES, YES LORD AMEN

LINK: https://youtu.be/YYRc0JeQuC0

AWESOME GOD, MIGHTY GOD

AWESOME GOD, MIGHTY GOD!
AWESOME GOD, MIGHTY GOD!
AWESOME GOD, MIGHTY GOD!
WE GIVE YOU PRAISE, AWESOME GOD!
WE GIVE YOU PRAISE, MIGHTY GOD!
YOU'RE HIGHLY LIFTED UP, AWESOME GOD!
YOU'RE HIGHLY LIFTED UP, MIGHTY GOD!

LINK: https://youtu.be/V5dcczS2GsE

MIXED – CONTEMPORARY/AFRICAN: PRAISE AND WORSHIP - SET 30

WORSHIP-:

THE STEADFAST LOVE OF THE LORD NEVER CEASES

PRAISE-:

1. YOU ARE GOOD AND YOUR MERCIES FOREVER, HALLELUJAH
2. YOU ARE GREAT, YES YOU ARE
3. ARISE, ARISE, ARISE
4. I KNOW YOU RESCUED MY SOUL
5. EVERY PRAISE TO OUR GOD

WORSHIP & PRAISE LYRICS

THE STEADFAST LOVE

THE STEADFAST LOVE OF THE LORD NEVER CEASES
HIS MERCIES NEVER COME TO AN END
THEY ARE NEW EVERY MORNING
NEW EVERY MORNING
GREAT IS THY FAITHFULNESS, O LORD
GREAT IS THY FAITHFULNESS

LINK: https://youtu.be/G3zbp6BU1S0

YOU ARE GOOD AND YOUR MERCY IS FOREVER

YOU ARE GOOD AND YOUR MERCY IS FOREVER, HALLELUJAH!
YOU ARE GOOD AND YOUR MERCY IS FOREVER, HALLELUJAH!
YOU ARE GOOD AND YOUR MERCY IS FOREVER, HALLELUJAH!

LINK: : https://youtu.be/Wyo3kqNgcYQ

YOU ARE GREAT, YES YOU ARE

YOU ARE GREAT YES YOU ARE HOLY ONE
WALKED UPON THE SEA RISE THE DEAD
YOU REIGN IN MAJESTY MIGHTY GOD
EVERYTHING WRITTEN ABOUT YOU IS GREAT
YOU ARE GREAT YOU ARE GREAT 4X
EVERYTHING WRITTEN ABOUT YOU IS GREAT

LINK: https://youtu.be/q2KiwKlG85s

ARISE, ARISE, ARISE

ONE THING WE ASK OF YOU, ONE THING THAT WE DESIRE
THAT AS WE WORSHIP YOU, LORD COME AND CHANGE OUR LIVES
SO, ARISE, ARISE, ARISE, ARISE, ARISE, TAKE YOUR PLACEBE ENTHRONED ON OUR PRAISE, ARISE
KING OF KINGS, HOLY GOD, AS WE SING ARISE
ARISE, ARISE, ARISE

LINK: https://youtu.be/RFoe8ZgNZEI

I KNOW YOU RESCUED MY SOUL

I KNOW HE RESCUED MY SOUL; HIS BLOOD HAS COVERED MY SIN
I BELIEVE, I BELIEVE, MY SHAME, HE'S TAKEN AWAY
MY PAIN IS HEALED IN HIS NAME, I BELIEVE, I BELIEVE,
I'LL RAISE A BANNER 'CAUSE MY LORD HAS CONQUERED THE GRAVE
MY REDEEMER LIVES (4X)

LINK: https://youtu.be/3glYEDzSyok

EVERY PRAISE TO OUR GOD

EVERY PRAISE IS TO OUR GOD
EVERY WORD OF WORSHIP, WITH ONE ACCORD
EVERY PRAISE, EVERY PRAISE
IS TO OUR GOD
SING HALLELUJAH TO OUR GOD
GLORY HALLELUJAH IS DUE OUR GOD
EVERY PRAISE, EVERY PRAISE, IS TO OUR GOD

LINK: https://youtu.be/X48B8AbkmbA

MIXED – CONTEMPORARY/AFRICAN: PRAISE AND WORSHIP- SET 31

WORSHIP-:

YOU DO MIGHTY THINGS; YOU DO GLORIOUS THINGS

PRAISE-:

1. I WILL LIFT UP MY VOICE I WILL JOYFULLY SING
2. JEHOVAH SHAMMAH, JEHOVAH NISSI
3. THERE IS SOMETHING THAT MAKES ME COME IN TO YOUR PRESENCE
4. JOY OVERFLOWS IN MY HEART
5. HOLY ARE YOU LORD, ALL CREATION CALL YOU LORD

WORSHIP & PRAISE LYRICS

YOU DO MIGHTY THINGS

I STAND AMAZED IN YOUR PRESENCE
THERE IS NOTHING YOU CANNOT DO
I STAND AMAZED IN YOUR PRESENCE
THERE IS JOY, PEACE, AND HOPE
THERE IS NO ONE LIKE YOU, JESUS
THERE IS NO ONE LIKE YOU, IN ALL THE EARTH
YOU DO MIGHTY THINGS; YOU DO GLORIOUS
THINGS, YOU'RE A FAITHFUL GOD, AWESOME IS YOUR NAME x2

LINK: https://youtu.be/wEOFjFzXGK4

I WILL LIFT UP MY VOICE, I WILL JOYFUL SING

I WILL LIFT UP MY VOICE, I WILL JOYFUL SING
FOR WHAT YOU HAVE DONE
FOR WHO YOU ARE
YOU ARE THE REASON I SING
MELODY IN MY HEART
YOU ARE THE SONG THAT I SING
I WILL YOU PRAISE YOU LORD
YOU REIGN, YOU REIGN, YOU REIGN FOREVER MORE

LINK: https://fb.watch/hOCoHjyvzY/

JEHOVAH SHAMMAH, JEHOVAH NISSI, YOU ARE MY EBENEZER

JEHOVAH SHAMAH
JEHOVAH NISSI
YOU ARE MY EBENEZAR
YOU ARE MY ADONAI
I GIVE YOU GLORY HONOUR POWER MAJESTY
YOU ARE MY LORD

LINK: https://youtu.be/jul4xzRwMmw

THERE IS SOMETHING THAT MAKES ME COME INTO YOUR PRESENCE

THERE IS SOMETHING THAT MAKES ME COME INTO YOUR PRESENCE - MY HELPER
THERE IS SOMETHING THAT MAKES ME COME INTO YOUR PRESENCE - MY HELPER
MY HELPER O MY HELPER (2X)
THERE IS SOMETHING THAT MAKES ME COME INTO YOUR PRESENCE - MY HELPER

LINK: https://youtu.be/mT6B6eoAlug

JOY OVERFLOW IN MY HEART

JOY OVERFLOWS IN MY HEART
SING A NEW SONG TO THE LORD
I WILL PRAISE YOUR NAME
I WILL WORSHIP YOU
GLORY HALLELUYAH SING A NEW SONG TO THE LORD (2X)

LINK: https://youtu.be/Aq4UDCRRdJc

HOLY ARE YOU LORD (AWESOME GOD)

HOLY ARE YOU LORD
ALL CREATION CALL YOU GOD
WORTHY IS YOUR NAME, WE WORSHIP YOUR MAJESTY
AWESOME GOD, HOW GREAT THOU ART
YOU ARE GOD, MIGHTY ARE YOUR MIRACLES
WE STAND IN AWE OF YOUR HOLY NAME
LORD, WE BOW DOWN AND WORSHIP YOU

LINK: https://youtu.be/qnLvi392hhE

MIXED – CONTEMPORARY/AFRICAN: PRAISE AND WORSHIP – SET 32

WORSHIP-:

DAILY AS I LIVE

PRAISE-:

1. THERE IS SOMETHING THAT MAKES ME COME IN TO YOUR PRESENCE
2. JOY OVERFLOWS IN MY HEART
3. WHAT WILL I GIVE YOU, MY PRAISE
4. HOSSANA, HOSSANA, HOSSANA, IN THE HIGHEST
5. HALLELUJAH THAT'S WHAT MY SONG WILL BE

WORSHIP & PRAISE LYRICS

DAILY AS I LIVE

DAILY AS I LIVE, OFTEN AS I BREATH
LET MY WHOLE LIFE, BE EXPRESSIONS OF YOUR GRACE x2
WE CRY ABBA FATHER
HALLOWED BE YOUR NEME
HALLOWED BE YOUR NEME
HALLOWED BE YOUR NEME

LINK: https://youtu.be/dl5ruzWw-H

THERE IS SOMETHING THAT MAKES ME COME INTO YOUR PRESENCE

THERE IS SOMETHING THAT MAKES ME COME INTO YOUR PRESENCE - MY HELPER
THERE IS SOMETHING THAT MAKES ME COME INTO YOUR PRESENCE - MY HELPER
MY HELPER O MY HELPER (2X)
THERE IS SOMETHING THAT MAKES ME COME INTO YOUR PRESENCE - MY HELPER

LINK: https://youtu.be/mT6B6eoAlug

JOY OVERFLOW IN MY HEART

JOY OVERFLOWS IN MY HEART
SING A NEW SONG TO THE LORD
I WILL PRAISE YOUR NAME
I WILL WORSHIP YOU
GLORY HALLELUYAH SING A NEW SONG TO THE LORD (2X)

LINK: https://youtu.be/Aq4UDCRRdJc

WHAT WILL I GIVE TO YOU, MY PRAISE

WHAT WILL I GIVE TO YOU, MY PRAISE
WHAT WILL I GIVE TO YOU, MY PRAISE
I DON'T HAVE MONEY, MY PRAISE
WHAT WILL I GIVE TO YOU, MY PRAISE
WHAT WILL I GIVE TO YOU, MY PRAISE

LINK: https://youtu.be/ZAjhMlnXN1c

HOSSANA, HOSSANA IN THE HIGHEST

HOSSANA, HOSSANA, HOSSAN IN THE HIGHEST
HOSSANA, HOSSANA, HOSSAN IN THE HIGHEST
LORD WE LIGT UP YOUR NAME
WITH THE HEAT FULL OF PRAISE
BE EXALTED OH LORD MY GOD
HOSSANA IN THE HIGHEST

LINK: https://youtu.be/E1X-VDCMyA

HALLELUJAH THAT'S WHAT MY SONG WILL BE

HALLELUJAH
THAT'S WHAT MY SONG WILL BE
THAT'S WHAT MY SONG WILL BE
THAT'S WHAT MY SONG WILL BE
THAT'S WHAT MY SONG WILL BE
HALLELUJAH
THAT'S WHAT MY SONG WILL BE x2

LINK: https://youtu.be/eYJpUgTXOUk

MIXED – CONTEMPORARY/AFRICAN: PRAISE AND WORSHIP – SET 33

WORSHIP-:

YOU DESERVE THE GLORY

PRAISE-:

1. LORD YOU ARE GOOD AND YOUR MERCY IS FOREVER
2. WE GIVE YOU ALL THE PRAISE
3. HALLE, HALLE, HALLELUJAH, GLORY, GLORY WE PRAISE YOUR NAME
4. CREATOR OF THE UNIVERSE
5. TAKE ALL THE PAISE, I HAVE COME TO SAY THANK YOU LORD

WORSHIP & PRAISE LYRICS

YOU DESERVE THE GLORY

YOU DESERVE THE GLORY AND THE HONOUR
LORD, WE LIFT OUR HANDS IN WORHIP AS WE LIFT YOUR HOLY NAME
YOU ARE GREAT, YOU DO MIRACLE, SO GREAT
THERE IS NO ONE ELSE LIKE
THERE IS NO ONE ELSE LIKE OOOO

LINK: https://youtu.be/LLseRHq-dA0

LORD YOU ARE GOOD AND YOUR MERCY ENDURETH FOREVER

LORD YOU ARE GOOD AND YOUR MERCY ENDURETH FOREVER x2
PEOPLE FROM EVERY NATION AND TONGUE
FROM GENERATION TO GENERATION
WE WORSHIP YOU, HALLELUJAH, HALLELUJAH
WE WORSHIP YOU FOR WHO YOU ARE

LINK: https://youtu.be/Wyo3kqNgcYQ

WE GIVE YOU ALL THE PRAISE

WE GIVE YOU ALL THE PRAISE
WE GIVE YOU ALL THE PRAISE
YOU ARE THE LORD, THERE IS NO OTHER
WE GIVE YOU ALL THE PRAISE
YOU ARE THE LORD, THERE IS NO OTHER
WE GIVE YOU ALL THE PRAISE

HALLE, HALLE, HALLELUJAH,

HALLE, HALLE, HALLELUJAH,
GLORY, GLORY WE PRAISE YOUR NAME
YOU ARE THE KING OF KINGS
AND THE LORD OF LORDS
WE PRAISE YOUR NAME

LINK: https://youtu.be/2NszJzqbNlE

CREATOR OF THE UNIVERSE

CREATOR OF THE UNIVERSE WHAT CANT YOU DO
WHAT CAN'T YOU DO WHAT CAN'T YOU DO
WHAT CAN'T YOU DO JESUS, NAME ABOVE EVERY NAME ABOVE EVERY OTHER NAME EVERY OTHER NAME
WHAT CAN'T YOU CHANGE, WHAT CAN'T YOU CHANGE JESUS
LIFT YOUR HANDS AND SAY YOU'RE ABLE
YOU ARE ABLE GREAT AND MIGHTY GREAT AND MIGHTY GOD
YOU'RE ABLE JESUS

LINK: https://youtu.be/HPgDaKajSnQ

TAKE ALL THE PRAISE

I HAVE COME, TO SAY THANK YOU LORD
I HAVE COME, TO GIVE BACK TO YOU
I HAVE COME, TO SAY THANK YOU LORD
TAKE ALL THE PRAISE x3
TAKE ALL THE PRAISE, YOU DESERVE

LINK: https://youtu.be/07dgTV33pTA

MIXED – CONTEMPORARY/AFRICAN: PRAISE AND WORSHIP – SET 34

WORSHIP-:

OUR GOD IS INDESCRIBABLE, FROM THE PAGES OF MY HEART

PRAISE-:

1. WATER HE TURNED INTO WINE
2. YOU ARE GOD, YOU ARE NOT JUST BIG
3. YOU ARE GREAT, YES YOU ARE
4. PRAISE YE THE LORD, OH MY SOUL
5. COME LET'S PRAISE THE LORD

WORSHIP & PRAISE LYRICS

FROM THE PAGES OF MY HEART

OUR GOD IS INDESCRIBABLE
HIS NAME IS HALLOWED IN THE FIRMAMENT
HE'S THE PASSOVER LAMB THROUGH SPACE AND TIME
SO, FROM THE PAGES OF MY HEART
LET MY WORSHIP BEGIN BUT NEVER
TO THE GOD OF ALL FLESH
FOR HE'S MY GOD AND HIS NAME IS YAHWEH
HIS NAME IS YAHWEH, YAHWEH
LINK: https://youtu.be/K1PXqjGMMMM

WATER YOU TURN INTO WINE

WATER YOU TURNED INTO WINE, OPENED THE EYES OF THE BLIND
THERE'S NO ONE LIKE YOU, NONE LIKE YOU
INTO THE DARKNESS YOU SHINE, OUT OF THE ASHES
WE RISE, THERE'S NO ONE LIKE YOU, NONE LIKE YOU
OUR GOD IS GREATER, OUR GOD IS STRONGER
GOD YOU ARE HIGHER THAN ANY OTHER
OUR GOD IS HEALER, AWESOME IN POWER OUR GOD, OUR GOD
LINK: https://youtu.be/NJpt1hSYf2o

YOU ARE GOD

YOU ARE GOD, YOU ARE NOT JUST BIG OH
YOU ARE NOT JUST LARGE OH
YOU ARE A GREAT GOD
YOU ARE BIG, BIG, BIG, BIG, BIG, BIG, BIG
LARGE, LARGE, LARGE, LARGE, LARGE, LARGE
GREAT, GREAT, GREAT, GREAT, GREAT
YOU ARE A GREAT GOD

LINK: https://youtu.be/VZd2fQS8yLI

YOU ARE GREAT, YES YOU ARE

YOU ARE GREAT YES YOU ARE HOLY ONE
WALKED UPON THE SEA RISE THE DEAD
YOU REIGN IN MAJESTY MIGHTY GOD
EVERYTHING WRITTEN ABOUT YOU IS GREAT
YOU ARE GREAT YOU ARE GREAT 4X
EVERYTHING WRITTEN ABOUT YOU IS GREAT

LINK: https://youtu.be/q2KiwKlG85s

PRAISE YE THE LORD OF MY SOUL

PRAISE YE THE LORD OF MY SOUL
THIS IS THE DAY HE HAS MADE
HALLELUJAH
HALLELUJAJ
PRAISE YE THE LORD

LINK: https://youtu.be/n5bCj5VetwI

COME LET'S PRAISE THE LORD

COME LET'S PRAISE THE LORD
HE IS JEHOVAH (TALK ABOUT HIS FAITHFULNESS)
HE IS EL-SHADAI (TELL THE WORLD OF HIS SALVATION)
SPREAD THE NEWS AROUND (TELL THE WORLD OF HIS PRAISE)
LET US PRAISE LORD (PRAISE THE LORD)
FOREVER AND EVER MY GOS HEIS THE SAME
HE'LL NEVER CHANGE
FROM ETERNITY, TO ETRNITY
HE'LL BE MY GOD OOH
PRAISE HIM
LINK: https://youtu.be/YEXJ9N-qHSM

MIXED – CONTEMPORARY/AFRICAN: PRAISE AND WORSHIP – SET 35

WORSHIP-:

JEHOVAH IS YOUR NAME

PRAISE-:

1. ALMIGHTY FATHER, WE THANK, WE THANK OOH
2. HAIL MY JESUS, POWERFUL WARRIOR
3. JEHOVAH EEH EHH, JEHOVAH AAH AAH
4. JEHOVAH, YOU ARE THE MOST HIGH
5. ARISE, ARISE, ARISE

WORSHIP & PRAISE LYRICS

JEHOVAH IS YOUR NAME

JEHOVAH IS YOUR NAME
JEHOVAH IS YOUR NAME
MIGHTY WARRIOR, GREAT IN BATTLE
JEHOVAH, IS YOUR NAME

LINK: https://youtu.be/Ro9KtH6cSVU

ALMIGHTY FATHER, WE THANK, WE THANK OOH

ALMIGHTY FATHER
WE THANK, WE THANK
WE THANK
WE THANK
WE THANK, WE THANK,
WE THANK OOH, WE THANK OOH, WE THANK OOH
WE THANK OOH

HAIL MY JESUS, POWERFUL WARROIR

HAIL MY JESUS
POWERFUL, POWERFUL, WARRIOR
HAIL MY JESUS
POWERFUL, POWERFUL, WARRIOR

LINK: https://youtu.be/xh3yQKrjBls

JEHOVAH EEH EHH, JEHOVAH AAH, AAH

JEHOVAH EEH, EHH
JEHOVAH AAH, AAH
JEHOVAH EEH, EHH
JEHOVAH AAH, AAH

LINK: https://youtu.be/o8pGlMRqKMM

JEHOVAH YOU ARE THE MOST HIGH

JEHOVAH YOU ARE THE MOST HIGH!
YOU ARE THE MOST HIGH GOD
JEHOVAH, YOU ARE THE MOST HIGH!
YOU ARE THE MOST HIGH GOD

LINK: https://youtu.be/QPNlsEy7n5M

ARISE, ARISE, ARISE

ONE THING WE ASK OF YOU, ONE THING THAT WE DESIRE
THAT AS WE WORSHIP YOU, LORD COME AND CHANGE OUR LIVES
SO, ARISE, ARISE, ARISE, ARISE, TAKE YOUR PLACEBE ENTHRONED ON OUR PRAISE, ARISE
KING OF KINGS, HOLY GOD, AS WE SING ARISE
ARISE, ARISE, ARISE

LINK: https://youtu.be/RFoe8ZgNZEI

MIXED – CONTEMPORARY/AFRICAN: PRAISE AND WORSHIP – SET 36

WORSHIP-:

YOU ARE WORTHY TO BE GLORIFIED, YOU ARE WORTHY JEHOVAH

PRAISE-:

1. JEHOVAH SHAMMAH, JEHOVAH NISSI
2. THE LORD REIGNS, LET THE EARTH REJOICE
3. CREATOR OF THE UNIVERSE
4. CASTING CROWNS
5. HOLY ARE YOU LORD, ALL CREATION CALL YOU GOD

WORSHIP & PRAISE LYRICS

YOU ARE WORTHY TO BE GLORIFIED

YOU ARE WORTHY TO BE GLORIFIED
YOU ARE WORTHY JEHOVAH
YOU ARE WORTHY TO BE GLORIFIED
YOU ARE WORTHY LORD x2

LINK: https://youtu.be/nFpU1BlG-hA

JEHOVAH SHAMMAH, JEHOVAH NISSI, YOU ARE MY EBENEZER

JEHOVAH SHAMMAH
JEHOVAH NISSI
YOU ARE MY EBENEZAR
YOU ARE MY ADONAI
I GIVE YOU GLORY HONOUR POWER MAJESTY
YOU ARE MY LORD

LINK: https://youtu.be/jul4xzRwMmw

THE LORD REIGNS, LET THE EARTH REJOICE

THE LORD REIGNS., THE LORD REIGNS.
THE LORD REIGNS.MLET THE EARTH REJOICE.
LET THE EARTH REJOICE., LET THE EARTH REJOICE.
LET THE PEOPLE BE GLAD, THAT OUR GOD REIGNS

LINK: https://youtu.be/aAgVvh2WgMM

CREATOR OF THE UNIVERSE

CREATOR OF THE UNIVERSE WHAT CANT YOU DO
WHAT CAN'T YOU DO WHAT CAN'T YOU DO
WHAT CAN'T YOU DO JESUS, NAME ABOVE EVERY
NAME ABOVE EVERY OTHER NAME EVERY OTHER NAME
WHAT CAN'T YOU CHANGE, WHAT CAN'T YOU CHANGE JESUS
LIFT YOUR HANDS AND SAY YOU'RE ABLE
YOU ARE ABLE GREAT AND MIGHTY GREAT AND MIGHTY GOD
YOU'RE ABLE JESUS

LINK: https://youtu.be/HPqDaKajSnQ

CASTING CROWNS

CASTING CROWNS, LIFTING HANDS
BOWING HEARTS, IS ALL WE'VE COME TO DO
ADONAI, ADONAI, ADONAI, YOU REIGN ON HIGH
WE WILL RISE, IN YOUR NAME, ADONAI, YOU REIGN ON HIGH

LINK: https://youtu.be/2P-FlceZIDo

HOLY ARE YOU LORD (AWESOME GOD)

HOLY ARE YOU LORD
ALL CREATION CALL YOU GOD
WORTHY IS YOUR NAME, WE WORSHIP YOUR MAJESTY
AWESOME GOD, HOW GREAT THOU ART
YOU ARE GOD, MIGHTY ARE YOUR MIRACLES
WE STAND IN AWE OF YOUR HOLY NAME
LORD, WE BOW DOWN AND WORSHIP YOU

LINK: https://youtu.be/qnLvi392hhE

MIXED – CONTEMPORARY/AFRICAN: PRAISE AND WORSHIP – SET 37

WORSHIP -:

YOU ARE THE LORD, LET YOUR NAME BE GLORIFIED

PRAISE -:

1. YES LORD, YES LORD (AM TRADING)
2. EVERY PRAISE TO OUR GOD
3. LORD YOU ARE GOOD AND YOUR MERCY IS FOREVER, HALLELUJAH
4. COME AND SEE THE LORD IS GOOD, THERE IS NOTHING HE CANNOT DO
5. JEHOVAH REIGNS

WORSHIP & PRAISE LYRICS

YOU ARE THE LORD, LET YOUR NAME BE GLORIFIED

YOU ARE THE LORD,
LET YOUR NAME BE GLORIFIED
YOU ARE THE LORD,
LET YOUR NAME BE GLORIFIED
WE GIVE YOU GLORY AND HONOUR
YOU ARE THE LORD
LET YOUR NAME BE GLORIFIED
LINK: https://youtu.be/oZHX6Gugqe0

YES LORD, YES LORD (AM TRADING)

I'M TRADING MY SORROWS
I'M TRADING MY SHAME
I'M LAYING THEM DOWN
FOR THE JOY OF THE LORD
I'M TRADING MY SICKNESS
I'M TRADING MY PAIN
I'M LAYING THEM DOWN
FOR THE JOY OF THE LORD
YES LORD YES LORD
YES, YES LORD AMEN
LINK: https://youtu.be/YYRc0JeQuC0

EVERY PRAISE TO OUR GOD

EVERY PRAISE IS TO OUR GOD
EVERY WORD OF WORSHIP, WITH ONE ACCORD
EVERY PRAISE, EVERY PRAISE
IS TO OUR GOD
SING HALLELUJAH TO OUR GOD
GLORY HALLELUJAH IS DUE OUR GOD
EVERY PRAISE, EVERY PRAISE, IS TO OUR GOD

LINK: https://youtu.be/X48B8AbkmbA

LORD YOU ARE GOOD AND YOUR MERCY ENDURETH FOREVER

LORD YOU ARE GOOD AND YOUR MERCY ENDURETH FOREVER x2
PEOPLE FROM EVERY NATION AND TONGUE
FROM GENERATION TO GENERATION
WE WORSHIP YOU HALLELUJAH, HALLELUJAH
WE WORSHIP YOU FOR WHO YOU ARE

LINK: https://youtu.be/708opj5poOc

COME AND SEE THE LORD IS GOOD

COME AND SEE THE LORD IS GOOD
COME AND SEE THE LORD IS GOOD
THERE IS NOTHING HE CANNOT DO
COME AND SEE THE LORD IS GOOD
HE GAVE ME VICTORY, GAVE PEACE OF MIND
THERE IS NOTHING HE CANNOT DO
COME AND SEE THE LORD IS GOOD

LINK: https://youtu.be/w1dZGX0kGGs

JEHOVAH REIGNS

JEHOVAH REIGNS, JEHOVAH REIGNS
JEHOVAH REIGNS, JEHOVAH REIGNS
YOU ARE LIFTED UP, ABOVE OTHER GOD'S
YOU ARE LIFTED, ABOVE OTHER GOD'S
JEHOVAH REIGNS, JEHOVAH REIGNS

LINK: https://youtu.be/SK9Qh_EV-b0

MIXED – CONTEMPORARY/AFRICAN: PRAISE AND WORSHIP – SET 38

WORSHIP-:

WE BOW DOWN AND WORSHIP YAHWEH

PRAISE-:

1. WE WANNA SEE JESUS LIFTED HIGH
2. BLESSED JESUS, WE'VE COME TO GIVE YOU PRAISE
3. HOSSANA, HOSSANA, HOSSANA IN THE HIGHEST
4. WE GIVE YOU ALL THE PRAISE, YOU ARE THE LORD THERE IS NO OTHER
5. ASWESOME GOD, MIGHTY GOD

WORSHIP & PRAISE LYRICS

WE BOW DOWN AND WORSHIP YAHWEH

WE BOW DOWN AND WORSHIP, YAHWEH
WE BOW DOWN AND WORSHIP, YAHWEH
YAHWEH, YAHWEH, YAHWEH
YAHWEH, YAHWEH, YAHWEH

LINK: https://youtu.be/q0A6nHOspkc

WE WANNA SEE JESUS LIFTED HIGH

WE WANNA SEE JESUS LIFTED HIGH
THE BANNER THAT FLIES ACROSS THE LAND
THAT ALL MEN MIGHT SEE THE TRUTH AND KNOW
HE IS THE WAY TO HEAVEN
WE WANT TO SEE, WE WANT TO SEE
WE WANT TO SEE JESIS LIFTED HIGH
STEP BY STEP WE ARE MOVING FORWARD
LITTLE BY LITTLE WE ARE TAKING GROUND
EVERY PRAYER A POWERFUL WEAPON
STRONGHOLDS COME TUMBLING DOWN AND DOWN AND DOWN AND DOWN

LINK: https://youtu.be/Glqypn3a9XE

BLESSED JESUS WE'VE COME TO GIVE PRAISE

BLESSED JESUS
WE'VE COME TO GIVE PRAISE
YOU SRE WORTHY
AND BLESSED BE YOUR NAME
WE LOVE YOU LORD
WE LOVE YOU LORD

LINK: https://youtu.be/tHQxyREYj-c

HOSSANA, HOSSANA IN THE HIGHEST

HOSSANA, HOSSANA, HOSSAN IN THE HIGHEST
HOSSANA, HOSSANA, HOSSAN IN THE HIGHEST
LORD WE LIGT UP YOUR NAME
WITH THE HEAT FULL OF PRAISE
BE EXALTED OH LORD MY GOD
HOSSANA IN THE HIGHEST

LINK: https://youtu.be/E1X-VDCMyAc

WE GIVE YOU ALL THE PRAISE

WE GIVE YOU ALL THE PRAISE
WE GIVE YOU ALL THE PRAISE
YOU ARE LORD THERE IS NO OTHER
WE GIVE YOU ALL THE PRAISE

YOU ARE LORD THERE IS NO OTHER
WE GIVE YOU ALL THE PRAISE

AWESOME GOD, MIGHTY GOD

AWESOME GOD, MIGHTY GOD!
AWESOME GOD, MIGHTY GOD!
AWESOME GOD, MIGHTY GOD!
WE GIVE YOU PRAISE, AWESOME GOD!
WE GIVE YOU PRAISE, MIGHTY GOD!
YOU'RE HIGHLY LIFTED UP, AWESOME GOD!
YOU'RE HIGHLY LIFTED UP, MIGHTY GOD!

LINK: https://youtu.be/V5dcczS2GsE

MIXED - CONTEMPORARY/AFRICAN: PRAISE AND WORSHIP - SET 39

WORSHIP-:

OH LORD MY GOD, HOW GREAT THOU ARE

PRAISE-:

1. I KNOW HE RESCUED MY SOUL
2. BLESSED BE THE NAME OF THE LORD
3. YOU ARE YAHWEH, ALPHA, AND OMEGA
4. COME LTET'S PRAISE THE LORD
5. HAIL MY JESUS, POWERFUL, POWERFUL

WORSHIP & PRAISE LYRICS

HOW GREAT THOU ARE

OH LORD, MY GOD
WHEN I, IN AWESOME WONDER
CONSIDER ALL THE WORLDS THY HANDS HAVE MADE,
I SEE THE STARS, I HEAR THE ROLLING THUNDER, THY
POWER THROUGHOUT THE UNIVERSE DISPLAYED
THEN SINGS MY SOUL, MY SAVIOR GOD TO THEE
HOW GREAT THOU ART, HOW GREAT THOU ART
THEN SINGS MY SOUL, MY SAVIOR GOD TO THEE
HOW GREAT THOU ART, HOW GREAT THOU ART
LINK: https://youtu.be/Cc0QVWzCv9k

I KNOW YOU RESCUED MY SOUL

I KNOW HE RESCUED MY SOUL; HIS BLOOD HAS
COVERED MY SIN
I BELIEVE, I BELIEVE, MY SHAME, HE'S TAKEN AWAY
MY PAIN IS HEALED IN HIS NAME, I BELIEVE, I BELIEVE,
I'LL RAISE A BANNER 'CAUSE MY LORD HAS
CONQUERED THE GRAVE
MY REDEEMER LIVES (4X)

LINK: https://youtu.be/3glYEDzSyok

BLESSED BE THE NAME OF THE LORD

BLESSED BE THE NAME OF THE LORD x2
BLESSED BE THE NAME OF THE LORD, MOST HIGH
THE NAME OF THE LORD IS, A STRONG TOWER
THE RIGHTEOUS RUN INTO IT AND THEY ARE
SAVED
THE NAME OF THE LORD IS, A STRONG TOWER
THE RIGHTEOUS RUN INTO IT AND THEY ARE
SAVED
LINK: https://youtu.be/bYrcrP1ysjw

YOU ARE YAHWEH, ALPHA, AND OMEGA

YOU ARE YAHWEH
YOU ARE YAHWEH
YOU ARE YAHWEH, ALPHA, AND OMEGA
YOU ARE YAHWEH, ALPHA, AND OMEGA

LINK: https://youtu.be/gDQAr3gmSqY

COME LET'S PRAISE THE LORD

COME LET'S PRAISE THE LORD
HE IS JEHOVAH (TALK ABOUT HIS FAITHFULNESS)
HE IS EL- SHADAI (TELL THE WORLD OF HIS SALVATION)
SPREAD THE NEWS AROUND (TELL THE WORLD OF HIS PRAISE)
LET US PRAISE LORD (PRAISE THE LORD)
FOREVER AND EVER MY GOS HEIS THE SAME
HE'LL NEVER CHANGE
FROM ETERNITY, TO ETRNITY
HE'LL BE MY GOD OOH
PRAISE HIM
LINK: https://youtu.be/YEXJ9N-qHSM

HAIL MY JESUS, POWERFUL, POWERFUL

HAIL MY JESUS
POWERFUL POWER WARROIR
HAIL MY JESUS
POWERFUL POWER WARROIR

LINK: https://youtu.be/xh3yQKrjBls

MIXED – CONTEMPORARY/AFRICAN: PRAISE AND WORSHIP – SET 40

WORSHIP -:

WORTHY, YOU ARE WORTHY KING OF KINGS, LORD OF LORDS, YOU YOUR WORTHY

PRAISE -:

1. JEHOVAH TURNED MY LIFE AROUND
2. JEHOVAH REIGNS
3. CASTING CROWN
4. I SEARCHED ALL OVER
5. YES YOU ARE THE LORD, MOST HIGH

WORSHIP & PRAISE LYRICS

WORTHY YOU ARE WORTHY

WORTHY, YOU ARE WORTHY
KING OF KINGS
LORD OOF LORDS
I WORSHIP YOU

LINK: https://youtu.be/xZpmwquJgBo

JEHOVAH, HE TURNED MY LIFE AROUND

JEHOVAH TURNED MY LIFE AROUND (2X)
HE MAKES A WAY WHERE THERE SEEMS NO WAY, JEHOVAH
JEHOVAH, TURNED MY LIFE AROUND
JEHOVAH TURNED MY LIFE AROUND OOOHH.
HE MAKES A WAY WHERE THERE SEEMS NO WAY

LINK: https://youtu.be/PYnt_KhKodA

JEHOVAH REIGNS, JEHOVAH REIGNS

JEHOVAH REIGNS, JEHOVAH REIGNS
JEHOVAH REIGNS, JEHOVAH REIGNS
YOU ARE LIFTED UP ABOVE OTHER GOD
YOU ARE LIFTED UP ABOVE OTHER GOD
YOU ARE LIFTED UP ABOVE OTHER GOD
YOU ARE LIFTED UP ABOVE OTHER GOD

LINK: https://youtu.be/SK9Qh_EV-b0

CASTING CROWNS

CASTING CROWNS, LIFTING HANDS
BOWING HEARTS, IS ALL WE'VE COME TO DO
ADONAI, ADONAI, ADONAI, YOU REIGN ON HIGH
WE WILL RISE, IN YOUR NAME, ADONAI, YOU REIGN ON HIGH

LINK: https://youtu.be/2P-FlceZIDo

YOU ARE MY STRENGHT

YOU ARE MY STRENGTH, STRENGTH LIKE NO OTHER
STRENGTH LIKE NO OTHER, REACHES TO ME
YOU ARE MY HOPE, HOPE LIKE NO OTHER
HOPE LIKE NO OTHER, REACHES TO ME
IN THE FULLNESS OF YOUR GRACE, IN THE POWER OF YOUR NAME
YOU LIFT ME UP, YOU LIFT ME UP (LET'S SING)

LINK: https://youtu.be/LA4eKhj-2ic

YES, YOU ARE THE LORD, MOST HIGH

YES, YOU ARE THE LORD, MOST HIGH
YES, YOU ARE THE LORD, MOST HIGH
YES, YOU ARE THE LORD, MOST HIGH
YES, YOU ARE THE LORD, MOST HIGH
YES, YOU ARE THE LORD, MOST HIGH

LINK: https://youtu.be/MpCKY9WfaA8

MIXED – CONTEMPORARY/AFRICAN: PRAISE AND WORSHIP – SET 41

WORSHIP-:

GLORIOUS GOD, BEAUTIFUL KING, EXCELLENCE GOD, WE BOW BEFORE YOUR THROW

PRAISE-:

1. YOU ARE GOD, YOU ARE NOT JUST BIG
2. YOU ARE GREAT YES YOU ARE
3. CREATOR OF THE UNIVERSE
4. EVERY PRAISE TO OUR GOD.
5. WATER HE TURNED INTO WINE

WORSHIP & PRAISE LYRICS

GLORIOUS GOD, BEAUTIFUL KING

GLORIOUS GOD, BEAUTIFUL KING
EXCELLENT GOD, WE BOW BEFORE YOUR THRONE
BOW BEFORE YOUR THRONE
WORSHIP AT YOUR FEET
BOW BEFORE YOUR THRONE
YOU'RE THE GLORIOUS GOD
YOU NAME IS ALPHA, OMEGA, AGESLESS,
CHANGELESS, AMIGHTY, JEHOVAH
GLORIOUS GOD, WE BOW BEFORE YOUR THRONE
LINK: https://youtu.be/xYCI11VD4dQ

YOU ARE GOD

YOU ARE GOD, YOU ARE NOT JUST BIG OH
YOU ARE NOT JUST LARGE OH
YOU ARE A GREAT GOD
YOU ARE BIG, BIG, BIG, BIG, BIG, BIG, BIG
LARGE, LARGE, LARGE, LARGE, LARGE, LARGE
GREAT, GREAT, GREAT, GREAT, GREAT
YOU ARE A GREAT GOD
LINK: https://youtu.be/VZd2fQS8yLI

YOU ARE GREAT, YES YOU ARE

YOU ARE GREAT YES YOU ARE HOLY ONE
WALKED UPON THE SEA RISE THE DEAD
YOU REIGN IN MAJESTY MIGHTY GOD
EVERYTHING WRITTEN ABOUT YOU IS GREAT
YOU ARE GREAT YOU ARE GREAT 4X
EVERYTHING WRITTEN ABOUT YOU IS GREAT
LINK: https://youtu.be/q2KiwKlG85s

CREATOR OF THE UNIVERSE

CREATOR OF THE UNIVERSE WHAT CANT YOU DO
WHAT CAN'T YOU DO WHAT CAN'T YOU DO
WHAT CAN'T YOU DO JESUS, NAME ABOVE EVERY
NAME ABOVE EVERY OTHER NAME EVERY OTHER NAME
WHAT CAN'T YOU CHANGE, WHAT CAN'T YOU CHANGE JESUS
LIFT YOUR HANDS AND SAY YOU'RE ABLE
YOU ARE ABLE GREAT AND MIGHTY GREAT AND MIGHTY GOD
YOU'RE ABLE JESUS
LINK: https://youtu.be/HPqDaKajSnQ

EVERY PRAISE TO OUR GOD

EVERY PRAISE IS TO OUR GOD
EVERY WORD OF WORSHIP, WITH ONE ACCORD
EVERY PRAISE, EVERY PRAISE
IS TO OUR GOD
SING HALLELUJAH TO OUR GOD
GLORY HALLELUJAH IS DUE OUR GOD
EVERY PRAISE, EVERY PRAISE, IS TO OUR GOD
LINK: https://youtu.be/X48B8AbkmbA

WATER YOU TURN INTO WINE

WATER YOU TURNED INTO WINE, OPENED THE EYES OF THE BLIND
THERE'S NO ONE LIKE YOU, NONE LIKE YOU
INTO THE DARKNESS YOU SHINE, OUT OF THE ASHES WE RISE, THERE'S NO ONE LIKE YOU, NONE LIKE YOU
OUR GOD IS GREATER, OUR GOD IS STRONGER
GOD YOU ARE HIGHER THAN ANY OTHER
OUR GOD IS HEALER, AWESOME IN POWER OUR GOD, OUR GOD
LINK: https://youtu.be/NJpt1hSYf2o

MIXED – CONTEMPORARY/AFRICAN: PRAISE AND WORSHIP – SET 42

WORSHIP-:

FROM THE PAGES OF MY HEART

PRAISE-:

1. I WILL LIFT UP MY VOICE, I WILL JOYFUL SING
2. BLESSED BE THE NAME OF THE LORD
3. MY GOD IS A GOOD GOD
4. PRAISE JEHOVAH, HE HAS TURNED MY LIFE AROUND
5. ONLY CAN DO WHAT NO MAN CAN DO JEHOVAH

WORSHIP & PRAISE LYRICS

FROM THE PAGES OF MY HEART

OUR GOD IS INDESCRIBABLE
HIS NAME IS HALLOWED IN THE FIRMAMENT
HE'S THE PASSOVER LAMB THROUGH SPACE AND TIME
SO, FROM THE PAGES OF MY HEART
LET MY WORSHIP BEGIN BUT NEVER
TO THE GOD OF ALL FLESH
FOR HE'S MY GOD AND HIS NAME IS YAHWEH
HIS NAME IS YAHWEH, YAHWEH

LINK: https://youtu.be/K1PXqjGMMMM

I WILL LIFT UP MY VOICE, I WILL JOYFUL SING

I WILL LIFT UP MY VOICE, I WILL JOYFUL SING
FOR WHAT YOU HAVE DONE
FOR WHO YOU ARE
YOU ARE THE REASON I SING
MELODY IN MY HEART
YOU ARE THE SONG THAT I SING
I WILL YOU PRAISE YOU LORD
YOU REIGN, YOU REIGN, YOU REIGN FOREVER MORE

LINK: https://fb.watch/hOCoHjyvzY/

BLESSED BE THE NAME OF THE LORD

BLESSED BE THE NAME OF THE LORD x2
BLESSED BE THE NAME OF THE LORD, MOST HIGH
THE NAME OF THE LORD IS, A STRONG TOWER
THE RIGHTEOUS RUN INTO IT AND THEY ARE SAVED
THE NAME OF THE LORD IS, A STRONG TOWER
THE RIGHTEOUS RUN INTO IT AND THEY ARE SAVED

LINK: https://youtu.be/bYrcrP1ysjw

MY GOD IS A GOOD GOD

MY GOD IS A GOOD GOD YES HE IS
HE LIFTS ME UP (HE LIFTS ME UP)
HE TURNS ME AROUND (HE TURNS ME AROUND)
HE SETS ME FEET, UPON THE SOLID ROCK
I FEEL LIKE DANCING, I FEEL LIKE CLAPPING

LINK: https://youtu.be/3WLAAl98kLQ

PRAISE JEHOVAH, HE TURNED MY LIFE AROUND

JEHOVAH TURNED MY LIFE AROUND (2X)
HE MAKES A WAY WHERE THERE SEEMS NO WAY, JEHOVAH
JEHOVAH TURNED MY LIFE AROUND
JEHOVAH TURNED MY LIFE AROUND OOOHH...
HE MAKES A WAY WHERE THERE SEEMS NO WAY

LINK: https://youtu.be/PYnt_KhKodA

ONLY CAN DO WHAT NO MAN CAN DO JEHOVAH

ONLY CAN DO WHAT NO MAN CAN DO JEHOVAH
ONLY CAN DO WHAT NO MAN CAN DO JEHOVAH
ONLY YOU ARE CAPABLE, ONLY YOU DEPENDEABLE GOD x 2
YOU ARE JEHOVAH, EEH YOU ARE JEHOVAH EEE x2

LINK: https://youtu.be/MdQINUBlPno

PART
D

HIGH PRAISE - THANKSGIVING

HIGH PRAISE
- WE GIVE YOU ALL THE PRAISE
- YOU ARE HIGHLY LIFTED UP
- YOU ARE GOOD, AND YOUR MERCY IS FOREVER.
- SHOUT ALLELUIA TO THE LORD
- SHOUT ALLE ALLELUIA, SHOUT ALLE ALLELUIA.
- PRAISE JEHOVAH, HE HAS TURNED MY LIFE AROUND

HIGH PRAISE
- HEY HEY MY GOD IS GOOD OH
- COME LET'S PRAISE THE LORD JEHOVA, JEHOVA, JEHOVA JEHOVA) -JEHOVA YOU ARE THE MOST HIGH
- JEHOVA JIRE
- I WILL LIFT UP MY VOICE
- EVERYBODY LIFT HIM UP/HIGHER...

HIGH PRAISE
- I WILL EXAULT YOU LORD, FOR THOU HAS LIFTED ME.
- HOLY ARE YOU LORD
- I WILL BLESS THE LORD OH MY SOUL.
- YOU ARE GOD
- AWESOME GOD
- YOU ARE YAWHEH, YOU ARE YAWHEH

HIGH PRAISE
- THANK YOU, LORD.
- OH, LORD WE PRAISE YOU
- PRAISE JEHOVAH HE HAS TURNED MY LIFE AROUND
- ALL THE GLORY MUST BE ON TO THE LORD IN THE HIGHEST
- ALLE ALLE ALLELUIA, GLORY, GLORY. GLORY, GLORY
- SHOUT ALLELUIA TO THE LORD

HIGH PRAISE
- ALMIGHTY GOD ALL POWERFUL GOD.
- JEHOVAH REIGNS HE REIGNS HE REIGNS.
- I WILL LIFT UP HIS NAME HIGHER.
- THERE IS SOMETHING/ MY HELPER.
- YOU ARE GOD YOU ARE NOT JUST BIG OH
- FOR THE GLORY MUST BE UNTO THE LORD..

HIGH PRAISE
- WHO HAS THE FINAL SAY
- ALMIGHTY FATHER, WE GIVE YOU GLORY.
- GIVE HIM PRAISE, GIVE HIM PRAISE. (WE'RE HERE TO GIVE ALL THE PRAISE TO THE LORD)
- AT THE MENTION OF YOUR NAME.
- WHAT WILL L GIVE TO YOU, MY PRAISE
- HAIL MY JESUS...

HIGH PRAISE
- ALLE, ALLE, ALLELUIA GLORY, GLORY WE PRAISE YOUR NAME
- YOU ARE A MIGHTY GOD THE GREAT L AM
- HOLY ARE YOU LORD
- YOU ARE THE REASON WHY L LIFT MY VOICE
- YES YOU ARE THE LORD MOST HIGH.
- MASTER OF THE UNIVERSE

HIGH PRAISE
- SHOUT ALLELUIA TO THE LORD
- SHOUT ALLE ALLELUIA, SHOUT ALLE ALLELUIA.
- PRAISE JEHOVA, HE HAS TURNED MY LIFE AROUND.
- YOU ARE GREAT YES YOU ARE
- I WILL PRAISE YOU FOR THE REST OF MY LIFE
- EVERYBODY LIFT HIM UP/HIGHER..

HIGH PRAISE - THANKSGIVING

HIGH PRAISE
- (JEHOVA, JEHOVA, JEHOVA JEHOVA) -JEHOVA YOU ARE THE MOST- HIGH
- JEHOVA JIRE
- I WILL LIFT UP MY VOICE
- EVERYBODY LIFT HIM UP/HIGHER...
- PRAISE JEHOVAH, HE HAS TURNED MY LIFE AROUND
- ALL THE GLORY MUST BE ON TO THE LORD IN THE HIGHEST.

HIGH PRAISE
- HIGHER HIGHER, EVERYDAYI LIFT JESUS HIGHER
- YOU ARE HIGHLY LIFTED UP
- ONLY YOU CAN DO
- I WILL LIFT UP HIS NAME, HIGHER
- I WILL PRAISE YOU FOR THE REST OF MY DAYS
- HAIL MY JESUS

HIGH PRAISE
- I WILL LIFT UP HIS NAME HIGHER.
- THERE IS SOMETHING/ MY HELPER.
- YOU ARE GOD YOU ARE NOT JUST BIG OH
- WHAT WILL L GIVE TO YOU, MY PRAISE
- HAIL MY JESUS...
- FOR THE GLORY MUST BE UNTO THE LORD

HIGH PRAISE
- WHAT SHALL WE SAY UNTO THE LORD, ALL WE HAVE TO SAY IS THANK YOU LORD
- WE ARE SAYING THANK YOU, JESUS THANK YOU< JEHOVAH THANK YOU
- JEHOVAH, TURNED MY LIFE AROUND, HE MADE A WAY...
- WE WILL HAIL, HAIL YOUR NAME
- HAIL MY JESUS, POWERFUL, POWERFUL WORRIOR
- ONLY YOU CAN DO, WHAT NO MAN CAN DO JEHOVAH

HIGH PRAISE
- AT THE MENTION OF YOUR NAME.
- WHAT WILL L GIVE TO YOU, MY PRAISE
- HAIL MY JESUS...
- EVERYBODY LIFT HIM UP HIGHER
- HIGHER, HIGHER, EVERYDAY, I LIFT MY JESUS EVERYDAY
- GLORY BE TO THE LORD IN THE HIGHEST, HALLELUJAH

HIGH PRAISE
- YOU ARE GOD...
- AWESOME GOD
- YOU ARE YAWHEH, YOU ARE YAWHEH.
- JEHOVA REIGNS HE REIGNS HE REIGNS.
- I WILL LIFT UP HIS NAME HIGHER.
- THERE IS SOMETHING/ MY HELPER

HIGH PRAISE
- YOU ARE THE REASON WHY L LIFT MY VOICE
- YES YOU ARE THE LORD MOST HIGH.
- MASTER OF THE UNIVERSE
- HEY HEY MY GOD IS GOOD OH
- (JEHOVA, JEHOVA, JEHOVA JEHOVA) -JEHOVA YOU ARE THE MOST HIGH
- JEHOVA JIRE

HIGH PRAISE
- JEHOVA REIGNS HE REIGNS HE REIGNS.
- I WILL LIFT UP HIS NAME HIGHER.
- THERE IS SOMETHING/ MY HELPER
- AT THE MENTION OF YOUR NAME.
- WHAT WILL L GIVE TO YOU, MY PRAISE
- HAIL MY JESUS

HIGH PRAISE - THANKSGIVING

HIGH PRAISE

- EVERYBODY LIFT HIM UP HIGHER2
- HIGHER, HIGHER, EVERYDAY, I LIFT MY JESUS EVERYDAY
- GLORY BE TO THE LORD IN THE HIGHEST, HALLELUJAH
- HEY HEY MY GOD IS GOOD OH
- (JEHOVA, JEHOVA, JEHOVA JEHOVA) -JEHOVA YOU ARE THE MOST HIGH
- JEHOVA JIRE

HIGH PRAISE

- JEHOVAH, TURNED MY LIFE AROUND, HE MADE A WAY...
- WE WILL HAIL, HAIL YOUR NAME
- HAIL MY JESUS, POWERFUL, POWERFUL WORRIOR
- ONLY YOU CAN DO, WHAT NO MAN CAN DO JEHOVAH
- YOU ARE GOD...
- AWESOME GOD

PART E

KINGDOM ADVANCEMENT SONGS

1. WE ARE MARCHING IN THE LIGHT OF GOD
2. GOD'S GOT AN ARMY, MARCHING THROUGH THE LAND
3. OH WHEN THE SAINTS MARCHING ON.
4. GO TELL IT ON THE MOUNTAIN
5. HE IS THE KING OF KINGS
6. OH WHAT A MIGHTY GOD WE SERVE

SONG LYRICS

WE ARE MARCHING IN THE LIGHT OF GOD

WE ARE MARCHING IN THE LIGHT OF GOD
WE ARE MARCHING IN THE LIGHT OF GOD
WE ARE MARCHING, MARCHING, WE ARE MARCHING OH HO
WE ARE MARCHING IN THE LIGHT OF GOD

LINK: https://youtu.be/gI24_27wW1E

OH, WHEN THE SAINTS GO MARCHING

OH, WHEN THE SAINTS GO MARCHING ON
OH, WHEN THE SAINTS GO MARCHING ON
LORD, I WANT TO BE IN THE NUMBER

LINK: https://youtu.be/kG6ZVNzqQ8M

GODS GOT AN ARMY

GODS GOT AN ARMY, MARCHING THROUGH THE LAND
DELIVERANCE IS THE SONG, HEALING IN THEIR HANDS
EVERLASTING JOY , LIFE FOR EVERMORE
IN THIS ARMY I'VE GOT A PART, IN THIS ARMY I'VE GOT A PART

LINK: https://youtu.be/3MLnZ2qZw0M

GO TELL IT ON THE MOUNTAIN

GO TELL IT ON THE MOUNTAIN
OVER THE HILLS AND EVERYWHERE
GO TELL IT ON THE MOUNTAIN

LINK: https://youtu.be/UAfIKeh04KU

HE IS THE KING OF KINGS

HE IS THE KING OF KINGS
HE IS THE LORD OF LORDS
HIS NAME IS JESUS, JESUS, JESUS, JESUS
J. E. S. U. S., HE IS THE KING

LINK: https://youtu.be/Gb98b10JqmY

WHAT A MIGHTY GOD WE SERVE

WHAT A MIGHTY GOD WE SERVE, OH, WHAT A MIGHTY GOD WE SERVE
OH, WHAT A MIGHTY GOD WE SERVE, OH, LET US SHOUT AND PRAISE THE LORD
I WILL SHOUT
OH, LET US SHOUT AND PRAISE THE LORD

LINK: https://youtu.be/rc5Ehy57P5E

KINGDOM ADVANCEMENT SONGS

1. GO TELL IT ON THE MOUNTAIN
2. HE IS THE KING OF KINGS.
3. OH WHAT A MIGHTY GOD WE SERVE
4. ABIDING IN THE VINE
5. THE ZEAL OF GOD HAS CONSUMED ME
6. VICTORY IS MINE

SONG LYRICS

GO TELL IT ON THE MOUNTAIN

GO TELL IT ON THE MOUNTAIN
OVER THE HILLS AND EVERYWHERE
GO TELL IT ON THE MOUNTAIN

LINK: https://youtu.be/UAfIKeh04KU

HE IS THE KING OF KINGS

HE IS THE KING OF KINGS
HE IS THE LORD OF LORDS
HIS NAME IS JESUS, JESUS, JESUS, JESUS
J. E. S. U. S., HE IS THE KING

LINK: https://youtu.be/Gb98b10JqmY

WHAT A MIGHTY GOD WE SERVE

WHAT A MIGHTY GOD WE SERVE, OH, WHAT A MIGHTY GOD WE SERVE
OH, WHAT A MIGHTY GOD WE SERVE, OH, LET US SHOUT AND PRAISE THE LORD
I WILL SHOUT
OH, LET US SHOUT AND PRAISE THE LORD

LINK: https://youtu.be/rc5Ehy57P5E

ABIDING IN THE VINE

I FOUND A NEW WAY OF LIVING
I FOUND A NEW LIFE IN CHRIST
I BEAR THE FRUITS OF THE SPIRIT
AM ABIDING, ABIDING IN THE VINE

LINK: https://youtu.be/Y6AWYLBdL-0

THE ZEAL OF GOD HAS CONSUMED ME

IT BURNS WITHIN MY SOUL A DRIVING FORCE
THAT CANNOT BE STOPPED
A FIRE THAT CANNOT BE QUENCHED
OH HALLELU, HALLELUJAH
HELLE, HALLE, HALLELUJAH
HALLELUJAJ

LINK: https://youtu.be/T3uTDTstJ6w

VICTORY IS MINE

VICTORY IS MINE
VIVTORY TODAY IS MINE
I TOLD SATAN TO GET THEE BEHIND
VICTORY TODAY IS MINE

LINK: https://youtu.be/f-IgTEetLkA

KINGDOM ADVANCEMENT SONGS

1. OH WHAT A MIGHTY GOD WE SERVE
2. HE IS THE KING OF KINGS.
3. GOD'S GOT AN ARMY, MARCHING THROUGH THE LAND.
4. WE ARE MARCHING IN THE LIGHT OF GOD
5. GO TELL IT ON THE MOUNTAIN
6. ABIDING IN THE VINE

SONG LYRICS

WHAT A MIGHTY GOD WE SERVE

WHAT A MIGHTY GOD WE SERVE, OH, WHAT A MIGHTY GOD WE SERVE
OH, WHAT A MIGHTY GOD WE SERVE, OH, LET US SHOUT AND PRAISE THE LORD
I WILL SHOUT
OH, LET US SHOUT AND PRAISE THE LORD

LINK: https://youtu.be/rc5Ehy57P5E

HE IS THE KING OF KINGS

HE IS THE KING OF KINGS
HE IS THE LORD OF LORDS
HIS NAME IS JESUS, JESUS, JESUS, JESUS
J. E. S. U. S., HE IS THE KING

LINK: https://youtu.be/Gb98b10JqmY

GODS GOT AN ARMY

GODS GOT AN ARMY, MARCHING THROUGH THE LAND
DELIVERANCE IS THE SONG, HEALING IN THEIR HANDS
EVERLASTING JOY , LIFE FOR EVERMORE
IN THIS ARMY I'VE GOT A PART, IN THIS ARMY I'VE GOT A PART

LINK: https://youtu.be/3MLnZ2qZw0M

WE ARE MARCHING IN THE LIGHT OF GOD

WE ARE MARCHING IN THE LIGHT OF GOD
WE ARE MARCHING IN THE LIGHT OF GOD
WE ARE MARCHING, MARCHING, WE ARE MARCHING
OH HO
WE ARE MARCHING IN THE LIGHT OF GOD

LINK: https://youtu.be/gI24_27wW1E

GO TELL IT ON THE MOUNTAIN

GO TELL IT ON THE MOUNTAIN
OVER THE HILLS AND EVERYWHERE
GO TELL IT ON THE MOUNTAIN

LINK: https://youtu.be/UAfIKeh04KU

ABIDING IN THE VINE

I FOUND A NEW WAY OF LIVING
I FOUND A NEW LIFE IN CHRIST
I BEAR THE FRUITS OF THE SPIRIT
AM ABIDING, ABIDING IN THE VINE

LINK: https://youtu.be/Y6AWYLBdL-0

PART F

CONTEMPORARY ANOINTING SONGS

1. ANOINTING FALL ON ME
2. THIS IS THE AIR I BREATHE
3. NEW WINE
4. SPIRIT OF THE LIVING GOD
5. ANCIENT OF DAYS
6. HOLY SPIRIT MOVE ME NOW

SONG LYRICS

ANOINTING FALL ON ME

ANOINTING FALL ON ME, ANOINTING FALL ON ME
LET THE POWER, OF THE HOLY GHOST
FALL ON ME, ANOINTING FALL ON ME
TOUCH MY HANDS MY MOUTH
AND MY HEART, FILL MY LIFE LORD
EVERY PART, LET THE POWER
OF THE HOLY GHOST, FALL ON ME
ANOINTING FALL ON ME
LINK: https://youtu.be/zk9UPOBu50g

THIS IS THE AIR I BREATHE

THIS IS THE AIR I BREATHE; THIS IS THE AIR I BREATHE
YOUR HOLY PRESENCE, LIVING IN ME /2X/
THIS IS MY DAILY BREAD, THIS IS MY DAILY BREAD
YOUR VERY WORD, SPOKEN TO ME
AND I... I'M DESPARATE FOR YOU
AND I... I'M LOST WITHOUT YOU

LINK: https://youtu.be/tzOz9oZVrtA

NEW WINE

IN THE CRUSHING, IN THE PRESSING
YOU ARE MAKING NEW WINE
IN THE SOIL, I NOW SURRENDER
YOU ARE BREAKING NEW GROUND
SO I YIELD TO YOU INTO YOUR CAREFUL HAND
WHEN I TRUST YOU I DON'T NEED TO UNDERSTAND
MAKE ME YOUR VESSEL, MAKE ME AN OFFERING
MAKE ME WHATEVER YOU WANT ME TO BE
I CAME HERE WITH NOTHING, BUT ALL YOU HAVE GIVEN
LINK: https://youtu.be/1ozGKlOzEVc

SPIRIT OF THE LIVING GOD

SPIRIT OF THE LIVING GOD, FALL FRESH ON ME
MELT ME, MOLD ME, FILL ME, USE ME
SPIRIT OF THE LIVING GOD, FALL FRESH ON ME
SPIRIT OF THE LIVING GOD, FALL FRESH ON ME
MELT ME, MOLD ME, FILL ME, USE ME
SPIRIT OF THE LIVING GOD, FALL FRESH ON ME

LINK: https://youtu.be/EiRV5Z4qFAU

ANCIENT OF DAYS

ANCIENT OF DAYS, AS OLD AS YOU ARE
AS OLD AS YOU ARE, YOU WILL NEVER CHANGE
ANCIENT OF DAYS AS OLD, AS OLD AS YOU ARE
AS OLD AS YOU ARE, YOU WILL NEVER CHANGE

LINK: https://youtu.be/5M1MFO4vOUg

HOLY SPIRIT MOVE ME NOW

SPIRIT MOVE ME NOW
SPIRIT MOVE ME NOW
MAKE MY LIFE WHOLE AGAIN, SPIRIT MOVE OVER ME
SPIRIT MOVE OVER ME

LINK: https://youtu.be/fFJvpNik9r0

CONTEMPORARY ANOINTING SONGS

1. BLESSED ASSURANCE
2. EAGLES WINGS
3. BOW DOWN AND WORSHIP HIM
4. LET IT RAIN
5. NEW WINE
6. OPEN THE EYE OF MY HEART, LORD

SONG LYRICS

BLESSED ASSURANCE

BLESSED ASSURANCE, JESUS IS MINE!
OH, WHAT A FORETASTE OF GLORY DIVINE!
HEIR OF SALVATION, PURCHASE OF GOD
BORN OF HIS SPIRIT, WASHED IN HIS BLOOD
THIS IS MY STORY, THIS IS MY SONG
PRAISING MY SAVIOR ALL DAY LONG
THIS IS MY STORY, THIS IS MY SONG
PRAISING MY SAVIOR ALL DAY LONG
LINK: https://youtu.be/FfVPnEhjKB4

EAGLES WING

HERE I AM WAITING, ABIDE IN ME I PRAY
HERE I AM LONGING, FOR YOU
HIDE ME IN YOUR LOVE, BRING ME TO MY KNEES
MAY I KNOW JESUS, MORE AND MORE
COME LIVE IN ME, ALL MY LIFE
TAKE OVER, COME BREATHE IN ME
AND I WILL RISE, ON EAGLE'S WINGS

LINK: https://youtu.be/MKyPgigDt3k

BOW DOWN AND WORSHIP HIM

BOW DOWN AND WORSHIP HIM
WORSHIP HIM, OH WORSHIP HIM!
BOW DOWN AND WORSHIP HIM
BOW DOWN AND WORSHIP HIM
WORSHIP HIM, OH WORSHIP HIM!

LINK: https://youtu.be/q0A6nHOspkc

LET IT RAIN

LET IT RAIN, LET IT RAIN
OPEN THE FLOOD GATES OF HEAVEN (SING IT!)
LET IT RAIN, LET IT RAIN
OPEN THE FLOOD GATES OF HEAVEN (SING IT AGAIN: LET IT!)
LET IT RAIN, LET IT RAIN
OPEN THE FLOOD GATES OF HEAVEN

LINK: https://youtu.be/AG7v8jJKAOk

NEW WINE

IN THE CRUSHING, IN THE PRESSING
YOU ARE MAKING NEW WINE
IN THE SOIL, I NOW SURRENDER
YOU ARE BREAKING NEW GROUND
SO I YIELD TO YOU INTO YOUR CAREFUL HAND
WHEN I TRUST YOU I DON'T NEED TO UNDERSTAND
MAKE ME YOUR VESSEL, MAKE ME AN OFFERING
MAKE ME WHATEVER YOU WANT ME TO BE
I CAME HERE WITH NOTHING, BUT ALL YOU HAVE GIVEN
LINK: https://youtu.be/1ozGKlOzEVc

OPEN THE EYES OF MY HEART LORD

OPEN THE EYES OF MY HEART
I WANT TO SEE YOU
I WANT TO SEE YOU
TO SEE YOU HIGH AND LIFTED UP
SHININ' IN THE LIGHT OF YOUR GLORY
POUR OUT YOUR POWER AND LOVE
AS WE SING HOLY, HOLY, HOLY

LINK: https://youtu.be/fadU7b9aa78

CONTEMPORARY ANOINTING SONGS

1. HERE IN YOUR PRESENCE, LET IT RAIN
2. WE BOW DOWN AND WORSHIP YAHWEH
3. ANCIENT OF DAYS
4. LET YOUR LIVING WATERS FLOW OVER MY SOUL
5. SEND YOUR POWER OH LORD OUR GOD5.
6. ANOINTING FALL ON ME

SONG LYRICS

WE ARE IN YOUR PRESENCE, LET IT RAIN

WE ARE IN YOUR PRESENCE, LET IT RAIN
OHH YOUR RAIN (JESUS), LET IT FALL ON ME
WE ARE IN YOUR PRESENCE, LET IT RAIN
OPEN THE FLOOD GATES IN ABUNDANCE
AND CAUSE YOUR RAIN TO FALL ON ME
BABA OH... OH , BABA OH... OH-OH-OH-OH

LINK: https://youtu.be/63nyGawcJbQ

WE BOW DOWN AND WORSHIP YAHWEH

WE BOW DOWN AND WORSHIP, YAHWEH
WE BOW DOWN AND WORSHIP, YAHWEH
YAHWEH, YAHWEH, YAHWEH
YAHWEH, YAHWEH, YAHWEH
WE BOW DOWN AND WORSHIP, YAHWEH

LINK: https://youtu.be/q0A6nHOspkc

ANCIENT OF DAYS

ANCIENT OF DAYS, AS OLD AS YOU ARE
AS OLD AS YOU ARE, YOU WILL NEVER CHANGE
ANCIENT OF DAYS AS OLD, AS OLD AS YOU ARE
AS OLD AS YOU ARE, YOU WILL NEVER CHANGE

LINK: https://youtu.be/5M1MFO4vOUg

LET YOUR LIVING WATER FLOW OVER MY SOUL

LET YOUR LIVING WATER FLOW OVER MY SOUL
LET YOUR HOLY SPIRIT COME AND TAKE CONTROL
OF EVERY SITUATION THAT HAS TROUBLED MY MIND
ALL MY CARES AND BURDENS ON TO YOU I ROLL
JESUS, JESUS, JESUS, SING TO THE FATHER
FATHER, FATHER, FATHER, HOLY SPIRIT
SPIRIT, SPIRIT, SPIRIT

LINK: https://youtu.be/_y3-zDtT_nl

ANOINTING FALL ON ME

ANOINTING FALL ON ME
LET THE POWER, OF THE HOLY GHOST
FALL ON ME, ANOINTING FALL ON ME
TOUCH MY HANDS MY MOUTH
AND MY HEART, FILL MY LIFE LORD
EVERY PART, LET THE POWER
OF THE HOLY GHOST, FALL ON ME

LINK: https://youtu.be/zk9UPOBu50g

SEND YOUR POWER OH LORD OUR GOD

SEND YOUR POWER OH LORD OUR GOD
SEND YOUR POWER OH LORD OUR GOD, OUR GOD.

LINK: https://youtu.be/kA8OrTji8hl

CONTEMPORARY ANOINTING SONGS

1. ALL GLORY, ALL HONOR, ALL POWER TO YOU
2. REFINERS FIRE
3. I SURRENDER ALL
4. GLORY TO THE LAMB
5. MOVE OVER ME, SPIRIT MOVE OVER ME
6. ANOINTING FALL ON ME

SONG LYRICS

ALL HONOUR

ALL HONOR, ALL GLORY
ALL POWER, TO YOU (REPEAT SEVERAL TIMES)
HOLY FATHER, WE WORSHIP YOU
PRECIOUS JESUS OUR SAVIOR
HOLY SPIRIT WE WAIT ON YOU
HOLY SPIRIT WE WAIT ON YOU

LINK: https://youtu.be/aE_bMzMH_1w

REFINERS FIRE

PURIFY MY HEART, LET ME BE AS GOLD
AND PRECIOUS SILVER, PURIFY MY HEART
LET ME BE AS GOLD, PURE GOLD
REFINER'S FIRE, MY HEART'S ONE DESIRE
IS TO BE HOLY, SET APART FOR YOU LORD
I CHOOSE TO BE HOLY, SET APART FOR YOU MY
MASTER READY TO DO YOUR WILL

LINK: https://youtu.be/VG3NaUZSnFI

I SURRENDER

ALL TO JESUS I SURRENDER
ALL TO HIM I FREELY GIVE
I WILL EVER LOVE AND TRUST HIM
IN HIS PRESENCE DAILY LIVE, I SURRENDER ALL
I SURRENDER ALL, ALL TO THEE
MY BLESSED SAVIOR, I SURRENDER ALL

LINK: https://youtu.be/SW8EA7DEQ2M

GLORY, GLORY, GLORY TO THE LAMB

GLORY, GLORY, GLORY TO THE LAMB
FOR YOU ARE GLORIOUS
AND WORTHY TO BE PRAISED
THE LAMB UPON THE THRONE
AND UNTO YOU, WE LIFT OUR VOICE IN PRAISE
THE LAMB UPON THE THRONE

LINK: https://youtu.be/wtR_vNTP61k

ANOINTING FALL ON ME

ANOINTING FALL ON ME, LET THE POWER
OF THE HOLY GHOST, FALL ON ME
ANOINTING FALL ON ME, TOUCH MY HANDS MY MOUTH
AND MY HEART, FILL MY LIFE LORD, EVERY PART
LET THE POWER, OF THE HOLY GHOST
FALL ON ME, ANOINTING FALL ON ME

LINK: https://youtu.be/zk9UPOBu50g

HOLY SPIRIT, MOVE ME NOW

HOLY SPIRIT, MOVE ME NOW
MAKE MY LIFE, WHOLE AGAIN
SPIRIT MOVE OVER ME, SPIRIT MOVE OVER ME

LINK: https://youtu.be/fFJvpNik9r0

CONTEMPORARY ANOINTING SONGS

1. AS THE DEER PANTETH FOR THE WATER
2. BLESSED ASSURANCE
3. LET YOUR LIVING WATERS
4. ITS NOT BY POWER, NOT BY MIGHT, BUT BY MY SPIRIT
5. ANOINTING FALL ON M
6. HOLY SPIRIT, THOU ART WELCOME

SONG LYRICS

AS THE DEER PANTETH FOR THE WATER

AS THE DEER PANTETH FOR THE WATER
SO MY SOUL LONGETH AFTER THEE
YOU ALONE ARE MY HEART'S DESIRE, AND I LONG TO WORSHIP THEE
YOU ALONE ARE MY STRENGTH, MY SHIELD
TO YOU ALONE MAY MY SPIRIT YIELD
YOU ALONE ARE MY HEART'S DESIRE
AND I LONG TO WORSHIP THEE
LINK: https://youtu.be/1Y2_63qfUkg

BLESSED ASSURANCE

BLESSED ASSURANCE, JESUS IS MINE!
OH, WHAT A FORETASTE OF GLORY DIVINE!
HEIR OF SALVATION, PURCHASE OF GOD
BORN OF HIS SPIRIT, WASHED IN HIS BLOOD
THIS IS MY STORY, THIS IS MY SONG
PRAISING MY SAVIOR ALL DAY LONG
THIS IS MY STORY, THIS IS MY SONG
PRAISING MY SAVIOR ALL DAY LONG
LINK: https://youtu.be/FfVPnEhjKB4

LET YOUR LIVING WATER FLOW OVER MY SOUL

LET YOUR HOLY SPIRIT COME AND TAKE CONTROL
OF EVERY SITUATION THAT HAS TROUBLED MY MIND
ALL MY CARES AND BURDENS ONTO YOU I ROLL
JESUS, JESUS, JESUS
SING TO THE FATHER
FATHER, FATHER, FATHER
HOLY SPIRIT
SPIRIT, SPIRIT, SPIRIT
LINK: https://youtu.be/_y3-zDtT_nI

IT'S NOT BY MIGHT, IT'S NOT BY POWER

ITS NOT BY MIGHT, ITS NOT BY POWER
BY MY SPIRIT SAYS THE LORD
THIS MOUNTAIN SHALL BE REMOVED (X4)
BY MY SPIRIT SAYS THE LORD
YOU ARE HIGH AND LIFTED UP;
THERE'S NO ONE LIKE YOU
HALLE-LUJAH!, HALLELUJAH, HALLELUJAH, AMEN (X2)
HALLEJUHAH HOSSANAH (X4)
LINK: https://youtu.be/cpWuTidMK2I

ANOINTING FALL ON ME

ANOINTING FALL ON ME
LET THE POWER, OF THE HOLY GHOST
FALL ON ME
ANOINTING FALL ON ME

LINK: https://youtu.be/zk9UPOBu50g

HOLY SPIRIT, THOU ART WELCOME IN THIS PLACE

HOLY SPIRIT THOU ART WELCOME IN THIS PLACE
HOLY SPIRIT THOU ART WELCOME IN THIS PLACE
OMNIPOTENT FATHER OF MERCY AND GRACE
THOU ART WELCOME IN THIS PLACE
LORD IN THY PRESENCE THERE'S HEALING DIVINE
NO OTHER POWER CAN SAVE LORD, BUT THINE
HOLY SPIRIT THOU ART WELCOME IN THIS PLACE
THOU ART WELCOME IN THIS PLACE
LINK: https://youtu.be/zqMg5gPxcdQ

PART G

MINISTRATION SONG RECOMMENDATION
ALL ROUND REST

1. No longer a slave
   https://youtu.be/OWCS_2uICjU

2. I call you faithful
   https://youtu.be/5VMAdu-HKQ8

3. Hallelujah you have won the victory
   https://youtu.be/ZA1BSK_MudQ

4. Jireh
   https://youtu.be/mC-zw0zCCtg

5. Made a way
   https://youtu.be/_EIr61s4gb8

6. Good, Good Father
   https://youtu.be/-ak0OoFBw3c

7. Goodness of God
   https://youtu.be/y81yIo1_3o8

ENOUGH IS ENOUGH

1. No bondage
   https://youtu.be/3H_NwhsAqwM

2. We are victorious
   https://youtu.be/OIun53iz6s4

3. Cornerstone
   https://youtu.be/izrk-erhDdk

4. Do it again
   https://youtu.be/ZOBIPb-6PTc

5. My Help
   https://youtu.be/RgcVM5Gb1w4

6. You are able
   https://youtu.be/WGum4RVkAb8

7. No more veil
   https://youtu.be/xT-h04UCEYA

SHOWERS OF BLESSINGS

1. The Blessing
   https://youtu.be/Zp6aygmvzM4

2. King of Glory
   https://youtu.be/2BXQvE2BYKQ

3. Goodness of God
   https://youtu.be/y81yIo1_3o8

4. Do it again
   https://youtu.be/ZOBIPb-6PTc

5. What a beautiful Name
   https://youtu.be/nQWFzMvCfLE

6. What a beautiful Name
   https://youtu.be/nQWFzMvCfLE

7. Good, Good Father
   https://youtu.be/-ak0OoFBw3c

COVENANT DAY OF FAVOUR

1. Jireh
   https://youtu.be/mC-zw0zCCtg

2. Nothing is impossible
   https://youtu.be/nuBA5YSsWUI

3. A million tongues
   https://youtu.be/rQQMnF_DH6o

4. Do it again
   https://youtu.be/ZOBIPb-6PTc

5. My Help
   https://youtu.be/RgcVM5Gb1w4

6. There's an overflow
   https://youtu.be/bq-Wv_KeQMw

7. It's working
   https://youtu.be/c_bhYOV7p0w

NEW DAWN BANQUET

1. No higher calling
   https://youtu.be/1Zs0K7RPND0

2. Set my life on fire
   https://youtu.be/YYms-CKS1WA

3. There's an overflow
   https://youtu.be/bq-Wv_KeQMw

4. Fragrance of Fire
   https://youtu.be/gqIwEbCyxBo

5. Believe for it
   https://youtu.be/fd24fpsF1Qw

6. That's what I believe
   https://youtu.be/gpTxpnbPPTU

7. No more veil
   https://youtu.be/xT-h04UCEYA

FINANCIAL FORTUNE BANQUEST

1. Nothing is impossible
   https://youtu.be/nuBA5YSsWUI

2. We are victorious
   https://youtu.be/OIun53iz6s4

3. Am free indeed
   https://youtu.be/bDouR8J6-X0

4. Do it again
   https://youtu.be/ZOBIPb-6PTc

5. My Help
   https://youtu.be/RgcVM5Gb1w4

6. You are able
   https://youtu.be/WGum4RVkAb8

7. Jireh
   https://youtu.be/mC-zw0zCCtg

COVENANT FAMILY DAY

1. The Blessing
   https://youtu.be/Zp6aygmvzM4

2. Made a way
   https://youtu.be/_Elr61s4gb8

3. My God is Awesome
   https://youtu.be/3-q_3U7M-Pg

4. Too Faithful
   https://youtu.be/YA2Lxfw4SSw

5. YAH the Holy One
   https://youtu.be/ft5tSclSY90

6. Psalm 23 (I Am not alone)
   https://youtu.be/8OlMGnPUAdw

7. Good, Good Father
   https://youtu.be/-ak0OoFBw3c

COVENANT DAY OF FRUITFULNESS

1. Jireh
   https://youtu.be/mC-zw0zCCtg

2. Be Fruitful
   https://youtu.be/jOufzYaZSEk

3. The name of Jesus
   https://youtu.be/PZuxWHUdtLo

4. Do it again
   https://youtu.be/ZOBIPb-6PTc

5. My Help
   https://youtu.be/RgcVM5Gb1w4

6. You are able
   https://youtu.be/WGum4RVkAb8

7. Speak into my life
   https://youtu.be/82xYJntRQxk

BREAKING INVISIBLE BARRIERS

1. No bondage
   https://youtu.be/3H_NwhsAqwM

2. We are victorious
   https://youtu.be/OIun53iz6s4

3. Break every chain
   https://youtu.be/6vjlpg9i2Bg

4. That's what I believe
   https://youtu.be/gpTxpnbPPTU

5. Your Spirit
   https://youtu.be/BZT8jqsc8lQ

6. Atmosphere shift
   https://youtu.be/CvMSmpJiQiE

7. No more veil
   https://youtu.be/xT-h04UCEYA

NEXT LEVEL BANQUEST

1. Indescribable
   https://youtu.be/gpO3aI5RuMY

2. Free
   https://youtu.be/LOIQ4iz6jr8

3. Days of Elijah
   https://youtu.be/6qXNduBdL8I

4. No Longer a slave
   https://youtu.be/OWCS_2uICjU

5. For your Glory
   https://youtu.be/aKetXJjMUZ0

6. You are the living word
   https://youtu.be/OyTYEeZdhK8

7. Never lost
   https://youtu.be/ZPHXL8Poku0

COVENANT DAY OF MARITAL BREAKTHROUGH

1. Nothing is impossible
   https://youtu.be/nuBA5YSsWUI

2. We are victorious
   https://youtu.be/Olun53iz6s4

3. Hallelujah you have won the victory
   https://youtu.be/ZA1BSK_MudQ

4. Do it again
   https://youtu.be/ZOBIPb-6PTc

5. My Help
   https://youtu.be/RgcVM5Gb1w4

6. You are able
   https://youtu.be/WGum4RVkAb8

7. Trust in you
   https://youtu.be/fjwefyT4_80

ENCOUNTER WITH DESTINY

1. The name of Jesus
   https://youtu.be/PZuxWHUdtLo

2. It all belongs to you
   https://youtu.be/HHjO89tqG2I

3. Cornerstone
   https://youtu.be/izrk-erhDdk

4. Jireh
   https://youtu.be/mC-zw0zCCtg

5. I won't go back
   https://youtu.be/7ULY0uL0LWo

6. Let praises rises
   https://youtu.be/zP-9QKSqL9s

7. What a beautiful Name
   https://youtu.be/nQWFzMvCfLE

BREAKING GENERATIONAL CURESES

1. No bondage
   https://youtu.be/3H_NwhsAqwM

2. God of Vengeance
   https://youtu.be/727K1tRPI1s

3. Atmosphere shift
   https://youtu.be/CvMSmpJiQiE

4. Am free indeed
   https://youtu.be/bDouR8J6-X0

5. Hallelujah you have won the victory
   https://youtu.be/ZA1BSK_MudQ

6. No Weapon formed against me
   https://youtu.be/JJYFWWcTsr4

7. No more veil
   https://youtu.be/xT-h04UCEYA

COVENANT DAY OF VENGEANCE

1. God of Vengeance
   https://youtu.be/727K1tRPI1s

2. No Weapon formed against me
   https://youtu.be/JJYFWWcTsr4

3. Psalm 23 (I Am not alone)
   https://youtu.be/8OlMGnPUAdw

4. No bondage
   https://youtu.be/3H_NwhsAqwM

5. Hallelujah you have won the victory
   https://youtu.be/ZA1BSK_MudQ

6. Atmosphere shift
   https://youtu.be/CvMSmpJiQiE

7. Am free indeed
   https://youtu.be/bDouR8J6-X0

COVENANT DAY OF SETTLEMENT

1. New wine
   https://youtu.be/1ozGKlOzEVc

2. Atmosphere shift
   https://youtu.be/CvMSmpJiQiE

3. You alone deserve the praise(Eze)
   https://youtu.be/QDR_a4VDLzI

4. Do it again
   https://youtu.be/ZOBIPb-6PTc

5. Nothing like your presence
   https://youtu.be/N8zQuWTwk-Y

6. Goodness of God
   https://youtu.be/y81yIo1_3o8

7. Good, Good Father
   https://youtu.be/-ak0OoFBw3c

COVENANT DAY OF RESTORATION

1. Set my life on fire
   https://youtu.be/YYms-CKS1WA

2. There's an overflow
   https://youtu.be/bq-Wv_KeQMw

3. My God is Awesome
   https://youtu.be/3-q_3U7M-Pg

4. Let your presence fall
   https://youtu.be/yilGRPQ5FJc

5. Holy Spirit you are welcome
   https://youtu.be/2q7hMfmVL3I

6. Believe for it
   https://youtu.be/fd24fpsF1Qw

7. New wine
   https://youtu.be/1ozGKlOzEVc

BUSINESS & CARREER BREAKTHROUGH

1. Made a way
   https://youtu.be/_Elr61s4gb8

2. We are victorious
   https://youtu.be/OIun53iz6s4

3. I Believe
   https://youtu.be/vDLByAnQ93Q

4. Another Breakthrough
   https://youtu.be/W6R7PJrinjk

5. Too Faithful
   https://youtu.be/YA2Lxfw4SSw

6. You are able
   https://youtu.be/WGum4RVkAb8

7. Fragrance of Fire
   https://youtu.be/gqIwEbCyxBo

COVENANT DAY OF EXEMPTION

1. No bondage
   https://youtu.be/3H_NwhsAqwM

2. No more veil
   https://youtu.be/xT-h04UCEYA

3. Cornerstone
   https://youtu.be/izrk-erhDdk

4. No Longer a slave
   https://youtu.be/OWCS_2uICjU

5. No Weapon formed against me
   https://youtu.be/JJYFWWcTsr4

6. Trust in you
   https://youtu.be/fjwefyT4_80

7. The name of Jesus
   https://youtu.be/PZuxWHUdtLo

COVENANT DAY OF OPEN DOORS

1. There's an overflow
   https://youtu.be/bq-Wv_KeQMw

2. We are victorious
   https://youtu.be/OIun53iz6s4

3. Great are you Lord
   https://youtu.be/0ORTihWykSA

4. Great I am
   https://youtu.be/O1QwIpUatLw

5. Indescribable
   https://youtu.be/gpO3aI5RuMY

6. You are able
   https://youtu.be/WGum4RVkAb8

7. Jireh
   https://youtu.be/mC-zw0zCCtg

COVENANT DAY OF EXEMPTION

1. Create in me a clean heart
   https://youtu.be/bacXQPujfKI

2. I need you
   https://youtu.be/tzdQgjKUTwM

3. Fill me up
   https://youtu.be/OKWkYxikygQ

4. Worth
   https://youtu.be/UPiC6Xcfaz0

5. Hallowed be your name
   https://youtu.be/pDyRUuHCg2g

6. Order my steps
   https://youtu.be/eVzJiW26xDc

7. More
   https://youtu.be/JqpNwzvPsDU

8. Happy
   https://youtu.be/q65JunMhWO8

9. Set my life on fire
   https://youtu.be/YYms-CKS1WA

www.ingramcontent.com/pod-product-compliance
Lightning Source LLC
LaVergne TN
LVHW021559070426
835507LV00014B/1864